"*The Great Oklahoma Swindle* shows that Oklahoma's story is all-American in a compressed timeline. That Cobb stands toe to toe with his state and never blinks makes this project a compelling read."

—Matt Sutherland, *Foreword Reviews*

"This unflinching look at Oklahoma's singular past helpfully fills in lesser-known aspects of the historical record."

—*Publishers Weekly*

"For the geographer and layperson alike [*The Great Oklahoma Swindle*] is an outstanding, timely, and accessible primer for better understanding how much the U.S. is shaped by the converging legacies of neoliberal governance, settler colonialism, and systemic racism. Loving a place is not always easy, but Russell Cobb's *The Great Oklahoma Swindle* sets an exemplary and thought-provoking model for other writers to follow in the twenty-first-century American scene."

—Robert Briwa, *Journal of Geography*

"*The Great Oklahoma Swindle* should be required reading for every citizen of the state, especially schoolchildren. As a human geographer and writer of history, I am truly impressed by how Cobb has unwrapped the exaggerations, stereotypes, and hidden history of Oklahoma to present a refreshingly accurate account of this puzzling place that I love, warts and all."

—Michael Wallis, best-selling author of *The Best Land under Heaven: The Donner Party in the Age of Manifest Destiny*

D1284946

"A swindle is a fraudulent scheme or action taken by those with the intention of using deception to deprive someone of money or possessions, sometimes just dignity. Russell Cobb has penned one of the most direct, frank, rough, rustic, reasoned, and realistic approaches to a deep dark side of what was intended to be deep dark secrets at the core of Oklahoma's red soil, red soul, and redneck essence with regard to its grit, greed, grandeur, and contrived gravitas, based in faith, farce, and fraud. I found it profoundly and profanely revealing and educational. It should be required reading for every serious student of history or those who love the truth regardless of how painful or pitiful the honest truth can be."

—Rev. Carlton Pearson, progressive spiritual teacher, author of *The Gospel of Inclusion*, and subject of the Netflix film *Come Sunday*

The Great Oklahoma Swindle

RACE, RELIGION, AND LIES IN
AMERICA'S WEIRDEST STATE

RUSSELL COBB

UNIVERSITY OF NEBRASKA PRESS   LINCOLN

Acknowledgments for previously published material appear on page xv, which constitutes an extension of the copyright page.

The University of Nebraska Press is part of a land-grant institution with campuses and programs on the past, present, and future homelands of the Pawnee, Ponca, Otoe-Missouria, Omaha, Dakota, Lakota, Kaw, Cheyenne, and Arapaho Peoples, as well as those of the relocated Ho-Chunk, Sac and Fox, and Iowa Peoples.

Library of Congress Cataloging-in-Publication Data
Names: Cobb, Russell, 1974– author.
Title: The great Oklahoma swindle: race, religion, and
    lies in America's weirdest state / Russell Cobb.
Description: Lincoln: University of Nebraska Press, [2020]
    | Includes bibliographical references and index.
Identifiers: LCCN 2019020725
    ISBN 9781496209986 (cloth)
    ISBN 9781496230409 (paperback)
    ISBN 9781496220035 (epub)
    ISBN 9781496220059 (pdf)
    ISBN 9781496220042 (mobi)
Subjects: LCSH: Cobb, Russell, 1974– | Collective memory—
    Oklahoma. | Oklahoma—History. | Oklahoma—Social
    conditions. | Oklahoma—Religious life and customs.
Classification: LCC F694 .C63 2020 | DDC 976.6—dc23
LC record available at https://lccn.loc.gov/2019020725

Set in New Baskerville ITC by Laura Ebbeka.
Designed by N. Putens.

To all y'all Okies, with love.

oklahoma will be the last song
i'll ever sing
JOY HARJO

I grew up in Tulsa, Oklahoma, like an idiot in some book.
BILL HADER

CONTENTS

ILLUSTRATIONS

ACKNOWLEDGMENTS

Before the seedling of this book broke through the Oklahoma red dirt, I had a chance encounter with a history professor at the University of Iowa as an undergraduate. He expressed interest in my Oklahoma upbringing and told me stories about the Green Corn Rebellion, the leftist politics of Woody Guthrie, and the influence of the Socialist Party in Oklahoma. I could not believe that Oklahoma had brought forth such radicalism, and I feverishly related all I learned to Alex Wayne, who has remained a friend all these years later. Friends in graduate school at the University of Texas at Austin and later at *The Nation* internship program in New York also helped urge me along my path toward a total reassessment of Oklahoma history. Late-night discussions with William Lin, Kabir Dandona, Matthew Maddy, and Justin Vogt put Oklahoma's contradictions in context. Jonathan Shainin provided some early editorial guidance in various publications.

The staff at *This American Life*, especially Julie Snyder, Alex Blumberg, and Ira Glass, had faith that the story of a figure practically unknown in the secular world from the backwater of Oklahoma would resonate with a national audience. I am still amazed and honored that I was able to have a hand in writing and framing Carlton Pearson's story for the *This American Life* segment on "Heretics." Carlton remains a friend and a mentor. He helped me see another layer of complexity in the culture of evangelicalism.

This book started to take its current shape with the creation of *This Land Press*, a little magazine once labeled "the *New Yorker* with balls" by *Columbia Journalism Review*. From 2010 to 2015, Michael Mason provided a window into Oklahoma's weird reality that bucked all conventions. *This Land* was fearless, odd, unpredictable. I am very proud of my contributions to the magazine and indebted to Michael's support in getting an early version of many of the stories related here out into the world. Although the magazine has ceased publication, its free-spirited and contrarian nature lives on in the *Tulsa Voice* through the editorship of Jezy Gray, who has been particularly supportive of my research around Muscogee (Creek) Tulsa.

The Oklahoma Policy Institute is a state treasure that provides a reality-based check to some of the more ridiculous initiatives that come from the state's political class. The institute's director, David Blatt, not only helped me understand why, for all the depressing statistics, things could also be worse, but he also drew out interesting comparisons with my adopted homeland in Alberta, Canada. Chapter 2 was supported by the journalism nonprofit the Economic Hardship Reporting Project. The rage that fueled my article for the *Guardian* on Oklahoma as America's failed state was harnessed into a large-scale research project by Matthew Bokovoy, who has ably shepherded this project from its beginnings into a—hopefully—coherent story about how messed up Oklahoma is and how it got that way. Matt, and everyone at University of Nebraska Press, believed that there was an important story to be told and helped fill in my woeful gaps of knowledge about Five Tribes scholarship. Brian Hosmer at the University of Tulsa also provided crucial feedback along with the way.

A special shout-out to my Okie contrarian brethren who have provided inspiration and friendship over the years, especially Chris Hastings, Chris Sachse, Jeff Weigant, and Bob Blakemore. Music fueled our first rebellions, and our raucous, disjointed experiments in punk, hip-hop, and God knows what else helped us forge community and create survival strategies for growing up as black sheep in a conformist town on the Bible Belt.

Before the idea of this book came to fruition, I worked on a family memoir at the writers' utopia known as Literary Journalism at the Banff Centre. The mentorship and guidance of Ian Brown, Victor Dwyer, and Charlotte Gill were instrumental in getting the personal angle to this story down. I am thankful to the *Toronto Star* and Patricia Hluchy for believing in the Cobb story enough to publish it as a Star Dispatch known as "Heart in Darkness: The Genetic Defect That Could Kill Me." Céline Gareau-Brennan at the University of Alberta Library and the staff at the National Archives in Fort Worth, Texas, provided research assistance, as did Sheri Perkins at Tulsa City County Library, Marc Carlson at the University of Tulsa library, the staff of the Sand Springs Cultural and Historical Museum.

Some longtime friends who listened to my rants, provided tips, and helped me discover unseen connections include Michael Erard, Sunny Mills, Omar Mouallem, Marcello Di Cintio, Ted Bishop, and Curtis Gillespie. J. D. Colbert's research on Creek history was an inspiration and kick-start to chapter 3, "The Road to Hell in Indian Territory." Along with Gina Covington and Eli Grayson, Colbert helped me understand that Tulsa's Creek past is not dead; it is not even past. Allison Herrera's effort to tell Tulsa's Creek story provided a push to learn more on my part. Her audio-producing skills helped me hone my own interviewing techniques. Similarly, this book's coverage of indigenous history is indebted to many people working at the Muscogee (Creek) Nation, especially RaeLynn Butler and Veronica Pipestem. Even though they had a quieter background presence, Melissa Harjo-Moffer and Odette Freeman helped out a lot in the way of looking up info, printing it out, and talking about how a Creek woman like Millie Naharkey or Minnie Atkins might have thought and acted based on the era they lived in. *Mvto* (thanks) to the elders. Gano Perez put together those GIS maps of Tuckabache's land. Darla Ashton, the granddaughter of one the most tragic victims of the swindle of land allotments, guided me around northeastern Oklahoma, visiting important sites. Tallulah Eve Smith brought an eloquent voice to contemporary Creek perspective. Nehemiah Frank is an inspiring young Black voice embodying the resurgence of North Tulsa. His input on the Tulsa Race Massacre of 1921 was invaluable.

Apollonia Piña added a breath of fresh air and an indigenous female voice toward the end of the journey. Every page of this book has been subjected to Apollonia's bullshit detector, as well as her knowledge and passion for all things Mvskoke. We share a mutual curiosity about how us Okies got so damn weird. Apollonia was my "research assistant," but I consider her a creative and intellectual partner in this endeavor. She bailed me out more than once when I could have echoed some outdated assumption about indigenous traditions (she convinced me to cut the "Civilized" part out of the "Five Tribes"). I would not have been able to bring Apollonia's perspective to the project without the support of the Faculty of Arts and the vice president of research at the University of Alberta, facilitated by Steve Patten. Kerry Sluchinski assisted me getting all the details in order, fact-checking, double-checking citations, and finishing other important tasks. An invaluable last round of edits was provided by Sarah C. Smith of Arbuckle Editorial.

A special word of gratitude and *fraternité* to my Quebecois homie and colleague, Daniel Laforest, who once drove the length of Oklahoma on I-40 and maybe stopped for a Slurpee. For Daniel, Oklahoma blended seamlessly into Arkansas and Texas. But now he knows how truly unique we Okies are. Over beers, he was my sounding board for all sorts of ideas throughout this project. Daniel and other friends colleagues in Spanish and Latin American studies—too many to mention here—tolerated my detour into the American Heartland and gave me support as my research and publishing profile picked up steam. Chairs of my home department, Laura Beard and Carrie Smith, urged me on, even when this project seemed like a total break from the traditional profile of a Spanish professor.

My mother, Pat Cobb, was my biggest cheerleader when I started publishing. Dementia took hold of her ability to read, think, and function. But I know that some part of her would be proud of this book, even if it presents a damning portrait of her homeland and its people. My uncle Tim Cobb has always been a source of family lore, black humor, and support. I do not know if many people within the extended network of Cobbs will approve of the work in this book, but Tim has always been an inspiration for me as a Cobb black sheep. He is what family should be: tolerant, loving, supportive, nonjudgmental. Same goes for my cousins Carey Calvert and Kay Kittleman and their children.

Rachel Hertz Cobb has been my constant and patient companion on voyages to the darker side of the Heartland, to Dementiatown, and back to our adopted home of Canada. Rachel has been my wise counsel, my editor, and best friend. I do not think I would have had the fortitude to make it here without her. Along the way, we ate, we drank, we danced, we argued, and made two wonderful children, August and Henry, who mainly know Tulsa for its signature mini hot dog, the chili cheese Coney Islander. I have thought about my sons throughout this project, hoping that they inherit a more just, inclusive, and honest world than the one I was raised in. Finally, to the people of Oklahoma, a place that will always be my sort-of home, I extend a huge embrace to y'all in all your contradictions, foibles, brilliance, and madness. *Mvto, gracias,* thanks.

Take it easy, but take it, Okies.

An earlier version of chapter 2 appeared as "Oklahoma Isn't Working: Can Anyone Fix This Failing American State?" in the *Guardian*, August 29, 2017.

An earlier version of chapter 4 appeared as "South by Midwest: Or, Where Is Oklahoma?" in *This Land Press*, November 14, 2012.

An earlier version of chapter 5 appeared as "Shalom, Ardmore" in *This Land Press*, August 19, 2015.

An earlier version of chapter 7 appeared as "Among the Tribe of the Wannabes" in *This Land Press*, August 26, 2014.

An earlier version of chapter 8 appeared as "Backwards Christian Soldier" in *This Land Press*, November 30, 2012.

An earlier version of chapter 9 appeared as "Continuous Present" in *This Land Press*, November 21, 2011.

An earlier version of chapter 10 appeared as "Heart in Darkness" in the *Toronto Star*, February 22, 2014.

An earlier version of chapter 12 appeared as "Brave New Park" in *This Land Magazine*, Winter 2016.

THE GREAT OKLAHOMA SWINDLE

Prologue

Fake news. Alternative facts. The cultural landscape of the early twenty-first century is littered with deformations of the truth and outright lies. The culprits are legion: internet culture, Donald Trump, big tech companies, Russian trolls, white nationalism, postmodern relativism. Collins Dictionary selected *fake news* as the word of the year for 2017. Long think-pieces have proliferated about "America's misinformation problem." Economists have been marshaled to quantify the impact of fake news on elections and the biases of the American public. Facebook, from which much of the fake news originates, has undertaken an ad campaign to warn users about how to spot false information. Universities are gearing up for more media literacy courses, alarmed by the supposed rise in unverifiable information. And yet we lack awareness of the history of fakery, swindles, and legally executed frauds that make up the U.S. colonization of its own territories.

This book is about how one state in the union—Oklahoma—was founded and maintained on false information and broken promises from its very beginning. Rather than seeing fake news as a contemporary media problem, in other words, I see it as the touchstone for our political culture. A swindle was at the heart of Oklahoma's state-building project. From the massive legalized theft of Native land in the early twentieth century, to a decades-long conspiracy of silence about one of the country's worst acts of racial violence, to a former governor who believes a statewide day of Christian prayer is a solution for social problems and a former attorney general who continues to deny the reality of climate change, the state of Oklahoma was built and is still maintained on a bedrock of lies.

The dean of Oklahoma history, Angie Debo, wrote that the story of her native state could be seen as a compressed history of the United States: "The one who can interpret Oklahoma can grasp the meaning of America in the modern world."[1] Native American assimilation and treaty-making, slavery, large-scale white settlement, and a massive economic boom followed by industrialization all took place over the course of half a century, making Oklahoma an American story run at 4× speed. The fact that Oklahoma is a deep red state, a reactionary state, leads some people to conclude that there is something un-American about it. I am not sure about that. Whether the state is an American exception or a microcosm—or a little bit of both—is a question I revisit throughout this book.

What I am sure of, however, is that the story the political class and economic elite of Oklahoma has told about itself has laid the groundwork for the continued exploitation and misery of not only its minority populations but its poor and working-class white population as well. Fake history is so baked into the state's religiosity, its political structures, and its education system that we do not even recognize it as such. This is just the way things are.

Take the most popular sports team in the state, the University of Oklahoma football team, whose mascot is the Sooner. The Sooner Schooner is pulled by horses around the Owen Field after every touchdown, a symbol of that pioneer pluck that embodies the state's spirit. Sooner imagery is ubiquitous: even the state's frayed Medicaid system is known as Sooner-Care. I learned to scream "Boomer Sooner!" at the television during football games around the time I could toddle, ignorant until recently about who the actual Boomers and Sooners were. These nicknames were given to white settlers who claimed to have titles to "surplus lands," the term given to land that was not taken up by Native American allotments in Oklahoma and Indian Territories. The Boomers and Sooners literally jumped the gun on the land rush, camping out on the edges of townsites with fake certificates for 160-acre plots of land. They often shot and killed each other, as well as the Native Americans who legally owned the land. As the early cities of Oklahoma took shape, the Boomers became the focus of the ire of city leaders. They disregarded local laws and handed out rough justice—including lynchings—to anyone who questioned their legal right to the land. They were, in the words of Danney Goble, little more than squatters.[2] Boomers appropriated Native American tribal names (one such group of white men called itself the Seminoles) and then proceeded to issue themselves fake land deeds.

That such figures could be transformed from their origins in land-based piracy to wholesome all-Americanness says a lot about the swindle at the heart of the Oklahoma project. For that is what the historical lies amount to: a broad-based movement to defraud disenfranchised people (Native Americans, African Americans, sharecropping Okies, migrant workers) of their land and, indeed, their very identities. These are not simple misstatements about the nature of empirically verifiable facts. Would that it were so. If simply correcting the historical record led to social justice, my task would be simple; however, it is much more profound than that.

When I was about nine years old, my mom took me on a drive through Tulsa's predominately Black North Side. Even though the North Side was only two miles from our home in tony Maple Ridge, we almost never went north of the train tracks downtown. But I wanted a puppy, and the animal shelter was on the North Side. As we drove across the tracks, my mom clicked down the door locks on our '83 Cutlass Ciera. Along streets near North Main, I saw sidewalks and driveways leading to nothing. The area around the crosstown expressway was particularly derelict. Husks of red brick buildings and boarded-up houses predominated the scenery. I asked about why so much of the North Side looked like a wasteland. My mom said that some people were too poor to take care of their property. This was the conventional wisdom: the poor lacked the basic personal responsibility to take care of their own property. Decades later, when I was well into my twenties, I chanced upon Scott Ellsworth's *Death in a Promised Land* at a library in Austin, Texas. The destitution of North Tulsa had nothing to do with Black neglect, as white Tulsa would have it, and everything to do with the Tulsa Race Massacre of 1921, perhaps the deadliest incident of racial violence in American history since the Civil War.[3]

Fully grown-up me was angry at my mom for never mentioning the massacre. Around this time—the turn of the millennium—she worked on the North Side and had hired an African American woman as an assistant manager at the bookstore she managed. By the standards of white Tulsa, she had become a progressive. But her attitudes about the massacre were a product of white Tulsa's silence. My high school history teacher did not mention the event in my Oklahoma history class, nor did it appear in our textbooks. White Tulsa wanted nothing to do with an event that flew in the face of its "Magic City" image, the supposed Oil Capital of the World with its world-class museums and small-town vibe.

Later in life, I learned more startling facts not taught or celebrated in Oklahoma's official narrative. The neighborhood I grew up in—the Sunset Terrace addition of Maple Ridge, in Tulsa—had been a Muscogee (Creek) allotment owned by a warrior named Tuckabache in the early twentieth century. When Tuckabache died in 1910, prominent Tulsans stepped in to make sure the land did not pass down to his grandchildren but was instead deeded over to land speculators. Tuckabache's family cemetery, where at least seventeen of his kin were buried, was a football toss from my backyard. No one in the neighborhood had even heard of Tuckabache. Our history is not so much forgotten as it is suppressed.

When I bring my wife, from a secular Jewish liberal family, to Tulsa, we know there are certain things *you just do not talk about.* Religion is supposed to be taboo, except that a common conversation starter is "What church y'all go to?" Politics are also supposed to be avoided, except that snide comments about Barack Obama being an African-born socialist go uncontested. The truth is that *some views* about politics and religion are not to be discussed, namely those that challenge the prevailing orthodoxy. We need to have deep conversations about the foundations of Oklahoma to understand the mess the state finds itself in. The massive margin of victory for Donald Trump—the second-widest in the nation—seems to confirm the view that Okies have completely fallen for the swindle. To many liberals in academia and the media, Oklahoma is the heart of Flyover Country, a place that deserves its own misery. But while the state may be based on a swindle, not everyone has bought in to the lie. Oklahoma has a venerable tradition of radicalism and social experimentation that we do not teach in our state-mandated curriculum. Debunking the notion of Oklahoma (and, by extension, large parts of the Midwest and South) as nothing more than a redneck wasteland occupies a large portion of this book. Just because its contemporary political and economic structure is based on a historical swindle does not mean that the state has not produced an incredible array of dreamers, radicals, visionaries, and weirdos. From the otherworldly architecture of Bruce Goff, to the prose of Ralph Ellison, to the socialist protest songs of Woody Guthrie, and to the jazz-blues-country fusion of Bob Wills, JJ Cale, and Leon Russell, the richness of the state's culture is both underappreciated and unparalleled. The local culture is characterized by a slow burn, like the state's barbecue, of racial mixture and genre-bending. I tell those stories too. The stories of the brave souls, like Carlton Pearson, who have met the charge of heresy squarely on and refused to back down or leave. Those stories deserve to be told and remembered.

There is a plaque at the John Hope Franklin Reconciliation Memorial that commemorates not only the death and destruction of the Massacre of 1921 but the spirit that rebuilt Greenwood after the violence despite threats from the KKK and Jim Crow laws. One part of the memorial reads:

> For this land, this Oklahoma, is our land, too. We have built its cities and worked its farms, raised its children and fought in its wars. On its altars of freedom you will find our blood as well. For hundreds of

years, beneath its endless skies, we have lived and worked, laughed and wept, loved and died. And as we have climbed, so have you.

Now, we must all climb together.

"We must all climb together." It is a phrase that our folk poet Woody Guthrie could have sung. Words that the Socialist Party of Oklahoma—once the nation's largest socialist party—would have endorsed. It is the spirit of solidarity that united the thousands of public school teachers who decided in the spring of 2018 that they had finally had enough of tax cuts and days of prayer for the oil patch; they walked off the job. Later in the year, some ran for the state legislature, defeating incumbents in the primary. Many teachers won their elections during the primaries of 2018, prompting national media to take notice of a "revolution" in America's Heartland. I never held my breath. A spirit of fatalism hangs heavy over the land. When you grow up believing the Boomers were the heroes, rather than the land pirates they were, it is hard not to be cynical about social progress. But it is not for nothing that Oklahomans adopted the state motto *Labor omnia vincit.* Labor conquers all. Oklahoma has witnessed periods of insurgency and solidarity, from the Crazy Snake to the Green Corn Rebellions of early statehood to the teacher walkout of 2018 and the unexpected victories of progressive women in the midterm elections post-Trump.

At its core, this book is about how one place in the heart of America got very, very messed up. But it is not only about that. This book is also about the beauty and genius of the place, a testament to the hybrid culture of a place of visionaries and dreamers. A complicated story, in other words. I sometimes find myself lost in the paradoxes of place, race, and religion. Oklahoma seems to embody Walt Whitman's famous lines: "Do I contradict myself? Very well then, I contradict myself. I am large. I contain multitudes."

Consider, for example:

In 1914, 175 candidates from the Socialist Party of Oklahoma won elections.

Oklahoma has led the nation in per-capita executions since 1980.

Some of the most prosperous all-Black townships in the nation were located in Oklahoma, prompting leaders like Booker T. Washington and Ida B. Wells to tout Oklahoma as "the Black promised land."

In 2016 the starting wage at QuikTrip, an Oklahoma-owned convenience store, was higher than the starting salary for a teacher in the state's schools.

The Native American preacher Oral Roberts grew up in poverty to eventually build a futuristic hub for evangelical Christianity in the Tulsa suburbs, where he once saw a nine-hundred-foot Jesus.

America's greatest folk singer, Woody Guthrie, was once a persona non grata in his hometown of Okemah because of his leftist politics.

Guthrie's father, Charley Guthrie, may have participated in one of the most horrific lynchings in American history, when a mother and son were hung from a bridge in Okemah.

In 2018 Oklahoma became the first state in the Bible Belt to legalize medical marijuana.

The nation's largest noodling tournament (catfishing by hand) is held in Oklahoma.

Cherokee is the fourth-most-spoken language in Oklahoma, though it is on the endangered languages list.

In 2015 there were more earthquakes in Oklahoma than in California.

At least thirty-nine Native American nations call Oklahoma home.

Tulsa and Oklahoma City are consistently ranked among the most affordable places to live among U.S. metro areas.

Franz Kafka wrote a story called "The Nature Theater of Oklahoma." He never visited the place.

The second deadliest terrorist attack and the worst episode of racial violence in the United States both took place in Oklahoma.

The largest gift to a public park in American history happened in Tulsa in 2014, when billionaire George Kaiser gave $350 million to create Gathering Place for Tulsa.

The Strawberry Capital of the World (at least as named by the state legislature in the 1940s), Stilwell, Oklahoma, also has the lowest life expectancy of any town in the nation (56.3 years).

Klansman David Duke and Black radical intellectual Cornel West were both born in Tulsa in the 1950s.

Very well then. We contain multitudes.

CHAPTER 1

Voyage to Dementiatown

Witnessing the unmaking of a human being is a hell of a thing. Western ideology stresses the continuous improvement of the self. We progress from a blank slate at infancy to a repository of wisdom by the time we enter our golden years. Supposedly. When my mom reached retirement age, she started to come undone the way Hemingway described rich people going broke: gradually at first, and then all of a sudden. After a few years of slow decline, she could not distinguish her hairbrush from her iPhone.

At the same time I was teaching my son to tie his shoes, I had to buy my mom slip-ons. She had unlearned how to tie a bow. Every couple of months or so, I suspended all disbelief and visited my mom in a place I called Dementiatown, Oklahoma. My mom's window out of Dementiatown to the place we call Reality was still there for a long time, but it was frosted over. You had to scratch your fingernail through the ice if you wanted to see anything clearly.

"You came all the way from Kansas," my mom said.

"Canada, Mom. Canada. I have been there for almost ten years."

My mom is literally an Okie from Muskogee, a small city in eastern Oklahoma where her dad ran a barbecue joint and drove a beer truck. I know little about the man, but I do know his barbecue never measured up to the legendary Slick's BBQ across town. Shortly before my grandfather's restaurant went out of business in the 1950s, my grandmother took my mom and split Muskogee for Tulsa. My grandfather's ill-fated turn as a barbecue pitmaster ended, and he somehow joined up touring the nation with a variety show as a figure skater. It occurs to me now that my mom's life was like a country song. But she hated country music. Unlike the narrator of the Merle Haggard song, my mom would never be caught dead pitchin' wool, drinkin' white lightning, or wavin' Old Glory down at the courthouse. "That's country" was her all-encompassing takedown of everything associated with her rural, working-class white upbringing.

No matter how steep the declines in her cognition, her judgment of social class stayed sharp. *Your mom is a lady*, people at the assisted living facility said. She preferred pinot grigio and Caesar salad to beer and smoked brisket. Even in Dementiatown, Oklahoma, there was such a thing as good taste. It took her half a lifetime to achieve her social status, and she was not going to give it up quietly. Invitations to bingo, lunch at Cracker Barrel, or services at the Southern Baptist church were rebuffed. "Too country," she said.

We wandered around a newly expanded Whole Foods and marveled at all the fancy cheeses and prepackaged sushi. "This place used to be a Bud's Supermarket," she reminded me. "You bagged groceries for Garth Brooks's parents here."

Sometimes I would put a bunch of high-end food in a shopping cart and push it around for a while. Then I would leave the cart in the pet food aisle. "How much am I paying to stay at that place?" she would ask on the way back to the assisted living facility.

"We've got it covered" was all I could say.

I did not have it covered at all.

My mom spent her teenage years trying to escape her poor upbringing. She seemed to have found the ticket when she met my dad, who came from one of the wealthiest families in Tulsa. His grandfather—Russell Cobb—had been a champion boxer at Harvard, the son of the architect Henry Ives Cobb, a builder of massive civic institutions like the University of Chicago and the state capitol of Pennsylvania. Russell Cobb I counted himself among a handful of men who ruled over Tulsa's ascension to Oil Capital of the World. The title is self-bestowed and since the 1950s, no one has taken it seriously. Russell Cobb was everywhere during Tulsa's golden age. He founded the Tennis Club. He was campaign manager for the Republican candidate for governor. He was police commissioner for Tulsa. But most importantly, he was an oil man, acquiring mineral rights from Oklahoma to Wyoming to California.

Russell Cobb's grandson, Candy Cobb, had swagger: solid gold cufflinks, a black Benz, and an uncanny resemblance to Elvis. He was a tennis champion and a Vegas gambler. He was my mom's ticket out of her poor, rural Okie upbringing. It would be just my mom's luck that my dad fell ill with a rare heart disease shortly after they married. The oil money dried up. They spent the next five years trying out every new treatment in cardiology, only to have my dad end up with a rejected heart transplant and a quack Pentecostal doctor praying over him on his deathbed. By the time my dad died, my mom's main inheritance was $200,000 in unpaid medical bills. She also had a restless five-year-old boy to contend with: me. I recently asked her why she never went on welfare or food stamps during that time.

"Welfare is for poor people," she said. "We weren't them."

Outside Dementiatown, it does not take much symbolic effort to read the code of welfare; it signifies not only poverty but nonwhiteness. The very word *welfare* connotes an Otherness that remained vivid in her mind. With reason: as the writers Thomas Byrne Edsall and Mary D. Edsall discovered decades ago, race "is no longer a straightforward, morally unambiguous force in American politics" but rather a series of codes.[1] My mom's family came from a small town in the middle of the old Muscogee (Creek) Nation, settled by her grandparents, who had been sharecroppers in Tennessee. We are both dark-complexioned and frequently mistaken for Latino or even Native American. One of her ancestors had Native blood, a dangerous proposition in a state that adopted all the racist laws of the Old South. Many of her aunts and uncles lit out for California in the 1930s and 1940s, only to be labeled "Okie scum," a subset of white trash. A few of them came back, bitter over the California experiment. In the company of her in-laws, she has often been treated as an extension of "the help."

My mom spent the next thirty years after my dad's death clawing herself back up the social ladder, paying off a mortgage and building a little nest egg. Now it was all being wasted on some "country" retirement home? She would not stand for it. She wanted out of the place.

Fine, I said.

We toured the nicest retirement home in town. Imagine an Italian villa recreated on the southern plains, complete with marble fountains, grottos, and pastels. The place even had a wine bar. She recognized a lot of the residents. They were members of the country club and the Episcopal church. High WASPs in white pants. My mom never had enough money to join the country club and went to church mainly on holidays. Still, she had a social network that invited her to the country club or the Petroleum Club on occasion. An Easter brunch at Southern Hills was, for her, a sign that she had put Muskogee and her mother's three-room house behind her.

She liked this Italian place. I did the math and calculated that her savings would have lasted approximately two years there. Her residence in Dementiatown, meanwhile, could last for three years. Or thirteen years. No one understood the severity of the illness or how it would come to ravish her over a decade. I inquired whether the fancy place accepted Medicaid, the public health care of last resort for Americans who have spent down all their savings.

No, sir, they said.

For a while, life at the "country" retirement home rolled on by without incident. My mom could still cruise around town in her Toyota Camry. Then one morning, she pulled out of a garage sale and crushed the side-view mirror of a pickup truck. She kept on going. I got a text from a neighbor, telling me two cops were snooping around the condo. They took down notes about the Camry. I called her. She had no idea why the police were there. She put them on the line. She had been suspected of a hit-and-run and could be slapped with a $500 fine. But she seemed like a nice lady, so they told her to be more cautious next time.

I had to go to Oklahoma and take the car away. We sold it to a man who just happened to be the father of the then–attorney general of Oklahoma, a guy who went on to become a very prominent member of the Trump administration before resigning in the summer of 2018. When he told me who he was, I recoiled. But he was driving a Prius! He turned out to be a kind man, a gentle soul who commiserated with me about aging parents and the perils of dementia. He pointed out that the Camry had suffered damage from the side-mirror accident as well as a few other scrapes and dents. And hail damage. Still, he cut me a check for the damaged car, for a few hundred dollars less that we had previously agreed upon.

I told my mom about the incident, thinking she would be impressed that the father of an up-and-coming political star had bought her old Camry. She was unimpressed. Anyone in the used car business, she thought, was a bit of a hick.

I called a distant cousin—all of her other relatives are dead—to complain about her lost checks, unpaid bills, and missed doctor's appointments. "She's fine" was the only response I got. I took her to a neurologist who wrote in his report that "Mrs. Cobb presented as an attractive, well-dressed woman" with some signs of cognitive disorder. It would get worse, he said. Way worse. But she seemed to be doing great for now, so why worry? My mom liked this neurologist. When things got uncomfortable, he changed the conversation. That was how I was taught to deal with unpleasantness: talk about something else. I took her to another neurologist. The next one gave her a battery of tests that showed evidence of vascular dementia. "So I have Alzheimer's?" my mom said.

"Similar, yet different," I said.

What was the point? All types of dementia—from Lewy Body to Alzheimer's—erase the very identity of the person afflicted. What used to be small tasks—pouring a cup of tea, tying a shoe, rolling down a car window—become challenges and finally impossibilities. Different dementias attack the mind from different angles, but the effect is the same: you gradually unlearn basic functions, slowly and inexorably vanishing until nothing is left. There are miraculous stories of cancer survivors, AIDS survivors, a heart attack that should have killed someone. There are no miraculous dementia survivor stories because no one has ever survived. My mom understood all this. She had survived two bouts of lung cancer, so she knew how to face mortality. But what she could not countenance was a slide back into poverty, back into countrydom.

Several years before she started developing symptoms of dementia, my mom and I went to visit her aunt in a nursing home outside Muskogee. It was a sprawling faux-colonial building that smelled like stale bread and bleach. The aunt had once been feted as the Queen of McIntosh County and now she was wasting away with Alzheimer's in a nursing home on Medicaid, having exhausted her life savings in three years. When we got back to Tulsa my mom made me promise her something. "Tell me you will take me out and shoot me before I go into a home like that," she said. I felt like it was a standard line parents issue to their children. No one wants to contemplate decline. "I just don't think I'm allowed to shoot you," I said. We laughed. Then we never spoke of it again.

I looked into bringing my mom to Canada. Friendly and compassionate Canada. I found out the Canadian system screens out elderly and sick parents of immigrants, requiring that they buy expensive private insurance to cover medical expenses. Fine, I thought. Private insurance in Canada would still be cheaper than the United States. There was a catch, though. There are a handful of preexisting conditions that no Canadian insurance company will cover, including AIDS, kidney disease, and, yes, dementia.

Her only option was to stay at the country home with more advanced care. The people there are nothing short of saints, I told her. They are always positive, telling us to have a blessed day, when death and disease loom around every corner. The majority of the staff are people of color. The patients are all white. I am still not sure how they do it, the nurses at the facility. They seem to be having *fun*. But my mom was not buying it. She wanted the impossible—a move back to her old house. I took a page from her playbook: guilt. "You should count your blessings. You have a spot in a facility with such advanced care," I said. "Think about all those old folks wasting away with bed sores in nursing homes where everyone's on welfare. They have to use food stamps just to have dinner!"

"I suppose it could be worse," she said.

I can understand why the prospect of a return to poverty troubled her. My mom lives in a state where the social safety net has been torn so badly, it is hard to know how far she could fall. Oklahoma has recently fallen to near the bottom of almost all social and health indicators in the United States. The state ranks among the worst in education outcomes and public education funding. It leads in obesity, incarceration, and executions. Throw in high rates of premature death, smoking, and terrible roads, and CNBC ranks it as the third-worst state to live in. Cutbacks to Medicaid and Health and Human Services mean that nursing homes across the state are closing.[2]

It takes ten years just to get on a waiting list for a waiver to help people with severe disabilities like my mom. As Republicans continue to cut taxes, that waiting list grows longer. List these facts to an Oklahoma conservative, however, and you are likely to get a number of culprits: government bureaucracy, Barack Obama, or the moral failings of individuals. Sometimes it feels like the whole state has become an extension of Dementiatown, where empirical reality is warped by some distant dream of a former time when everything was fine.

My mom, by the way, remains a Republican even though she has not voted for one for president since George H. W. Bush. Why? As my mom's friend explained to me when I was eight years old, Republicans are the party of rich people and Democrats are the party of poor folks. If you aspire to wealth, vote Republican; if you are content with poverty, vote Democrat. As the generation that suffered the indignities of the Dust Bowl, the California exodus, and the Great Depression has passed from living memory to history, their children and grandchildren have abandoned the networks of solidarity that saved their forebears from total ruin. In exchange for tax breaks, they have embraced a gospel of individualism: if your life is messed up, you probably did something to deserve it. It is no wonder that my mom's extensive network of friends from the Episcopal church and other pillars of WASP society has almost disappeared. No one wants to visit Dementiatown, not even for an hour. There is nothing to be gained there. Networking would be an exercise in futility. There is no cultural capital in a *country* retirement facility.

But if there was one blessing to life in Dementiatown, it was that these facts were abstractions. My mom did not really understand how deep her social isolation went. She gets glimpses of her former life when her few remaining friends take her to brunch, to see her graceful old house in Maple Ridge, and to check out the latest offerings at Whole Foods. And she has company in Dementiatown. As the U.S. population grows older, our collective risk for dementia increases. Our hyper-capitalistic system provides no benefits for taking care of our aging parents, but it has created a market for long-term care facilities where we can offload the burden to low-wage workers. It is a deal with the devil, but I was left with no choice but to accept the terms.

DUMB OKIE LOGIC

I arrived in Tulsa to move my mom to a higher level of care on the same day the governor of Oklahoma proclaimed a statewide day of Christian prayer over the price of oil. The decline in the price of oil led to a state revenue failure and a teacher exodus to Arkansas and Texas, of all places. It was only weeks before the election in November 2016. I took an Uber from the airport to the assisted living place. The driver wore a tight ponytail and silver-rimmed glasses. He had an intellectual vibe and he told me he played in a classic rock cover band. He asked where I was coming in from.

"Canada," I said.

"You don't have any of them Syrian refugees there, do you?"

"Oh, yeah," I said proudly. "Canada is taking in tens of thousands."

"Well, Trump is going to get rid of them all down here." I laughed it off. An Uber driver with long hair and glasses? He was being sarcastic.

"Right! And he's going to build that wall too."

"Damn straight."

I learned from my driver that as soon as Oklahoma got rid of the illegals, the Jihadis, and the liberals, the state would arise from its financial crisis and become the oil capital of the world again. God as his witness.

The state was in tatters because its politicians run it like a laboratory for radical tax cuts, and this guy was blaming Muslims and Mexicans. I grew taciturn. "You in ISIS?" he said after a while. "With that beard and dark skin, man, you could be in ISIS."

I laughed it off but I was rattled. *You dumb Okie,* I muttered as he pulled away.

Dumb Okie. It is a stock phrase with a painful history that haunts me. In the late 1930s, Lillian Creisler, a junior college English professor in Modesto, California, had her students write essays about their new neighbors in the Upper San Joaquin Valley. The historian James N. Gregory recounts some of the descriptions of the residents of "Little Oklahoma" in California. Students wrote that Okies were "a relief problem." They "lower the standards of living." Adjectives included "shiftless," "lazy," and "ignorant." Finally, Okies "take away our jobs."[3] As Gregory noted, many of these adjectives were stereotypes for Mexicans or African Americans; the same words Californians used to describe Okies in the 1930s Okies employ to describe minorities in 2018. The fact that middle-class Californians had put white migrants in the same category as people of color meant that the racial codes for the term *Okie* signified the erasure of their white privilege. I think this is why the term *white privilege* does not always sit well with me. Not that I am afraid to own the privileges I have—I have never been stopped by the police for anything other than speeding and have always been treated fairly by law enforcement—but I know that Okies have not always gotten the same privileges associated with middle-class suburban white kids. In fact, as in other versions of "white trash," there is a sort of racial subtext working against Okies: they have failed at whiteness. Consider, for example, the words of H. L. Mencken. Okies, he said, "are simply, by God's inscrutable will, inferior men, and inferior they will remain until, by a stupendous miracle, he gives them equality among His angels."[4] Mencken was considering why, when the novel *The Grapes of Wrath* was released, Oklahomans staged book burnings. John Steinbeck had revealed an economic and social crisis created by capitalist greed, and rather than addressing the truth of Steinbeck's vision, Dumb Okies burned the book without even reading it. We do not only shoot the messenger; we shoot ourselves in the foot while we are at it. In fact, Steinbeck portrayed Okies, Mexicans, Filipinos, and other minorities as equally exploited by the California landowners, who played the different groups off each other to lower wages and block labor movements. Some Okies—most famously Woody Guthrie—saw through the attempt to stoke white resentment by pitting Okies against Mexicans, for example, but the false hope that white supremacy would elevate Okies above other workers makes the universal idea of white privilege grate against the historical reality.

The spirit of Mencken is alive and well on my Facebook feed. Friends from California to Texas—people who would be appalled by racial or ethnic slurs—seem to take a special delight in digs at Okies and other sundry "deplorables." A few choice examples have stayed with me. One occurred after I posted a link to the opening of downtown Tulsa's first independently owned bookstore. "Finally," I wrote, "some good news out of my hometown. We have a bookstore downtown!"

"People there will have to learn to read first," Peter wrote.

The label *Okie* might not have the same freight it had in previous generations, but the animus of racism and classism motivating it is still very much alive. I have been called a "dumb Okie" several times. (I have lived in California and Texas, where anti-Oklahoma bias is so common no one even thinks about it, or if they do, they consider it a harmless jab. Talk about microaggression.) Part of the reason this phrase hurts is that it is, at some level, true. So let us call this particular form of conservative Christian confirmation bias for what it is: Dumb Okie logic.

There are many examples of Dumb Okie logic in action, and many such instances have led to national embarrassment. Such was the case of a 2015 bill—HB 1380—that would have ended the teaching of Advanced Placement U.S. history in state schools. State Representative Dan Fisher said the new framework for U.S. history represented the country as a "nation of oppressors and exploiters" and failed to show "American exceptionalism." The new framework (a nonconfrontational, middle-of-road and peer-reviewed take on American history) only showed, in Fisher's opinion, "what is bad about America." In 2015 HB 1380 passed the legislature's education committee but was ultimately defeated by a grassroots network of teachers, students, and parents.[5]

When all else fails and the realities of constant budget cuts, climate change denial, and racism become too much to bear, Dumb Okie logic turns to God. The Christian God of white evangelical Protestants was tailor-made for compartmentalization. Religion has become a dumping ground to offload anything that causes cognitive dissonance. While Florida and other states have taken small steps to address mental health and gun violence in schools, Oklahoma has come up with another solution: mandate the posting of the phrase "In God We Trust" in every classroom in the state, along with images of both the American and Oklahoma flags.[6] In 2010 a Republican legislator introduced a ballot measure for a constitutional amendment known as Save Our State. It had nothing to do with restoring the drastic cuts to education and social services that began during the Great Recession but rather addressed the "threat" of Sharia law. No one could demonstrate a single instance in which Sharia law had been invoked in Oklahoma, but no matter: Islamic doctrine was an existential threat to Christian values in the Heartland. The amendment passed overwhelmingly only to be struck down by a district court, which pointed to the clear violation of the U.S. Constitution on establishment of a religion.[7]

SHOOTING THE MESSENGER IN THE FOOT

You might remember how, in the movie *Chinatown*, private detective Jake Gittes unravels a conspiracy in the death of Hollis Mulwray, the Los Angeles water commissioner. Mulwray had tried to stop the nefarious businessman Noah Cross from parching the land of California farmers, but the farmers believed the government to be the agent of the drought. As Gittes inspects an orange grove, finding more evidence of a conspiracy, he is confronted by a man in overalls. "Mulwray," the farmer says in an Oklahoma twang. "That's the son of a bitch that's done it to us."[8] When Gittes presents the farmer with evidence that he has got the wrong man, the farmer angrily insists that the government, not the wealthy business-man, is to blame. Gittes replies, "You don't know what you're talking about, you dumb Okie. Mulwray's dead."

It is a throwaway line in terms of plot development; we never see the Okie again. He is a stock character, a backward hick who cannot see how the very system he supports undermines his own best interests. But the Dumb Okie is not just a stock character from a movie about California in the Great Depression anymore. He is a stand-in for the deplorable: white, male, working to middle class, without a college degree, and a resident of Flyover Country. He suffers, yes, but he cannot see through the haze of substance abuse, religion, and toxic masculinity to find a way forward. A Marxist would say he suffers from false consciousness, unable to identify how his alienation stems from exploitation by the owners of capital. I think it is more complicated than that.

Many of these "Dumb Okies" are like my childhood friend Dan, who owns a small HVAC servicing company and a little plot of land outside Bristow. Dan is not poor, but he is steeped in debt. When he drives his F-250 to Tulsa's resurgent downtown, he feels like he does not belong in the hip new bars and boutique hotels. I ran into Dan at a drive-through taco stand on Tulsa's rundown East Side after the 2016 election. We danced around political topics, a difficult series of steps. Dan fits the model of the conservative Okie, someone who chafes at the idea of white privilege since he would say that he has not only worked hard but also confronted significant class prejudice to build his own business. I had followed his expressions of right-wing outrage against Barack Obama with curiosity on Facebook. Dan was not, on the surface, a racist. We played on the same integrated basketball team in middle school, and I had never heard him voice any racial animus toward our Black teammates. Why was he so mad?

Dan is, to paraphrase Arlie Russell Hochschild, a stranger in his own land. Or what he thought was his own land. He is told by Fox News, his buddies, and the president that it is not his land anymore. His nation has been taken over by Mexicans willing to work for a fraction of what he used to charge as a licensed AC repairman. He had to plunge himself into debt to start his own company, and now these "illegals" were going to get amnesty for breaking the law? Something needed to be done. Yes, he agreed with me, public schools were failing and something had to be done, but raising taxes would put his already small margins in jeopardy.

Okies (like pikers, hillbillies, and clay eaters before them) do not feel privileged, especially during a time of increasing inequality and a raging epidemic of opioid abuse. Mortality rates for Dan's social class (white males without a college degree) are increasing, even as they decrease for college-educated whites and minorities.[9] Over the past couple of years, Dan and I have seen many of our mutual acquaintances die deaths of despair in their thirties and forties. Two guys I remember as talented musicians shot themselves just as they seemed to be entering the steadiness of middle age. Another friend took too many prescription pills and wrapped his car around a telephone pole, possibly on purpose. Two others died from a combination of booze and pills. Where were the social justice warriors to advocate for these guys? Dan wanted to know.

Rather than rubes suffering from false consciousness, these "deplorables" are the natural product of political, educational, media, and religious structures that have cemented white supremacy, xenophobia, and anti-intellectualism into every aspect of life. I complained about Oklahoma's dubious distinction of coming in last in teacher pay. The modern education system was obsolete. "Cut teachers by 80 percent and have them learn online," he said. "The teachers are controlled by their union."

Dumb Okie, I thought. We finished our tacos and went our separate ways.

Bill Maher hinted at the resurgence of the Okie on *Real Time* shortly after the inauguration of Donald Trump in January of 2017. "Remember the country anthem from the hippie era that put the counterculture in its place?" Maher asked. "Merle Haggard. Okie from Muskogee? 'We don't smoke marijuana in Muskogee. We don't take our trips on LSD.' Yeah, today, Muskogee, population 38,000, has nine drug treatment centers. They should change the lyrics to: 'We don't share our needles in Muskogee. We don't mix our smack with PCP.'"[10]

For Maher, "the Okie" was useful shorthand for the uneducated working class: white trash. Maher likes to rile up progressives with his anti-religion rants that at times veer into Islamophobia and racism. But there was little backlash from liberals when the subject of his derision was Trump-voting white people. Maher's crowd hooted in approval when he rejected the idea of reaching out to this demographic. It was time, he said, to call them what they are: "fucking drug addicts." What sort of progressive was going to stick up for meth heads from Mobilehoma? Certainly none of my academic or journalist friends with their advanced degrees.

"Who's stoned all the time now? Not us," Maher continued. "We've moved on to kale smoothies and an occasional craft beer. Meanwhile, you've got meth mouth and are taking your dog's arthritis pills. Live free or die? More like press down and twist."

I am a huge Merle Haggard fan. I know Merle thought of the song as a parody of the "America First crowd" and openly smoked dope for years. Maher, of course, never entertained the idea that an Okie like Merle Haggard might have a sense of irony more subtle than his own. I happen to have fond memories of going back to Muskogee with my mom and grandma. But I have also been to Muskogee and seen the despair of the place up close. A few years ago, I took my wife there to try to find my grandfather's barbecue place. It was gone. In fact, most of the town seemed gone. Even the legendary Slick's barbecue place was no more. Downtown was mostly a ghost town; the action was out on an interstate access road lined with pawn shops, fast food restaurants, and used car lots. Maher was right on target about the town's drug problem, but that was not the whole story. It also has a high crime rate and a teenage pregnancy rate twice the national average. Its poverty rate is worse than Baltimore's.[11] But my Okie brethren were much more upset that Bill Maher had made fun of them than they were about the actual conditions in their state.

"Fuck that guy," an Oklahoman friend of mine said on Facebook. The *Tulsa World*, my hometown's local paper, ran a whole story on Maher's rant, which, predictably, elicited calls for a boycott of HBO. I sort of sympathized with the outraged Okies, not with their calls for a boycott but with the charge of a double standard when it came to punching down at working-class whites in the Heartland. But why was my reaction to Maher similar to the farmer's in *Chinatown*: get angry at the messenger rather than consider the veracity of his claims?

I realized it was Maher's rhetorical formulation of *not us* that disturbed me. As a liberal, cosmopolitan professor with an upper-middle-class lifestyle, I was part of Maher's *us*, sipping craft beer and eating kale in Canada, of all places. But I was also an Okie and, therefore, *not us*. As Roxanne Dunbar-Ortiz notes in *Red Dirt*, many white Oklahomans have suffered class prejudice along with a fear of being labeled *Indian*. Even if they did not experience it directly, most Okies know of the animosity and derision directed toward them in California during the Great Depression.

Being an Okie is not something I was ever taught to be proud of. And yet it is the closest thing I have to an ethnicity. My grandmother grew up in rural Oklahoma in a three-room cracker box with eight siblings and no running water. My mom remembers her mother frying up squirrel when money was tight. They picked collard greens—actually weeds on the side of the highway—for dinner. My grandmother, a woman who helped raise me, was disgusted with the relatives who abandoned the state for California during the Dust Bowl. Oklahoma was her home. She refused to leave, even to go bass fishing. My weekends with her were structured around Oklahoma Sooners football games, and I cried when they lost to the hated tea-sippers from Austin. She was, as my mom would say, *very country*.

In the Trump era, social and political issues pivot on questions of identity as much as they do on policy. My politics are decidedly left of center. My identity, however, is hopelessly bifurcated. And no matter how disgusted and appalled I am by my Trump-voting, climate-changing-denying, just-pray-on-it, hypocritical Okie brethren, some part of my core self is still with them. To turn my back completely on all the Okies in my life would mean denying an essential part of my identity. And not only my identity, but the identities of millions of people who still feel some connection to their Okie, Arkie, cracker, clay-eater, or hillbilly relatives. There are real grievances among the white working class, yes, but they are enmeshed and entangled with a history of racism and class prejudice. That is what makes this subject so difficult to talk about. Disentangling the contradictions of white privilege, class prejudice, racism, and evangelical Christianity cannot be done in a Tweetstorm or an angry blog post. Understanding these contradictions, while coming to terms with what Chenjerai Kumanyika called the "false promise of white supremacy," should be where our efforts lie, not in demonizing people from Flyover Country.

Every Okie, if they bother to do a cursory look into history, realizes their state is founded on a massive swindle. Broken treaties with Native American tribes led to the state's first large-scale settlement. Then came more broken treaties, legalized fraud, lynchings, widespread theft, and ethnic cleansing in Black townships, culminating in the Tulsa Race Massacre of 1921. The sheer scale of what happened in Tulsa in 1921 puts it on par with acts of ethnic cleansing in the former Yugoslavia, with untold scores dead, and an entire district burned to the ground. Then came generations of silence about the event. No one wanted to talk about this and many other dark chapters in our local history. Any mention of it was erased from school textbooks. Change the conversation. Blame the Other. When all else fails, turn to God. "Don't forget the pulpit," said one corrections officer when I told him I was writing a book about the dismal state of affairs. "You can't account for the particularity of Oklahoma without the church."

The evangelical movement normalizes injustice by substituting a hyperindividualism for the social gospel that once guided Heartland socialism. *If things seem messed up, well, that's just God's plan.* When pressed on the hard science that demonstrates that carbon emissions from human activity are causing climate change, Senator Jim Inhofe has said it is all the work of God. When a collapse in global oil prices triggered a budget crisis in Oklahoma, Governor Mary Fallin called for a statewide day of prayer for the oil patch. This is the core of the Great Oklahoma Swindle: rationalize profit-taking as divine right and tell losers in the equations that it is their own fault. It is maddening to watch this swindle drive Oklahoma to the very bottom of almost every measurable social indicator, yet a relief to see that Okies have started to see through it.

How did we get here in the first place? The much-overlooked historian Angie Debo wrote that historical processes of colonization, treaty abrogation, and industrialization that took place in the United States over two hundred years took place in Oklahoma in a few years before and after the turn of the twentieth century. The fact that everything happened in a short time span meant that history has seemed unimportant to a lot of Oklahomans. We either glorify our history along the lines of *Oklahoma!*, where there's "plenty of hope and plenty of room to swing a rope," or we look away entirely.

Sometimes I feel like Oklahoma is one big Dementiatown, suffering from some cerebral disease that is impeding blood flow to the brain. The steeper the declines in education spending, healthcare outcomes, and criminal justice, the more blame is placed on immigrants and the liberal media. The worse things get, the worse we sabotage ourselves. These problems, however, are symptoms of a history with roots in slavery and colonialism. It is not a simple story, and teasing out the hidden histories and contradictions of Oklahoma without losing my own mind has been my labor here. In the words of Woody Guthrie, "Take it easy, but take it."

CHAPTER 2

You're Not Doing Fine, Oklahoma

A third-grade teacher panhandles on the side of a highway for money to buy essential school supplies. Four straight years of budget cuts have pushed her to the brink of quitting. Entire school districts resort to four-day school weeks. A teacher exodus begins.[1]

A paralyzed and mentally ill veteran is left on the floor of a county jail. Guards watch for three days until the inmate dies, turning a medical cell into what a judge calls "a burial crypt." A death row inmate violently convulses on the gurney as prison officials experiment with an untested cocktail for execution. Prisons operate at 115 percent capacity.

Wildfires burn out of control. Cuts to forestry services mean that out-of-state fire-fighting crews must be called in. More than a dozen state parks are set be closed. A highway patrol chief announces a potential "public safety crisis" due to "sinister" budget cuts.

A city overpass crumbles, and swarms of earthquakes shake a region of gentle rolling hills and tallgrass prairie in the middle of the North American continent.

Even before Donald Trump assumed the presidency, the United States had its own failing state: Oklahoma.

Given the mess in which the state found itself after a whole decade of tax cuts failed to materialize into added state revenue, Oklahoma should have been an object lesson in trickle-down economics. But no. Other oil-rich states, including North Dakota, took their cues from Oklahoma in cutting gross production taxes for oil and gas producers. Governor Sam Brownback of Kansas employed an Oklahoma-style conservative revolution that blew up in his face. Yet tax cuts have been the signature "success" of the Republican Party since the election of Donald Trump. Tax cuts are the one issue that has united conservatives on the national stage.

"The state is dying a death of a thousand cuts," Oklahoma Policy Institute Director David Blatt told me. In the middle of 2017, the state was in the middle of a perfect storm: declining revenues from oil and gas, tax cuts, and a politically charged evangelical movement that justified it all as God's plan. Donald Trump tapped the state for national posts. Attorney General Scott Pruitt took his imperious disregard for regulation to his new position at the head of the Environmental Protection Agency. Governor Mary Fallin was on Trump's transition team. Another climate-change-denying Okie, Jim Bridenstine, became NASA's top administrator.[2] Oklahoma, in other words, seemed to be the canary in the coal mine of American democracy on full-tilt neoliberal policies with an evangelical bent.

It would seem Republicans had a political mandate to continue the neoliberal revolution. Trump won by a landslide in the state. Republicans held all statewide elected offices and super-majorities in both houses of the state legislature . The state has been used as a sandbox to test conservative policies—harsh anti-immigrant laws, health spending cuts—without facing any blowback. But while Oklahoma may look like just another red state from the outside, a closer look reveals a much more complicated picture. Since 2016 special elections have swung toward Democrats. A teacher walkout in 2018 was immensely popular and led to the first pay raise for teachers in over a decade. A referendum on medical marijuana was opposed by all the major Republican politicians in the state, as well as the oil and gas industry, but it passed by thirteen points. Mary Fallin's hand-picked successor for the governor's mansion came in third in the Republican primary. Fallin was dead last in a 2018 poll ranking the popularity of the nation's governors.

The issue was not, as some coastal liberal pundits would have it, that the middle of America was a brainwashed dead zone of Christian nationalists. By the end of 2018, it had become clear that the issue was civic engagement. In 2016 WalletHub used a variety of metrics, from voter participation to total political contributions, to measure the most politically engaged states. Oklahoma, all too commonly, came in dead last.[3] In 2018 all that changed as a record number of incumbents lost elections, many of them to public school teachers. The canary in the coal mine was still fluttering its wings.

When Okies first started grumbling about the decline in public health, infrastructure, and education, there was the usual "concern" voiced from the political class. Alas, there was no money. Except that there *was* money. There was a lot of money in this oil-rich state, which sits atop one of the largest shale reservoirs in North America. Oil is the substance that created modern Oklahoma at the beginning of the twentieth century. Despite rhetoric about diversification, oil is still the driver of the state's political culture. One in six jobs in Oklahoma is tied to the oil and gas industry, and that industry comes with a powerful lobby that has driven production taxes down to the lowest in the nation.

In the fall of 2016, faced with a scenario darker than a Depression-era dust storm, Governor Mary Fallin knew she had to do something. So she called for the state to pray. More specifically, she called on Christians to gather on October 13, 2016, for Oilfield Prayer Day to ask God for the price of oil to go up. But prayer day did not go according to plan. The official proclamation had to be hastily rewritten to include "people of all faiths," not just Christians, the price of oil did not budge, and the earthquakes continued, including one that hit the town of Cherokee shortly after a prayer day breakfast.

Years of tax cuts and budget shortfalls meant that Oklahoma had fallen to forty-ninth in teacher pay by 2017. Spending per pupil decreased by

23.6 percent from 2008 to 2018. The state led the nation in spending cuts to education for four years in a row. Entry-level employees with a high school diploma at the popular convenience store QuikTrip make more than teachers.

Oklahoma was becoming a national embarrassment. This deep red state has—paradoxically—one of the most progressive constitutions in the union, which allows for popular initiatives and referenda to be voted on directly. Okies channeled their progressive origins and put an initiative on the fall 2016 ballot to turn the tide. State Question 779 would have amended the state's constitution to hike the sales tax by 1 percent to pay for teacher pay raises, early childhood education, and programs to improve literacy and high school graduation rates.

The initiative was defeated by almost twenty points. Liberals did not like the regressive nature of the sales tax. Conservatives were allergic to any tax hike—as they are everywhere—and some said the state's low cost of living meant that teachers should not expect to be paid as much as they were in Arkansas or Texas. Still, many expected approval of SQ 779. "People told me they would vote for it," Lisa Newman, a high school teacher from El Reno, told me. "But there was some money in there for higher education, so I think some of my colleagues voted against it." Newman's voice quavered as she recounted a history of cutbacks to planning periods, increases in class sizes, and a stagnant salary since she started teaching. She moved back into her parents' house and, at age thirty-nine, contemplated a declining standard of living while she raised two boys and works around fifty hours a week. "It's completely demoralizing. I don't know what it's going to take for people to pay attention to what's happening to this state."

Shelby Eagan, Mitchell Elementary School's 2016 Teacher of the Year, decided she had had enough after SQ 779 was defeated. "I would like to have kids someday," she said. "I can't imagine a future in a state with no money for education. My rent has gone up. The cost of living has gone up. I have to buy my own supplies for the classroom."

Eagan is originally from Kansas City, but she loves Oklahoma. She came to Tulsa on a Teach for America program hoping to find work as a high school history teacher but found her calling teaching in an urban elementary school. It was not so much a job as an all-encompassing call to service. Eagan taught kids "how to tie their shoes, blow their nose." She fell in love: "The kids are innocent, sweet, and hilarious. Their jokes kept me going." Eagan is politically active, whip smart, passionate. She spent her free time mentoring after-school dance programs, although many of her colleagues work second and third jobs.

One hundred percent of Mitchell Elementary's students were on free or reduced-fee lunch programs. Many students had only one pair of pants. Eagan often went to Walmart on the weekend to buy extra pairs of pants for her students. She knew she could not last unless something drastic was done to save public education in Oklahoma.

Mitchell Elementary sat in a low-slung neighborhood of taco trucks, dollar stores, and weedy used car lots in northeast Tulsa. Around 60 percent of the school was Latino, with the rest of the population divided among African Americans, whites, and Native Americans. Mitchell was down to two buses for 540 children in 2016. To accommodate the overcrowding, children had to be placed three in a row on benches designed for two students. Eagan told me that the decline in funding was accompanied by a test-obsessed curriculum and a basic mistrust of teachers.

"We joke that we're stuck in a McClassroom," she said. Eagan is the kind of teacher administrators should be pushing hard to keep in the district, but "they don't care. There's a basic disrespect for teachers here."

So, after fall of 2016, Eagan decided to look elsewhere for a better gig. According to friends back in Kansas City, teachers there had vision and dental insurance, an employee-match pension program, and access to new fitness centers. Eagan found a job in the area that would increase her salary by $10,000 right off the bat. "I hope it gets better in Oklahoma," she said. "The children deserve better. But I can't keep putting my own needs in second place forever."

Oklahoma Policy Institute researcher Carly Putnam told me that everyone in the state knows how dire the education situation is. Things got so bad that the Cherokee Nation, a tribe systematically cheated out of its land allotments in the creation of the modern state of Oklahoma, donated $5 million to the state's education fund. Although education may be the most glaring failure of governance, Putnam said it was only part of the picture: "Our system has atrophied to the point that it's hard to know where to begin to build it back up."

Putnam cited the example of a popular support program for developmental disabilities. It takes ten years just to get on a waiting list to be considered for the support waiver to help a disabled person; Oklahoma Health and Human Services is now considering applications filed in 2008. Pay rates for providers have been slashed, leading many health insurance providers to pull out of the state. The state is down to three inspectors for all of the state's nursing homes and as many as one-quarter of nursing homes have closed since 2000. Many of the disabled are already dead by the time HHS starts to consider their file. Oklahoma experienced the slowest growth in life expectancy of any state from 1980 to 2014.[4] In one county, life expectancy has actually declined. The town of Stilwell has a life expectancy of 56.3 years, similar to that of the Congo. "Mental health, education, criminal justice, it's all tied together," Shelby Eagan said.

Eagan told me about a bipolar student at Mitchell who was nearly arrested and expelled. "He's my little baby. Well, he's thirteen now, not my baby anymore. No one had the training to deal with his manic or depressive days. One day, another student kicked him in the head during a manic day. Then he told my student he was going to lie to the teacher about what happened if he told."

This triggered something in Eagan's student, who punched the offending student. He was taken to the principal, and Tulsa police were called. Administrators decided to expel the student and charge him with assault. "I went on a tirade," Eagan said. "We don't fund mental health issues. And now we're going to give a fourth grader a criminal record?"

Eagan argued with administrators. They watched a tape of the incident, and she convinced them that suspension was sufficient. "But what if I hadn't been there? The school-to-prison pipeline. It weighs on my conscience."

FAILING STATE IN THE HEARTLAND

In a much-cited essay, the legal scholar Rosa Brooks wrote that failing states are characterized, above all, by a breakdown in the social contract. It is difficult to mark the exact point at which a political entity can be said to be "failing," but Brooks highlights a few commonalities across the globe. Failing states, she writes, "lose control over the means of violence, and cannot create peace or stability for their populations or control their territories. They cannot ensure economic growth or any reasonable distribution of social goods. They are often characterized by massive economic inequities, warlordism, and violent competition for resources."[5]

"If you call the police in Tulsa, they still come," David Blatt told me. "The trash still gets picked up. We're not Somalia or Haiti. Yet." Blatt is not the kind of guy prone to ideological hyperbole. He is studious, quiet, diminutive, and as the executive director of Oklahoma's only liberal think tank, Oklahoma Policy Institute, he has to pick his battles.

"Our unofficial motto is 'it could've been worse,'" Blatt said. He is happy to work with Republicans and spends a good deal of time trying to talk sense with anyone who will listen at the state legislature. Blatt also holds a PhD in political science from Cornell, so he is careful with terms like *failing state*. It is one matter to keep students home because of budget shortfalls, but it is quite another to have students stay home because of roving bands of warlords.

Looking at the situation as a social scientist, though, myriad data points suggest something has gone horribly wrong. Not only does Oklahoma lead the nation in cuts to education, but its rates of incarceration recently resulted in its designation as the "the world's prison capital." Oklahoma's incarceration rates outstrip authoritarian states like Cuba, Iran, and China by a longshot. Proportionally, Oklahoma imprisons five times as many people as Honduras, the world's murder capital.[6]

Measures to reform the criminal justice system are popular across the political system, but an entrenched law enforcement establishment of DAs, sheriffs, and police departments, have old school notions about law and order. Furthermore, many of the police departments fund themselves from civil forfeiture and fines, as state funding declines. Even the most reform-minded counties need to collect more in fines as state revenue decreases. OK Policy Institute has tracked rising amounts of court debt from 2011 to the present. A vicious cycle of unpayable fees leads to more fees, more debt, and much of it goes unpaid, leading to bad outcomes for citizens and departments. Blatt said that the confluence of mass incarcerations, police corruption scandals, education cutbacks, and denialism about the role of fracking in earthquake swarms sets Oklahoma apart. Put all of it together, and "you see a state that has failed at some fundamental level of governance."

People like to think of public policy in terms of discrete "issues": education, health care, mental health, criminal justice. But in a failing state, it becomes clear that social justice cannot be achieved without a comprehensive understanding of how all these things fit together. The case of Elliott Williams provides a case in point. Williams's lawyer, Bob Blakemore, told me that what should have been a mental health case ended up becoming a tragedy that revealed a shocking indifference to basic human decency in the Tulsa County Jail. Williams had been honorably discharged from the army but suffered from a diagnosed bipolar condition. After a few nights of insomnia at his parents' house in Owasso, he checked himself in at a hotel.

Williams threw a soda can in the lobby and walked into a door. Hotel staff called police. An officer who arrived at the scene found Williams "rambling on about God and eating dirt." The officer and the staff concluded that Williams was suffering from "some kind of mental breakdown." Rather than press charges, they decided to escort him out of the hotel and call his parents. At some point, while outside the hotel, Williams threatened to kill himself. A cop ordered him to stay seated on a curb. Williams got up and moved toward a police officer who pepper-sprayed him.

Williams was arrested. The small-town jail of Owasso was not equipped to deal with a case like Williams's. Rather than find a suitable mental health facility, the Owasso police sent Williams to Tulsa County Jail. It was Williams's bad luck to be transferred to a jail that only weeks before had been diagnosed with "a prevailing attitude of indifference." In the midst a total psychotic breakdown, Williams was body-slammed by an officer. He was transferred to a holding cell where he rammed his head against a wall, leaving him paralyzed.

The head nurse told him to "quit fucking faking." He defecated on himself and officers dragged him to a shower. He still did not move. To prove that he was faking, an officer put a small cup of water just outside Williams' grasp. He never reached it.

Williams was left in a medical cell for three days, where a video camera recorded him unable to move below the waist. Five days after he was put in the Tulsa County Jail, Williams was dead of complications from a broken neck and serious dehydration.

The jail was run by Sheriff Stanley Glanz, who would later become infamous as the man who assigned Bob Bates, a fishing buddy and insurance adjuster with no police training, to a violent crimes task force. Bates, it was revealed later, wanted in on some police action. In a confrontation with a suspected arms dealer, Bates reached for his Taser. He accidentally grabbed his pistol and shot and killed the suspect.

"Sorry," Bates said as the man died.

The rampant corruption and misuse of violence continued, even as lawsuits against Bates and Glanz piled up. Glanz was eventually forced out, but an even more shocking Tulsa police killing made the news after he resigned. In September 2016, officer Betty Jo Shelby shot and killed Terence Crutcher. Body cam footage showed Shelby shoot an unarmed Black man with his hands in the air as he walked back to his car. Shelby was later acquitted of a manslaughter charge. State actors, including police officers and jail officials, turned to violence as a means of social control, even as white, affluent citizens remained oblivious to the breakdown in public safety.

Loss of control over the means of violence. Check.

Shane Matson is a geologist whose family has been in the Oklahoma oil business for three generations. He gets downright giddy when talking about minerals and topography. He is an industry man. It is in his blood. He challenged Obama regulations on drilling in Osage County and remains optimistic about his industry in creating prosperity. Matson is appalled, however, by the state's mishandling of its reserves. "We let three companies in Oklahoma City dictate to the state," he said. Chesapeake, Devon, and Continental have pushed to lower the state's gross production tax from an already low 5 percent to 2 percent in 2014. As the budget crisis reached a fever pitch in 2018, Continental CEO Harold Hamm blamed subsidies for the wind industry, rather than record low gross production taxes on oil and gas, for Oklahoma's problems. Donald Trump tapped Hamm to be a special adviser on energy.

Matson saw the whole situation as reckless. "We've cheapened ourselves to the point where we might as well be Haiti cutting down our last forest to sell charcoal to the Dominican Republic," he said. "We are sitting on the best rock [geologist slang for oil-rich shale] in North America," Matson says. The biggest plays in horizontal drilling in North America right now are known as SCOOP and STACK—both in Oklahoma. "We are a resource-rich state. We ought to be treating this latest boom like it's going to be our last. Because this is it."

Risk-takers occasionally win big in Oklahoma. From the first wildcatters to Harold Hamm and Aubrey McClendon, there are many colorful characters who have staked it all on oil and struck it rich. Chesapeake Energy cofounder McClendon gambled on horizontal drilling when the technology was in its infancy and eventually grew his company to become the second-largest natural gas producer in the country after ExxonMobil. At the pinnacle of his career in 2012, *Marketplace* reporter Scott Tong found out that, in Oklahoma City, "if you don't like [McClendon], you'll have to whisper."

In early 2016 McClendon was indicted for violating antitrust laws. The Justice Department mounted evidence that Chesapeake orchestrated price-fixing schemes, cutting out any open competitive bidding with landowners. On March 2, 2016, the day after a federal grand jury announced its indictment of McClendon, OKC's most famous billionaire, drove his car seventy-eight miles per hour into a bridge and died instantly. In an effort to raise money to finance the hundreds of millions of dollars in claims against his estate, his wine collection was sold at auction for $8.4 million. Scholars have shown that development of oil leads directly to increased levels of violence, more social inequality, and less democratic governance.[7]

Violent competition for resources. Check.

I can hear the voices now. They are sitting courtside at Chesapeake Arena for an Oklahoma City Thunder basketball game. They are shopping and dining at Tulsa's newly resurgent downtown. Picking up their kids from a handsome college prep high school on the way to Whole Foods. *Failed state?!* they are scoffing at me. We have never had it so good. Central Oklahoma City and Tulsa are thriving after decades of neglect. Tulsa is a beautiful city of rolling hills, parks, and delicious barbecue. And to be sure, Oklahoma's cheap housing and wide-open western mentality encourages risk-takers of all sorts. Hipsters priced out of Portland and Austin have relocated to Tulsa and started high-end breweries and T-shirt shops.

Chad Warmington, the president of the Oklahoma Oil and Gas Association, stated that about 25 percent of the state's tax revenue comes from oil and gas while the industry employs about 13 percent of the state's workforce. Dependence on taxes from oil and gas "has left the state unprepared for inevitable price downturns of a cyclical industry," Warmington said in an email. The current downturn, then, "has led many to question the state's management of the tax dollar."

I ran my failing-state hypothesis by all the conservatives who would talk to me. "Hysterical and overwrought" was one response. Other people thought Oklahoma had not gone far enough, that more school choice, more tax breaks, more privatization would eventually create efficiency. For all its political foibles, the Oklahoma economy is doing fine—as the old song goes—and people continue to move here to reinvent themselves in a low-cost, business-friendly environment. And for those with means, the failures are hardly visible.

Tulsa People, a lifestyle magazine, features an extensive rundown of the city's excellent private schools. Truth be told, I attended one with a generous financial aid package. Cascia Hall Preparatory School boasted a 100 percent rate of graduates continuing on to college. Tulsa Community Foundation is just behind Silicon Valley Community Foundation as the richest community foundation in the nation. Okies can be generous people.

For those with the means, the multiple social ills in Oklahoma can be rendered invisible by a bubble of affluence. Some school districts are flourishing. Union High School, in suburban Tulsa, has its own planetarium. Mall parking lots are chocked full of new Lexuses, Audis, BMWs, many of them driven by teenagers. You could spend an entire life in a bubble of top-notch private schools, elegant neighborhoods, and PGA-rated country clubs and never feel the impact of the petro-Christian hegemony over the political structure of the state. Go from your four-thousand-square-foot home to your megachurch to the high school football game in a state-of-the-art new stadium, and Oklahoma seems to be working just fine, thank you very much. As a cousin confided in me recently, "I realized I never got outside my bubble growing up in Tulsa. Once you're outside, it's a whole different world."

The Oklahoma Policy Institute calculates that the current regime of tax breaks and refunds costs around half a billion dollars in decreased revenue every year. That figure, if correct, would cover the current $220 million budget gap in education but would still not be enough to make up for the state's entire budget shortfall in 2018. There is an eleven-year difference in life expectancy between Tulsa's richest and poorest zip codes. That poorest zip code—74126—has a life expectancy comparable to that of North Korea.[8]

They are often characterized by massive economic inequities. Check.

POLITICS BEYOND PARTY

When I was in elementary school, I remember seeing my mother struggle with hundreds of thousands of dollars of unpaid medical bills after my dad died of heart disease. She was suddenly a single mother with an incomplete college education, no professional training, and a mountain of debt. We depended on the generosity of friends and family to get by. When I asked her why she never went on welfare or food stamps while she worked as a daycare teacher and raised me, she laughed. "Welfare is for poor people," she said. "We weren't them."

Antigovernment ideology is so rooted into the consciousness here, it does not even register as ideology. Everyone I talked to for this story—lawyers, teachers, small business people—seemed so frustrated with the death spiral of basic social services that they were reticent to talk about any silver linings. I do not blame them. There is something so deeply ingrained and unyielding in the state's conservatism, it defies any logical explanation.

And yet Oklahomans have also demonstrated a willingness to buck ideology and take on reform. In fall 2016 Oklahomans approved State Question 780, which reclassified certain small-possession drug crimes from felonies to misdemeanors. Another state question would have amended the state constitution to prohibit any laws against agribusiness. A coalition of small farmers, Native American tribes, and animal rights groups came together to defeat the bill. David Blatt says there is still a strain of Heartland populism that is skeptical of Big Agra's attempt to rewrite the state's constitution. Another referendum authorizing public money for religious purposes was also defeated. In the end, Oklahomans voted against three referenda in the conservative mold by a surprisingly large margin.

Republicans wasted no time in mounting a challenge. Senator Ralph Shortey proposed a bill that would have essentially reversed most of the reforms passed by referendum. Voters, Shortey said, did not understand what they were voting for. Weeks after introducing his bill, Shortey was arrested at an OKC hotel for soliciting sex with a teenage boy and smoking marijuana. Cases like Ralph Shortey's reinforce a certain strain of cynicism about public affairs. Turnout in the 2014 gubernatorial election was the lowest ever recorded. Trump's vaunted drubbing of Hillary in 2016 meant little in terms of actual votes cast: in 2008 John McCain earned more votes than Trump in Oklahoma. Despite the outcry from highway patrol officers to teachers, Fallin pushed for even more tax cuts in the 2017 budget. The lack of a viable opposition meant that she did not need an official prayer day to get it done. As the state faced a $800 million budget shortfall, the Senate managed to push through a bill that decriminalized the seduction of virgins with promises of marriage.

Oklahoma declared a revenue failure in 2017 for the second year in a row. "Our situation is dire," Oklahoma finance director Preston Doer-flinger said at the time. "To use a pretty harsh word, our revenues are difficult at best. Maybe they fall into the category of somewhat pathetic."

Dumb Okie logic called for prayer. After the governor issued her Oil-field Prayer Day proclamation, people gathered in churches, hoping for a little divine intervention targeting worldwide falling oil prices. Prayer day came and went, and the price of oil barely budged. Three weeks after prayer day, however, the earth shook. A 5.0 magnitude earthquake hit the town of Cushing, the "Pipeline Crossroads of the World."

Maybe God had something to say about Oklahoma after all.

CHAPTER 3

The Road to Hell in Indian Territory

A forced marriage consummated in oil created the state of Oklahoma in 1907. The highly symbolic event doubled as a political reality. Oklahomans restage the event every so often. One particularly meticulous recreation was staged in the town of Guthrie in 2007. State officials restaged the wedding on the steps of the Carnegie Library. The bride, Miss Indian Territory, was given away to the groom, Mr. Oklahoma Territory. The original wedding marked the merger of the two territories into the nation's forty-sixth state. Governor Frank Keating, church leaders, and tens of thousands of Oklahomans turned out for the event in Guthrie. The *Daily Oklahoman* noted, without irony, that the event would replicate—down to the hand-set type on the program—the original festivities in which William Durant, a Choctaw legislator, "acted as the father of the bride and gave Miss Indian Territory away."[1]

In the original ceremony, Durant praised Miss Indian Territory as a "beauteous maiden" who is nevertheless "an orphan." Her dowry, Durant said, would be the "fertile fields" and "productive mines" of the land. The symbolism of the reenactment is not lost on Native American activists, who see the wedding as an act of cultural genocide. Celebrating this political nail in the coffin of tribal sovereignty was, in the words of Comanche activist Gerald D. Tieya, like asking Jews to celebrate Kristallnacht.[2] That modern-day Oklahoma replicates the original forced wedding without so much as an acknowledgment of the devastation to Native American lands and culture says a lot about the way the state's history is enacted. But it hides a more interesting story of hybrid cultures that is only now becoming visible to the white mainstream. Honoré de Balzac could have been speaking about the rise of the oil industry in Oklahoma when he wrote that "the secret of unexplained grand fortunes is a forgotten crime."

Indian Territory was one of the most linguistically and culturally diverse regions in the Americas before the land runs of the end of the nineteenth century. Thirty-nine nations with their own languages, cultures, and governmental institutions were relocated to Oklahoma. Not only the Five Tribes from the Southeast but nomadic Plains nations from the West and other tribes from the Midwest were all forcibly relocated with the promise that the land would be theirs without white encroachment. More languages were spoken in Indian Territory than in all of Europe. Many of the tribes were mixed race, intermarried with whites and African Americans. Black settlers poured into Indian Territory looking for a new promised land. White marauders took shelter in caves and sometimes intermarried with Native Americans. Some took sides with the Confederacy, others with the Union. Some held out for an all-Native American state. Still others entertained notions of the place as a Black homeland for freed slaves and their descendants. Wild and wooly, with dozens of hybrid cultures and languages uneasily coexisting next to the United States, the Oklahoma and Indian Territories were more akin to territories like Puerto Rico and Cuba than the American mainstream (as a side note, I think Oklahoma could really outdo its rival Texas by starting a Forty-Two Flags Over Oklahoma theme park).

In just a few short decades, however, Native Americans in Oklahoma lost around 90 percent of their land. Languages went extinct.

Protestant Christianity was imposed at Indian boarding schools where children were taken away from their parents to "kill the Indian and save the man." Contrary to what prevails in the popular imagination, Native Americans in Oklahoma did not lose their land in shootouts with cowboys in the Old West. They did not sell off their land and live high on the hog (with a few notable exceptions, which we will examine later). They were not confined to reservations in some forgotten corner. The foundation of Oklahoma was, in the words of one historian, "a perfectly legal invasion."

Despite the cultural genocide of Oklahoma's early years, the state still has the largest Native American population of any state outside California.[3] What happened in Oklahoma was nothing short of a legalized swindle that played out in boardrooms and courtrooms. Oil was—and is—the catalyst for it all. The courtroom is not the sort of setting that makes for a sexy Western, but it is starting to filter up into the national consciousness. David Grann, in *Killers of the Flower Moon*, documents how white businessmen sought to obtain title to Osage Indian land through marriage and other legal means in the 1920s. When that did not work, they resorted to violence, killing dozens of Osage in order to obtain oil leases. This period—known as the Osage Reign of Terror—needless to say was not a unit in state-mandated Oklahoma history courses.

Much of the promotional material for *Killers of the Flower Moon* revolves around the claim that in the 1920s, the wealthiest people per capita in the entire world were the Osage of northern Oklahoma. It is hard to fact-check such a statement and perhaps beside the point, since the mythology of illiterate and simple Native Americans suddenly living like royalty through pure dumb luck was already firmly ensconced in the American imagination. Hollywood picked up on journalistic accounts of Native Americans who just happened to be sitting on a fortune of black gold. Stories about Jackson Barnett, "the world's richest Indian," often came with a moral smugness and judgment about wealthy indigenous men who squandered their riches by drinking too much or buying all the wrong investments. While Grann tries to maintain a critical distance from the "rich Indian" trope, publishers have found it hard to resist. The supposed squandering of oil wealth suggests that maybe Natives did not deserve it in the first place.

Oklahoma is an American anomaly. Whereas other states were settled by white people who forced out indigenous people, the state was largely settled by tribes from elsewhere, some of whom owned slaves and adopted many European customs. The slaves then became part of the tribes, who intermarried and formed their own cultural practices. The discovery of oil, however, gave another twist to this American anomaly, injecting the place with white settlers of every regional background and religious persuasion: Italian coal miners, Jewish drygoods merchants, southern sharecroppers, and Pennsylvania oil men all flooded into the new state looking for a piece of one of the only noncolonized territories left in the continental United States.

Since the discovery of oil in Oklahoma at the turn of the twentieth century, Christian white men have seen it as not only their right but their divine duty to extract and sell as much oil as possible. Before he was ousted as EPA chief, Tulsan Scott Pruitt gave an interview to the Christian Broadcasting Network in which he said that oil was God's blessing: "The biblical world view with respect to these issues is that we have a responsibility to manage and cultivate, harvest the natural resources that we've been blessed with to truly bless our fellow mankind."[4] Governor Fallin's Oilfield Pray Day echoed the sentiment. Petroleum manifested God's blessing on Oklahoma. The proclamation asked Okies to "seek His wisdom" while praying for the price of oil to rise.[5] Although Fallin backtracked on the specific references to a Christian God, the message was clear: the citizens of Oklahoma should thank the patriarchal God—Him—of the Christian Bible for the geological patterns of dead organisms in the midcontinental substrata. Oil men have wedded petro-Christian theology to capitalism and Manifest Destiny. Not only did God bless humanity with petroleum products, but He (sic) anointed white men to seize the land from others, extract it, commodify it, and keep the proceeds for themselves. Jerald C. Walker, a Cherokee historian who was also a Methodist minister and university president, encapsulated this imperialistic rationale in an essay titled "The Difficulty of Celebrating an Invasion." Walker summed up

1. The Golden Driller's inscription is dedicated "to the men of the petroleum industry who by their vision and daring have created from God's abundance a better life for mankind." Photo by the author.

the petro-Christian logic: "The invaders (the Sooners) had a mandate, yes, and an overriding moral responsibility to foster private ownership of the land controlled by Indian peoples, and, in the process, to fully develop the agricultural and commercial potential of what would become Oklahoma."[6]

This ideology is now so ubiquitous that it registers as common sense in the state. But a look at other jurisdictions—even ones as culturally similar as Canada—reveals the particular form of capitalism at the heart of the petro-Christian project in Oklahoma. In places such as Canada and Norway, mineral rights are generally not owned by individuals. With some exceptions, publicly held lands and their minerals cannot be alienated to individuals; they are held for the public good.

Even though Oklahoma started to diversify away from overreliance on oil since the collapse of the industry in the 1980s, the oil industry is still a sacrosanct institution that Okies rarely question. *Tulsa, the Oil Capital of the World.* Tulsa is a place where the fourth-tallest statue in the United States—known as the Golden Driller—pays tribute to "men of the petroleum industry who by their vision and daring have created from God's abundance a better life for mankind," as stated on a plaque at the base of the oil derrick.

There is another oil derrick on the grounds of the state capitol in Oklahoma City, nicknamed Petunia No. 1. It was drilled into a bed of flowers in the 1930s and for many years towered over the capitol building until the state put a dome on the building in 2002. If Oklahoma is the product of a forced marriage brought into existence through the imposition of Christian and white supremacist doctrine, oil is the dowry seized by the patriarch. Ms. Indian Territory has not been an equal partner in her matrimony to Mr. Oklahoma.[7]

The capitalist divine right to oil is echoed in the words of Senator James Inhofe (former mayor of Tulsa), the infamous climate change denier who once threw a snowball in Congress, urging President Obama to catch it. Inhofe does not simply argue for continued oil exploration and extraction on economic terms; for him, it is a matter of divine right. Oil is "God's abundance," proof that He has blessed this land with riches,

Inhofe has said. In his book on climate change, *The Greatest Hoax*, Inhofe (who usually refrains from citing scripture in debates) describes a Christian God as the ultimate backstop against any negative consequences from burning fossil fuels. "God is still up there," Inhofe writes, "and He promised to maintain the seasons and that cold and heat would never cease as long as the earth remains." Oil is a cornerstone of Oklahoma's identity, anchored down in Protestant Christian theology. An oil rig is part of Tulsa's official seal, along with the date 1898.

What the talk about "blessings" and "God's gift" obscure, however, are the much more secular machinations by which the mineral rights to the land holding the oil passed from the communal property of sovereign Native American nations to the hands of a few men within the first twenty years of the twentieth century. What Angie Debo once deemed a "criminal conspiracy" on the part of Oklahoma politicians to transfer Native American land allotments to white oil men has been rewritten as divine providence or Manifest Destiny. The role of religion in papering over the violence of Native dispossession is something even someone as fearless as Debo did not touch.

How did we get here? And why has this foundational crime been forgotten? Tulsa's rise to prominence as the Oil Capital of the World reveals Oklahoma's particular unholy ruling alliance between the oil and gas industry, evangelical Christianity, and a reactionary wing of the Republican Party.

TULSA'S FORGOTTEN CREEK HERITAGE

Many towns in the old Creek Nation derive not from white settlers but from ancient tribal towns in the Southeast. Tulsa is one of those towns, even though the birth year on the city's seal is listed as 1898. Tulsa's deeper origins, however, had nothing to do with oil and everything to do with a frontier zone of indigenous, European, and African cultures. Tulsa's origins as a Mvskoke town in the Southeast are usually glossed over in one Oklahoma history lesson or a few pages of prologue. Recent work by historians and activists demonstrates, however, just how vital this early history is to how Tulsans became who we are.

In recent years, J. D. Colbert has been trying to awaken Tulsa to this deeper history. Colbert is a Muscogee (Creek) Native American who spent a career in banking before turning over his time to rediscovering the Creek roots of his hometown. He is struck by how little Tulsans know of the land they occupy. When I met him, Colbert told me that Tulsa's history began before the white man ever set foot in the Americas. I had to admit I was skeptical. Nothing in the history I learned in school predated 1898. I sought out Angie Debo's long-out-of-print *Tulsa: From Creek Town to Oil Capital.* What I read in it contradicted everything I had learned in school about the Magic City, everything inscribed on plaques and on the walls of museums. The first written chronicle of Tulsa dates back to 1540, when one of Hernando de Soto's men sat down to document its importance in the Creek Confederation. De Soto's chronicle turned the traditional name Tvlahasse (or Tullahassee) into Tallise, which Debo posits as a Spanish transliteration of the Creek shortened form, Tallasi.[8] In any case, Tulsa's original name derived from the Creek words *etvlwv* (town) and *ahassee* (something old). This means that in 1540, Creeks already considered Tulsa an "old town." De Soto wrote that "Tallise was large and was located near a deep river. On the other side of the river were other towns and many fields of maize. On both sides, it was a land very well supplied with maize in abundance."[9]

Creek towns in the ancestral homelands of the southeast were built uniformly, with individual houses built of sticks and clay, each with its own garden plot where the principal crops were corn, squash, beans, and tobacco (a form of farming similar to what was found in Mesoamerica in the *milpa*). The town would have had a main square for stick ball games, stomp dancing, and a roundhouse (*chokofa*) for town council meetings. Tallasi was a large town that may have held "imperial sway," in Debo's words. Like its modern equivalent in Oklahoma, the town's inhabitants dispersed from the main center to form smaller towns with names derived from a landscape feature or event connected to their founding. Tulsa, for example, has Sand Springs as a western neighbor and Broken Arrow to the east, monikers that testify to the naming patterns Creeks developed in the Southeast. Creeks had "mother towns" from which smaller towns formed. Rivalries and animosities existed as well, most principally between Upper and Lower Creek towns. Upper Creeks were known for their resistance to European culture, while Lower Creeks were ruled by intermarried Creek and European leaders who hybridized traditional Muscogee customs with Scottish, French, and Spanish ways. Another important division was between "white" and "red" towns, which had nothing to do with race but with their orientation toward peace or war (white towns were peaceful, red towns warlike).

At some point, a daughter city to Tallasi formed in Alabama, Locvpokv.[10] Locvpokv (also spelled Loachapoka) was an Upper Creek town that resisted white settler encroachment. The town grew rapidly, but it was situated at the northernmost boundary of the Creek Confederacy and was raided by white settlers in the Cumberland Valley after U.S. independence. The Tallasi-Locvpokv alliance was intended to form the bedrock of Creek resettlement in the Tulsa area, but the two towns, although sharing a common identity, did not always get along. Although they were mother-daughter towns, one was red and one was white, reflecting two different orientations toward conflict. This distinction further divided Creeks during the Red Stick War of 1813–14, when some sided with Andrew Jackson, and some sided with Shawnee leader Tecumseh, who fought to create a separate Native American nation under British protection. Creeks fought and negotiated with France, Spain, and the United States. They fought each other. They fought their neighbors, the Cherokees. Then, as white plantation society secured a hegemony in the U.S. South, Upper and Lower Creeks fought back. After two wars with the United States, the Creek Confederation finally relented to removal.

After losing around one-quarter of its population along the Trail of Tears, Tallasi-Locvpokv was reborn on a gentle bluff on the east side of the Arkansas River underneath a post oak tree in 1836. The ashes from a ceremonial fire, carried all the way from the ancestral home, were rekindled under the Council Oak tree. The name was difficult to pronounce for the white Indian agents, railroad builders, and outlaws who started filtering into the place, so it eventually became known as Tulsey Town, and then, finally, Tulsa.

Casting a shadow over the Council Oak tree, which still stands just south of downtown, is "the new roundhouse," as Colbert calls the University Club Tower. This new roundhouse is a Tulsa icon. For Colbert, the new roundhouse is a metaphor for Tulsa's Creek heritage in that it is hidden in plain sight.

The "official" date of the founding of Tulsa in 1898 also obscures the tragedy the town faced during the Civil War. When the war began, Confederates made promises to honor treaties broken by the Union. Southerners pointed to the cultural similarities between themselves and the Five Tribes, including slavery, overlooking key differences between plantation slavery and the practices of the Five Tribes. The Confederates said they would mend relations and keep promises that Washington had broken. As a result, many leaders from the Five Tribes sided with the Confederacy. Creek chief Opothleyahola urged his tribe to remain neutral, but backed into a corner, he remained loyal to the Union. For those Creeks with ties to the Old South, however, the Confederates' promises led them to commit to the lost cause. Creek Confederates, supported by Texas cavalry, attacked the Loyalists. Opothleyahola led civilians, traditionalists from various tribes, and some escaped slaves out of Tulsa and into battle with rebels north and west of the city. I was shocked to learn that at least one, if not two, Civil War battles took place in modern-day Tulsa County. Why was this never mentioned? Perhaps because the result of the conflict within the Creek Nation led to a humanitarian disaster known as the Trail of Blood on Ice. Tulsans do not like stories that contradict our image of a magic city blessed by God.

Opothleyahola led thousands of Creeks from Tulsa to Fort Row in Kansas, where they had been promised shelter, protection, and rations by Abraham Lincoln. The Union did almost nothing to support these Loyal Creeks, and they attacked repeatedly during their exodus to Kansas. Once they finally made it to Kansas, the fort was completely unprepared for the refugees. Thousands died from frostbite and starvation (including Opothleyahola), having staked their lives on the promises of the United States. Some residents of Tallasi-Locvpokv survived, including Tuckabache, who returned to his land just south and east of downtown Tulsa after the war.[11] The U.S. Civil War led to absolute destruction of the traditional town, which had been rebuilt from the model in Alabama. It was rebuilt, and Lower Creeks, led by Josiah Perryman, established a post office and trading outpost.

Then came the Dawes Commission, which aimed to assimilate Indians by teaching them English and instilling capitalist virtues. All members of the Five Tribes would receive an individual allotment of 160 acres of land in Indian Territory. The Five Tribes are often lumped together as a group of nations sharing a common history of displacement from the Deep South, journeying together along the Trail of Tears and settling in Oklahoma. Creeks, especially Upper Creeks, stood out among the other tribes as the least willing to go along with Washington's ideas for the future of Indian Territory. Even among the Creeks themselves, there were intense disagreements about slavery, Christianity, and removal. While other tribes reluctantly agreed to give up the communal nature of land ownership after the Civil War, many Creeks, under the leadership of Chitto Harjo (or Crazy Snake), refused. The Snake faction, as it was known, resisted the forced marriage until the bitter end.

Harjo had never been fond of the assimilationists. He saw the work of the Dawes Commission as a prelude to the devastation of the Creek Nation. Land ownership was anathema to traditionalist Creeks like Crazy Snake. After years of making concessions to the railroads and white settlers, Harjo had had enough. He fought off the assimilationists in a series of skirmishes around Okmulgee. As allotment proceeded and Oklahoma neared statehood, Harjo and his allies refused to back down. They were handed checks and titles for land. The checks were never cashed. Politicians in Washington simply could not understand.

On the eve of statehood in 1906, Chitto Harjo strode to the front of the Seaman Building in downtown Tulsa with an interpreter. Harjo made his most dramatic stand. In the company of U.S. senators and Oklahoma oil men crowded inside a meeting hall, Crazy Snake reminded everyone that the United States was still bound by a treaty. "As long as the sun shone and the sky is up yonder these agreements shall be kept," he said. "This was the first agreement that we had with the white man. He said as long as the sun rises it shall last; as long as the waters run it shall last; as long as the grass grows it shall last."[12]

Resistance to the dispossession of Creek lands was widespread after statehood as well. Even the *New York Times* weighed in on the issue. In 1909 the *Times* wrote dismissively of Harjo and his "murderous band . . . of half-breeds and lawless Negroes."[13] Harjo managed to elude arrest to the end, fighting off federal agents and white settlers until his death in 1915. Debo wrote that his rebellion "was the last flare of the Indian spirit in the white man's town of Tulsa."[14]

Debo, usually an astute observer of the subtle ways that Native culture thrives despite the odds, may have written the Creeks out of modern Tulsa prematurely. For the descendants of the Creeks who lost their lands in the early twentieth century, Native culture continued to echo through the town. According to Rob Trepp (a Muscogee descendant of the Perryman family), Creeks still held ceremonies near the Council Oak tree for many years, determined to keep Tulsa's roots alive. Sounds of Creek stomp dances and stickball games attracted hordes of white curiosity seekers well into statehood until finally the Creeks moved the stomp dance to a hidden location near their traditional capitol in Okmulgee. In recent years, Creeks have started coming back to Council Oak Park to stage stickball games and feasts. Trepp, until his death in late 2018, led tours of Creek sites around town. When we met at his forebears' ranch in Jenks in 2016, he was confident that a renaissance of Native culture would accompany Tulsa's rebirth in the twenty-first century. I hope his optimism bears out, but the continued silence of Tulsa's establishment about its Creek past does not give me hope. The case of Tuckabache is instructive in this regard.

Tuckabache, who had accompanied Opothleyahola during removal and the Trail of Blood on Ice, was allotted 160 prime acres just south of present-day downtown. He had mostly gone along with the dissolution of tribal government, granting an easement to a railroad through his land. Tuckabache lived in a cabin around the intersection of Hazel and Cincinnati, an area now graced by million-dollar homes (and one block away from my childhood home). Whites moved in, buying up his surplus land around his homestead in the early years of the twentieth century. He watched his way of life disappear and came to resent the railroad, calling the granting of the easement the biggest error of his life. In 1910, well into his nineties, he dictated a will leaving the land to his grandchildren. He died three days later. Oklahoma newspapers reported in his obituary that efforts were being made to break the will and open the land to developers.[15] Tuckabache died, one Tulsa paper said, "hating the white man."

Tuckabache's granddaughter, Jennie Hickory, was forced to sign over her land with an X; she was given $1,000 for the title. The land was sold a few years later for $52,400. Tuckabache's descendants realized that they had been swindled and sued to regain their family's land. The case went all the way to the Supreme Court of Oklahoma in 1919. While the lower courts had failed to properly consider the best interests of the minors, the highest court in Oklahoma confirmed the sale of the property. A cloud remained in the title, however, that plagues real estate deals down to the present day. By the late 1910s, the oil boom was in full swing, and reopening the question of landownership would be a Pandora's box.

Creeks had a few allies among white lawyers and activists, but the national and local press described dispossession of Native lands as inevitable. "Like the death of Geronimo," a State News wire service reported, "the demise of Tuckabache was the passing of one of the famous Indian characters of the Southwest."[16] Even Chief Pleasant Porter, who had tried to mitigate the white takeover of the Creek Nation, concluded in 1907 that "the destiny of the Creeks is their absorption with the white race as citizens of the United States."[17] The Creek Nation was on "the road to disappearance," as the title of another Debo book had it.

I related this little-known piece of Tulsa history to a realtor who had never heard the name Tuckabache. The story struck her as familiar. In Maple Ridge, she said, property transactions are complicated by "the dead Indian." She did not know who, exactly, the dead Indian was or when he died, but he was a thorn in the side of everyone who bought or sold property in the area. The "dead Indian" in the abstract meant that there was always a cloud in the title. Abstracts in south Maple Ridge revealed a contested line of succession in the 1910s. This was probably why I had never heard any actual names of any of the Creeks who had called my piece of Tulsa home. But now "the dead Indian" had a name: Tuckabache. When it came to Tulsa's past, my people have always preferred the nice and tidy version, the Oil Capital of the World borne out of the American wilderness.

I brought this matter up with J. D. Colbert. He showed me a map of modern Tulsa overlaid with Creek allotments. The result is an astonishing visualization of a city transformed in just a few short years. I searched the map to find the house I grew up in, in the Sunset Terrace addition of Maple Ridge, a place whose claim to fame is "Tulsa's first suburb." Today, it is a leafy and tony neighborhood where oil mansions sit next to charming 1920s cottages, all surrounded by mature trees. But Colbert's map shows it as the land of Tuckabache, of Tom Coney, of Wehiley Naharkey. Not only did Tuckabache spend around sixty-five years there, raising two generations of children and grandchildren, he had himself buried in his family cemetery, a plot of land that, according to an archeological survey, borders the backyard of my childhood home. Some seventeen members of Tuckabache's family were buried there, before their remains were moved in the 1920s to make way for the Sunset Terrace subdivision. I wrote to acquaintances who grew up in my neighborhood. I talked to my mom's friends, some of whom have been in the area for fifty years. Not a single person had ever heard the name Tuckabache or Chitto Harjo. The first settlers of the land had receded into oblivion.

Scenes of horse-mounted cowboys fighting off Indians in rugged landscapes dominate our collective imagination of colonization, but they have nothing to do with what happened in the Creek Nation. The story of the liquidation of tribal governance and Native lands in Oklahoma is very much a modern legal battle over mineral rights and land deeds. It is a story about American capitalism, one that echoes Balzac's quote about a hidden crime behind every great fortune. "People look at these gorgeous buildings in downtown Tulsa and see art deco monuments," Colbert said. "I see buildings splattered with the blood of Creek Indians."

Colbert's words haunt me. My great-grandfather moved to Tulsa in

1925 from New York City to join the oil rush. With his Harvard pedigree and ties to the Republican Party leadership, he quickly rose to the top of white society. Along with his son (yes, another Russell Cobb), he started an oil company that bought up mineral rights to dozens of tracts of land in Oklahoma. By the 1950s, the Cobbs were one of the wealthiest families in town.[18] Until now, it had never occurred to me that everything the Cobbs had helped found in Tulsa—the Tennis Club, the Petroleum Club, the Forest Hills neighborhood—would be unthinkable without the appropriation of Native allotments in the early twentieth century. It is hard to imagine the wholesale dispossession of Native American lands without the discovery of oil, which remains the driver of the state today. Even though the Cobb family fortune has dwindled to a handful of small checks paid out each year, I wonder why no one discusses how the oil came into the family's hands. We have skeletons in our closet, to be sure, but this is a larger story of an entire state that helped itself to Native land.

Nothing in Oklahoma happened in a vacuum, however. What took place was a logical—if tragic—extension of the Doctrine of Discovery originally promulgated by the Spanish crown and given legalistic and technocratic application in the U.S. Supreme Court in the nineteenth century. Petro-Christians have used the law and the Bible to write Native Americans out of history. When they appear at all, they are tragic passive figures who only serve as voiceless prologues to civilization. Or they are anachronistic figures who cannot adjust to modern capitalism.

To celebrate the centennial of the discovery of oil in the state, the glossy, boosterish magazine *Oklahoma Today* ran a special issue in 1997 dedicated to the commodity that made Oklahoma rich. A section on "Native American Women and Oil" tells the larger-than-life stories of Osage (they call themselves the Ni-u-kon-ska, "people of the middle waters") who drove cars until they ran out of gas, then ordered brand new cars rather than fill up the old ones.

Then there is Lucinda Pittman, a Muscogee (Creek) woman who did not like all the black Cadillacs on the showroom floor of her local dealership. She demanded that she have a brightly colored Cadillac, and soon she was driving "the gaudiest car in America."[19] Stories about Jackson

Barnett, "the world's richest Indian," have been of perennial interest to consumers of pulp journalism. But such stories never include the theft of Native wealth that took place in the first two decades of Oklahoma's history.

More numerous than the salacious stories of wealth, affairs, and crime among Oklahoma's rich Indians are, if you know where to look, the accounts of brazen but legal theft that began pouring out of Indian Territory as non-English-speaking Choctaws signed away vast tracts of timber-rich land in southeastern Oklahoma. As of 1903, federal courts had to ratify all documents involving minors. Courts appointed guardians for Native American minors, but the judges were often buddies with the guardians and assigned them without any regard to the Native Americans' welfare. Under this new regime, the scale of graft only escalated. One guardian could petition the court to become a guardian for dozens of Native children. Adults could be declared incompetent as well, but children made the easiest victims. A speculator in Antlers applied for the guardianship of 161 children, most of whom he had never even met.[20]

But before we go much further in this story, we need to consider the notion of historical trauma and collective memory. Many people disagree about how and why a historical tragedy affects succeeding generations of people who did not directly experience those events, but one thing is clear: historical tragedy leaves a legacy for succeeding generations. Not everyone is going to experience historical trauma the same way, and some may not experience it at all, but scholars who have studied historical trauma believe that many of the issues that plague Native communities such as substance abuse, suicide, poverty, and depression, can be traced back to the original trauma of displacement and colonization. Eli Grayson, a descendant of Creek Freedmen, told me that intergenerational trauma affected every relationship he had. "I grew up hating white people," he said. Grayson says he "glories in all things Creek," but coming to terms with history has been difficult. He did not even know that he was descended from slaves until he went to the Creek capitol in Okmulgee to inquire about his Creek family name.

Darla Ashton does not like to think about intergenerational trauma.

Ashton grew up with a vague notion that her grandparents had been swindled, but they did not like to talk about it. "Once something was over," Ashton said, "my grandma only looked to the future." It was a survival strategy, handed down from mother to son. "Stoic is the word I would use to describe my dad," Ashton said. The only glimpse she got as a child of any trauma happened during fights, which could trigger her normally quiet father and grandmother. "They would chase each other around and yell at each other in Creek."

I reached out to Ashton to try to connect with a descendant of the Naharkey family, whose allotments occupied a sizable portion of modern Tulsa. Ashton, who is an avid reader and proud of her Creek heritage, had little knowledge of early Tulsa history or what happened to the family's extensive land holdings throughout the city. Like everyone else I talked to, she had never heard of Tuckabache or Crazy Snake. This was not because Ashton ignored history. The stories were hidden. Tulsa's murals, plaques, and monuments celebrate the grandeur of the oil industry while completely omitting the graft and fraud of the early twentieth century. "I'm sure they don't want us to know," she said.

The Naharkeys were one of a few families that formed the core of the Locvpokv tribal town in Alabama before removal. This family, then, represented the longest-living direct linkage to Tulsa's ancestral beginnings. Approximately one-quarter of the Locvpokv town members died during the process of removal. When the time for allotment came, the Naharkeys received allotments in or near their refounded ancestral town. Naharkey's family had plenty of experience with white land speculators. Wehiley Naharkey, Ashton's great-grandmother, had been allotted land just outside of downtown Tulsa, a place where the first oil mansions arose on the eastern banks of the Arkansas River in the 1910s. Harry Sinclair, a high-roller with political connections that went all the way to the White House, built a house on Naharkey's land after she died. For a while, this Creek family was at least honored by a street name—Naharkey Place—until that, too, was erased from history in favor of Sixteenth Street.

Sinclair's mansion is now torn down, but it was the focus of scandal in his day. After Sinclair found riches in Oklahoma, he looked to potential oil fields in Wyoming owned by the navy. The interior secretary, Albert Fall, persuaded the navy secretary to lease the land to Sinclair. Fall, meanwhile, collected bribes from Sinclair and another oil buddy for the lands in Wyoming and California and became a very rich man. Until Watergate, this incident—the Teapot Dome Scandal—was considered one of the most egregious examples of government corruption in American history.

Millie Naharkey's land was not in as prime a location as Wehiley's, but a developer and oil man, Grant Stebbins, thought that it might be an oil play. Stebbins had been instrumental in developing Tulsa's first wealthy neighborhood south of downtown, Maple Ridge. He was flush with money and his oil company, Gladys Belle, sought to take control of Millie's allotment.

Stebbins was not the only one vying for Millie's land, however. With the discovery of oil in the Tulsa area the stakes over Native allotments had risen, as had the cunning of whites who competed over the disappearing lands. Of the thirty million or so acres allotted to Native Americans in Oklahoma after the Dawes Commission, only some three million would still be in Native hands by 1951. Today, the Cherokee Nation estimates that only 2 percent of the original allotments remain with descendants of the original allottee.

The tragedy of Millie Naharkey is bound up in the little-known, yet highly consequential institution of the young state of Oklahoma, guardianship. Before statehood, the Dawes Commission was formed to take a census of every Native American in Indian Territory and then proportion out individual tracts for private ownership. For those who did not want land, the government would pay out a fair price for the land and open it to white settlement.

Before 1907 Boomers and Sooners used fake certificates or the threat of violence to take possession of Native land. In response, the government created a guardianship program, ostensibly to "protect" Native American minors from grafters. It came out of the well-meaning intentions of people like Massachusetts Senator Henry Dawes. Dawes saw the transition from communally held property to private allotments as the sad but inevitable price of civilization. The road to hell was paved with good intentions: the state-court regulated system of guardianship became the go-to vehicle for dispossession of Native lands. In Creek and Cherokee lands, people with dubious claims to Native citizenship rushed in to take control while other white "philanthropists" acquired as their wards dozens if not hundreds of Native American children, considered by the courts incapable of managing their own lands.

Guardians were little more than facilitators of graft. Many had birthday books of Native American minors whose restrictions would be lifted as soon as they turned eighteen. Many of these guardians are seen as the founding fathers of Oklahoma, their names still gracing streets, buildings, and businesses throughout the state. But the guardianship program was not just limited to minors. Any Native American declared incompetent by a court would also be appointed a guardian. Non-English-speaking Natives were often presented in court by speculators and declared—without translation—to be lacking the mental faculties to conduct their own affairs. Angie Debo wrote that almost every Native American with a deed to land with a potential oil well was affected; "it was not until about 1913 that it began to be apparent that all Indians and freedmen who owned oil property were mentally defective."[21]

Native Americans who could walk and talk in the white man's ways had a better chance of resisting guardianship. By the same token, many tribal members who passed as white served as the linchpins in a fraudulent system. Again, Oklahoma's cultural and racial oddities defy easy generalizations. People like Senator Robert L. Owen, a Cherokee-speaking Confederate veteran, seemed to advocate on behalf of the tribes, then worked as a legal guardian to enrich himself and further the dissolution of Native sovereignty. In the case of Tuckabache, a similar pattern unfolded. After Tuckabache's death, his estate was divided among his common law wife and grandchildren. Sam Davis, a Creek of mixed ancestry, fluent in Muscogee and English, became the guardian for the grandchildren. In at least one case, Davis convinced one of the grandchildren to sign an X on her portion of the land to deed it over to his wife, Ethel. Ethel Davis, later in possession of a large portion of the Tuckabache estate, flipped it to the Travis brothers for $54,200 in 1917. The Travis brothers, along with the investor A. E. Z. Aaronson, built extravagant mansions in the area. Aaronson's home was valued at $750,000 in the 1920s. It later became the notorious party house for Leon Russell until that land was, once again, subdivided into smaller lots, each with an extravagant home gracing its grounds.

Millie Naharkey was born just as the Dawes Commission was wrapping up its work in 1906. Naharkey appeared on the Dawes Rolls as three-fourths Creek. It was a notable fraction. "Full bloods" had restrictions based on their 40-acre homesteads (their other 120 acres, known as a "surplus," could be bought and sold). It was a notable concession the federal government made to Creeks as they watched their tribal holdings dissolved. The Creeks held out against allotment for almost twenty years after the federal government first proposed it, and Crazy Snake's faction never accepted the new treaty. As a newborn Creek, Millie had her own allotment, in addition to land she inherited from her father, Mose (sometimes spelled Moses or Mooser in English), who died the year she was born. Millie's father had remarried in his later years to Martha Red, categorized as "half blood" Creek, meaning that the land deemed "surplus" (120 acres) could also be sold to non-Native speculators.

As a girl living with her widowed mother in west Tulsa, little Millie stood to inherit a lot of land around Tulsa, to be divided with her half brother Sammie. Just a couple of miles down the road from her mother's allotment stood the small town of Red Fork, the site of the first oil gusher in Tulsa County in 1901. The excitement around this oil well led Tulsa boosters to build the first bridge across the Arkansas River in 1904 and start a successful campaign to incorporate Red Fork into Tulsa proper.

THE CRIME BEHIND THE FORTUNE

By the time Millie Naharkey was set to become an adult in the early 1920s, most of the rich oil land in Oklahoma had made its way into white hands. Tulsa's claim as the Oil Capital of the World was more than mere booster hyperbole. Oklahoma led all other states in oil production, and many of the biggest names in the business (Harry Sinclair, J. Paul Getty, Waite Phillips, and others) were at least partially based in Tulsa. The remaining allotments in the 1920s were a matter of intense speculation and intrigue. To beat out the competition, oil men hired contractors to abduct Native Americans and take them across state lines, cutting them off from family members and their guardians. Charles Page, a revered oil man who built the town of Sand Springs, would often be declared a hero for miraculously locating a missing Native woman and serving as her benefactor. Page built a self-described "colony" for widows and orphans in Sand Springs. In later lawsuits, the attorney general's office, along with the Creek Nation, alleged that Page would have Native American women "disappeared" by his agents, only to have himself become their saviors, gaining their land as a reward for his work.

Page legally adopted the children in the colony, and they called him "daddy." He imposed a strict code of behavior that had to be followed in exchange for a free room and a quart of milk a day. Some alumni of Page's colony praised the man. The one biography of Page was written by a woman who spent part of her youth in the widows and orphans colony. With so many children passing through, it is possible that many had positive experiences. Others, however, experienced Page's social experiment as a purgatory on the road to dispossession. Such was the case of Millie Naharkey, who ended up as Page's ward for a while. But Naharkey ended up suing Page for illegally buying the family's allotment, which, she contended, had been illegally partitioned from her father. Naharkey was not the only one to see Page as a fraudster. Federal prosecutors contended that Page had a hand in manipulating the Dawes Rolls so that he could end up with oil-rich allotments.

One infamous case involved an allotment that turned out to be on top of one of the most productive oil fields in U.S. history. The allotment was just east of the town of Cushing, a place now known as the oil pipeline crossroads of the world. The land was at the western border of the Creek Nation, a place where the Dawes Commission allocated allotments to the Snake faction and others who seemed to have no interest in farming. It was a rocky place far from the major Creeks towns. One section was allotted to Tommy Atkins, who was listed by Dawes agents as a six year old boy in Wagoner, many miles to the east.

Land men from a small company called Gypsy Oil drilled on Tommy's allotment. It was wildly productive, churning out around ten thousand barrels a day.[22] But no one could locate Tommy Atkins to secure a lease. Royalties were held in a trust. Investigators concluded that Tommy had died and the land had passed on to his mother, Minnie Atkins, who also could not be located. Thus ensued a scramble of white oil men trying to find Minnie Atkins and her title to the land.

According to Opal Clark (Charles Page's biographer), Page heard the Atkins story over a cigar one day. He resolved to find the woman. He turned over all operations of his businesses to his assistant and caught a train for California. The best lead on Minnie's whereabouts had her hiding out in Mexico.[23] It was not a bad guess, as a number of Native Americans after the dissolution of tribal government set out for Mexico in hopes that cheap land and a nation founded on the idea of *mestizaje* between European and indigenous traditions might be hospitable for a rebirth of the Five Tribes.

While others followed a cold trail south of the border, Page located Atkins in California at a cowboy encampment washing dishes and brought her back to Oklahoma. The spoils of his victory were Minnie's concession of her inheritance to Page. Tommy Atkins's oil reserves were then valued at around $2 million in 1914 and $20 million eight years later. Page made a fanfare of promising that all the money would go to his widow and orphans colony.

Page's big win, however, was short-lived. Minnie's sister, Nancy, filed suit in a district court, saying she could prove that little Tommy was her son, not Minnie's. Nancy argued that Minnie borrowed the boy to get more land from the Dawes Commission. Minnie Atkins, as it turned out, was kicked off tribal roles after an 1895 census done by the Creek Nation. Nancy Atkins had big money backers of her own (including Thomas Gilcrease), and she initially won the lawsuit, but it was quickly appealed. With the title now in doubt, the courts sought to figure out who really was Tommy's mother.

As they deliberated, a curious figure appeared in Leavenworth, Kansas: a young man by the name of Henry Carter. Henry repeated the same story as Charles Page's lawyers in court but added an interesting twist: Tommy Atkins had not died but rather changed his identity to Henry Carter to get away from a bad reputation his mother had achieved in Leavenworth (Minnie had children by three different men). Henry had an enrollment card from the Dawes Commission itself for one Thomas Atkins. But then another Tommy Atkins appeared. And another. Some were Black, others mixed race. It was unclear whether Tommy Atkins was a freedman (a descendant of slaves held by Creek people and later absorbed into the tribe) or a "full-blood." It was unclear if he was alive or dead, or whether he had existed at all.

Witnesses did seem to agree on one thing. There was a Tommy Atkins who had been born in a brothel run by an African American woman in Leavenworth, Kansas, in the 1880s. But then a key witness showed evidence to the court that Charles Page had bribed scores of people to testify to Tommy's birth. After two years of lawsuits and investigations, the only thing that seemed certain was that whoever could claim the Atkins land would be extremely rich.

Meanwhile, the value of the Cushing-Drumright oil field continued to grow. In 1919 it accounted for 17 percent of all oil produced in the United States with some three thousand wells crowding out the rocky hills of western Creek County. Oil companies extracted hundreds of millions of barrels of oil and the place was crisscrossed with pipelines, presaging Cushing's modern status. The Atkins title, however, was in chaos. A woman named Sadie James said in a deposition that Charles Page paid her $1,000 to create witnesses that would verify that Minnie was the mother. These witnesses would testify in court that Atkins had been born and raised at the Kansas bordello. James, pressured by federal prosecutors, changed her story. Now she testified that she had worked at the bordello for years and the whole Atkins story was a fiction. She had told Page as much initially. However, the promise of thousands of dollars to manufacture witnesses had been too much for Sadie James to resist. Another witness also flipped to the government. He had previously stated that he knew Tommy Atkins as a baby at Leavenworth. In court, however, he said he needed to "get right with God" and tell the true story: Page's men had paid him for a fiction. Page's lawyer went after James's credibility and the other witness, both African American. Who was the jury going to believe, Page's lawyers countered: Oklahoma's most prominent oil man or a Black prostitute and a john with changing stories?

In the midst of all these competing claims, the Interior Department made a startling announcement: not only were all the Tommy Atkinses claiming to be alive frauds, but there had never been a Tommy Atkins in the first place. Atkins was invented by someone hoping to cash in on extra land. Such cases were common. Since everything went back to incomplete censuses done by the Creek Nation or the Dawes Rolls, there was lots of room for error. Some people were counted twice, and my research into the Dawes Rolls pulled up two Tommy Atkinses. Of course it is possible that they were separate people. But if, as the government alleged, the Tommy Atkins who received the Cushing allotment never existed in the first place, the royalties from the land in Creek County would go back to the tribe. The tribe had its own records showing that Minnie Atkins's own enrollment had been rejected by the Creek government because she had been absent from the territory for more than ten years. But in the transition from Indian Territory to Oklahoma, the Creek Nation had been rendered all but extinct by the federal government. Now, however, the Creeks had a chance to cash in on Oklahoma's black gold. But it was put in the strange position of having to prove the inexistence of one of its citizens to do so.

With so much at stake, many Native Americans—and whites pretending to be Indians—concocted schemes to get an allotment. Minnie Atkins herself had married a white man named Harry Folk, and the two had settled down in a comfortable house in Page's company town of Sand Springs. The legal proceedings had demonstrated Page's ruthless ways of paying off witnesses and altering facts. His story of finding Minnie Atkins in California was contradicted by numerous witnesses in court, who held that Minnie had been found in Seattle by a private investigator. Page then paid off the investigator so that he could secure the deed. If one believed Page's testimony, he never boarded the train to California and never "found" Minnie in a cowboy camp. The Atkins case, which ended up in the U.S. Supreme Court, ultimately upheld Page's claim on the deed, but not before Minnie herself had died in 1919. The Supreme Court's ruling did not so much vindicate Page as it did uphold the finality of the Dawes Commission in establishing, once and for all, who counted as an Indian in the Five Tribes. In the case of the Creek Nation, everyone knew the commission was hopelessly flawed. Page had found a way to exploit the flaws to turn himself into "Oklahoma's Rockefeller."

The *Tulsa World*, which had initially lauded the opening of Page's widows and orphans colony, smelled a rat. The *World* documented instances in which Page leaned on witnesses to alter their testimony to secure more oil leases. The *Tulsa World* depicted Charles Page in stark contrast to the benevolent philanthropist image the oilman cultivated for himself in his own paper, the *Tulsa Democrat*. This Charles Page roughed up opponents, bribed city officials, and hired street thugs as enforcers. He paid off prostitutes to frame up rivals and tried to monopolize the city's water and electricity supply through blackmail and extortion. The *World* exposed Page's bribes to city officials while denouncing him as Tulsa's "self-appointed dictator . . . who poses as a reformer and champion of honest government for the purpose of covering his secret debauchery."[24]

The *World* had it in for Page in part because the oil man had decided to challenge the local media structures by starting his own newspaper, the *Tulsa Democrat* (which later became the *Tulsa Tribune*). Page's ambition to control Tulsa's water, electricity, and widows came to an abrupt halt in 1926, when he died from influenza. After reading dozens of newspaper accounts, depositions, and other court documents, it remains very much an open question whether Tommy Atkins ever existed. After all, the Oklahoma Supreme Court had established that there was a Tommy Atkins on the Dawes Rolls, not that there had actually been a Tommy Atkins. Dawes was simply the law of the land. Whether it corresponded to reality, the court found, was another matter. What is for sure, though, is that the name Charles Page continues to grace everything from the main road from Tulsa to Sand Springs, to Sand Springs's high school, to his former widows colony, now the Charles Page Family Village.

Just across the river, the passing of the old warrior Tuckabache ushered in a real estate boom. Martha and Millie Naharkey, Creek-speaking women who lived according to traditional Creek values, were quickly becoming surrounded. For many Creeks, the idea of individual landownership was anathema to the traditional practice of cultivating land collectively. Following the death of Moses Naharkey, an Indian agent and Methodist pastor named J. H. N. Cobb (no relation to me) managed to establish himself as the Naharkey guardian.

As a federal Indian agent, Cobb was supposed to act in the best interests of his charges. His writings, however, reveal a man who saw Native Americans as inferior people who required the supervision of white Christian men. Like many guardians, Cobb took control of the affairs of multiple families. Regarding another branch of the Atkins family, Cobb testified that "that they are ignorant, speak little or none of the English language, that they are not strong mentally and are incompetent and unable to manage their affairs." Courts rarely questioned such assessments.

The death of Moses Naharkey, a Creek councilor, tested the Creek system of matrilineal inheritance against the new Anglo-American laws. Mooser Creek (a Mvskoke variant of Moses) in west Tulsa was named after him. Under the laws of the new state of Oklahoma, Sammie Naharkey felt that he was entitled to more of his father's land than the Creek system allowed. Whether Sammie truly felt that way or his guardian planted the idea in his head, we cannot know. In any case, Sammie sued his sister Millie and her mother for 160 acres. The case, the judge admitted, was rather complicated, in part because Moses Naharkey had named his daughter with Martha after his dead wife. Thus, the two Millies had to be differentiated as "Little" and "Old" Millie.

Only weeks after Sammie won his case, he signed a deal with Charles Page and the wife of his friend John Cleary, Alleyne Bechtel. The Notary Public in the deal was none other than Charles Page's personal lawyer, Benjamin F. Rice Jr., the son of an Arkansas senator who became Page's chief counsel for many years. Rice and Page were part of an emerging white elite that edged out all sorts of contenders for Indian allotments. The warranty deed also included a relinquishment of dower, an important aspect of the deal since Tulsa was technically still in Indian Territory, where, according to tribal custom, women had an important voice in land ownership. Sammie signed his name with an X, thereby transferring his inherited 160 acres to Page and Bechtel for $2,000. Page's hope that Sammie's land would become the next gusher was dashed. There was little oil in the west Tulsa allotment, but it was squeezed in between gushers at Red Fork, Drumright, and Cushing. Page would not give up. He wanted the rest of the Naharkey lands.

But by the 1920s, Charles Page had lots of competition. News of the "rich Indian heiress" Millie Naharkey had spread beyond the borders of Oklahoma. For most of her youth, Naharkey was away from her land at Chilocco Indian School near the Kansas border. It was a place designed to hammer white Christian and capitalist values into Native Americans. The harsh conditions led many students to liken it to a prison. Her granddaughter, Darla Ashton, says Naharkey never talked about the school or anything from her youth. It was something she spent the rest of her life trying to put behind her.

Millie Naharkey returned from Chilocco to Tulsa as a teenager to find that she had become famous. One suitor came from New York City, promising to take the teenage girl to Broadway, where she would become a star. The man was reportedly chased off by Indian agents from Muskogee as he telegraphed Naharkey from his hotel in Tulsa. Other handsome strangers showed up in new cars, all of them promising to wine and dine her. The press found the scene of the "destitute child of nature" juxtaposed with the oil mansions just across the Arkansas River a source of unending good copy.[25]

The Tulsa developer and oil man Grant Stebbins—a rival of Charles Page—also had a plan to get the Naharkey lands. But, as the New York suitor incident proved, not all Indian agents were corruptible. The tribes, after years of being defrauded by white men versed in legal matters, had figured out how to fight back through the courts. Activists such as Zitkála-Šá (also known as Gertrude Bonnin) toured the United States highlighting the abuses in Indian Country. Slowly, public opinion and government action started to change. The Indian Rights Association, which had previously seen allotment in Oklahoma as the only way to "civilize"

Native Americans, changed its course. Zitkála-Šá and others from the IRA traveled to Oklahoma to document what was happening. Their report was summed up in a small book titled *Oklahoma's Poor Rich Indians*. It caught the attention of federal lawmakers, who would eventually be pressured into enacting the Indian Reorganization Act of 1934.

According to the report and court documents, Grant Stebbins hired a Tulsa oilman, A. B. Reese, and a University of Oklahoma college student, W. R. McNutt, to develop a new plan to get the Naharkey lands. One of the men came up with an idea to separate Naharkey from her guardian, Charles Page, and the Indian agents based out of Muskogee. Page seemed to have had the inside track to getting Millie's lands because he already held Sammie's chunk of their father's allotment. But the feud between Sammie and Millie provided an opening for Stebbins. Still, as the Atkins case demonstrated, Charles Page would stop at nothing to obtain what he wanted.

Stebbins's men promised Millie and her mother, Martha, a fun and relaxing vacation a week before Millie's eighteenth birthday. When the Naharkeys mentioned they liked to fish, McNutt and Reese saw their opening. The other member of the party was Millie's half brother, a shady character known as Foxie Red, later alleged to be the connection between the Naharkey women and Stebbins's oil men. In June Reese and McNutt picked up the Naharkeys to tour the Ozarks and fish to their heart's content. After days of driving around the Oklahoma countryside, the oil men gained the Naharkeys' trust. Assured that the Naharkeys would not call Indian agents to rescue them, the oil men took the Naharkeys across state lines into Missouri, stopping at a small town in the Ozarks. The idea, as Reese and McNutt later testified, was to cajole Millie into signing over the deed to Stebbins on her eighteenth birthday. They pressured Millie to have Robert F. Blair become her new attorney. Millie wanted to know if she was leasing or selling her allotment. Blair insisted that it was a mere oil lease, but Millie sensed something was off. She was interested in a lease of her mineral rights but balked at a sale.

When Blair showed up in a county court claiming to represent Millie, alarm bells went off. Millie's guardian was connected to the most powerful bank in town, First National Bank of Tulsa. Indian agents were alerted and the search was on. The attorney general of Missouri would later allege that the pair of oil men, the attorney, and Stebbins engaged in a criminal conspiracy to kidnap, defraud, and rape Millie Naharkey. Federal prosecutors attempted to have Blair disbarred.[26]

Sensing that agents were on the trail, McNutt and Reese moved the group deeper into the Ozarks. Reese and McNutt used liquor to soften Millie up. Then they gave her two checks for a total of $2,000 from the Gladys Belle Oil Company. The pair drove her to a bank to deposit the checks, trying to prove their good faith. At least one check was later determined to be a forgery. When Millie pressed them for more details about the transaction, Reese and McNutt emphasized that she was only signing a lease to drill for oil and that she would continue to own the land.[27] The men and the Naharkeys decamped at a resort called Roaring River, deep in the Ozarks. The odd grouping of Native women and white oil men created a sensation in the little town of Caseville. They had "nature parties" that involved copious amounts of booze.

A few days in, things took an ugly turn. Naharkey later testified to the Native American writer Zitkála-Šá that after she was plied with alcohol, McNutt made advances on her, which she refused. At one point, McNutt said he would marry her. The couple took a room together at Roaring River. Martha, Millie's mother, approved, thinking that the story would have a happy ending. Martha returned to Tulsa, leaving Millie alone with McNutt, Reese, and her half brother Foxie Red. In her interview with Zitkála-Šá, Millie struggled to recall the details, either because it was too painful or because she had been forced to drink so much she blacked out.

After Martha left, the oil men tried to convince Millie that Indian agents from Muskogee wanted to kidnap her. It was a classic case of gaslighting. At one point, Reese gave Millie a knife and told her to stab any Indian agent that came looking for her. At the same time, Reese gave small payments to Foxie Red, who was supposed to talk Millie into transferring the deed, not just allowing a drilling lease. During this time, McNutt repeatedly raped Millie, who occasionally cried out for help. None came. Under constant harassment, Millie signed a transfer of title which

Blair then took to Joplin, Missouri. Millie was assured that some $25,000 would eventually be deposited into her bank account, which would fund her education at a well-to-do private school in Kansas City.

After obtaining the lease, the oil men drove Millie to Kansas City, where she thought she would finish high school. In Kansas City, Indian agents finally caught up with the group and learned the whole story. Reese and McNutt were arrested in Joplin and charged with a long list of crimes, including kidnapping. The case against them would drag on for years, as federal prosecutors tried to disentangle the web of conspiracies that went from law firms, to real estate developers, to unethical family members. The superintendent for the Five Tribes, Shade Wallen, saw a report on the affair and declared it "one of the most revolting in the history of the Indian Service." Wallen wrote that "the conspirators not only attempted to deprive this innocent Indian girl of her property, but one of them, according to the evidence, made an unlawful assault on her."

The salacious nature of the kidnapping and rape, along with the high stakes of the oil money, made the case a brief national news item. Press reports state that the attorney general considered prosecuting the men for "white slavery," a euphemistic term for the forced prostitution of white women. Naharkey was not white, and in the trial, it was her word against Reese and McNutt's. As all of this played out in the courts, Zitkála-Šá wrote:

> I personally met Millie Naharkey, and was struck by her smallness of stature, her child's voice and her timidity. It was difficult to believe that she was of legal age, for she appeared in every way to be a girl of only thirteen or fourteen years. . . . After a long private conference with this girl, I grew dumb at the things she rehearsed, much of which is of official record at Union Agency, Muskogee. There was nothing I could say. Mutely I put my arms around her, whose great wealth had made her a victim of an unscrupulous, lawless party, and whose body was mutilated by a drunken fiend who assaulted her night after night.[28]

Naharkey's story was shocking even by the standards of the day, but the scandal resulted in no justice for her family. Reese and McNutt were found guilty of providing liquor to an Indian, but the more serious charges of kidnapping and rape were dropped. Stebbins relocated to Kansas City and died in 1925. He is remembered to this day as upstanding founding father of Tulsa. Blair, however, seems to have disappeared; after running a highly visible law practice through the 1910s and early 1920s, all mention of him in Oklahoma papers ceases after 1925. He may have legally escaped trouble, but his good name was ruined.

Naharkey never got to the private school in Kansas City. She returned to her west Tulsa homestead, trying to put the whole incident behind her. Darla Ashton says her grandmother never spoke about the kidnapping but did complain about continued problems with her white guardian. Millie Naharkey's guardian at First National Bank gave her a modest weekly stipend that increased by $5 to $10 every few years. She eventually married a part German, part Creek man named Arthur Yeatman. Yeatman was listed on the 1940 Census as a full-time farmer, with two kids by Millie, John Richard and Mary Jane.

After half a life of abuse and bad luck, Naharkey won a resounding victory in the Oklahoma Supreme Court in 1936. In a landmark case that would slow the theft of Five Tribes lands, the court ruled that Page's partition of the Naharkey lands was done in violation of the restrictions on "full-blood" Indians. Naharkey recovered eighty acres of land that would eventually become near-lakefront property around Keystone Lake west of Tulsa. However, her good fortune was short-lived. Naharkey still did not control her own assets. She wanted to open a gas station or motel on her recuperated property. Her guardian at First National Bank disagreed. In a letter to the federal government, he stated that Naharkey was almost broke and that the sale of the land on the open market would yield her a nice nest egg, from which she could collect interest. Naharkey sold her slice of Mose's land and received $50,000, though this, too, stayed in the hands of her guardian at First National. Any purchase she wanted to make from this sum had to be approved by the guardian.

Darla Ashton took me to Arthur and Millie's house in a working-class subdivision built mostly after World War II. The Yeatman house itself was tiny, as Ashton recalled. Surrounded by overgrown shrubs and displaying signs of rotting wood, the house still stood, a testament to the legacy of this painful period. Sheets hung in the windows in place of curtains, but with the owners kept the lawn tidy and had added a patio. The house symbolized the sort of social class that struggled to stay just above the poverty line.

At some point, Arthur and Millie split up, and having raised her two children, Millie found herself alone again. All this time, she was still classified as "incompetent" by her guardian at First National. A banker there oversaw many Native American accounts, signing off on the smallest purchases. Even items as trivial as Band-Aids had to be reported, eventually, to the Interior Department. Any purchases beyond basic foodstuffs had to be documented and reported. The whole process made Naharkey feel dehumanized, Darla said. Only in 1966 did First National start documenting its allowance, which in that year amounted to $55 a week. Guardians could also pay themselves out of their wards' accounts for their "services." There was nothing to stop them from paying themselves at stiff rates.

Although Darla Ashton did not know much about how her grandmother was defrauded, she remembers her bitterness over the pettiness of the allowances from First National. "She begged to have them fix her refrigerator," Ashton said. Since it was a bigger expense than usual, the guardian hesitated to approve the expense. "Finally, she just smashed the thing to bits with an icepick. That way they had to buy her a new one. She had to beg for things like that. It pissed her off."

The trap of poverty and continued subjugation of guardianship led her son Richard to demand that Millie be rid of her guardian once and for all. Richard and Millie came up with a plan to develop their land near I-44 and U.S. Highway 75 into a motel and convenience store, one last shot at the American Dream. Richard wrote the Interior Department detailing his plans, but a review of her case led to no changes. Ashton remembers these last years of her grandmother's life with a mix of warmth and bitterness. Ashton would come to visit and find her grandmother neglected, her hair a mess. Nearly blind and destitute, Naharkey spent most of her time watching television. Another woman, Lillie, lived with her for a while and promised to take care of her but ended up siphoning off large amounts of Millie's monthly payment. Naharkey wrote an angry

2. Darla Ashton grew up with little notion of the tragedy her grandmother faced. Here she examines the Tullahassee Indian Cemetery in a Sand Springs parking lot. Photo by the author.

letter to the Interior Department complaining that Lillie had been taking her mail and cashing her checks. "I never gave consent for you people to do that," she wrote in a shaky hand in 1978.

Ashton loved her grandmother dearly, but Naharkey was quick to anger and quiet about her past. And she was poor. "My grandma died without a pot to piss in," Ashton told me as we drove out to a Creek burial site in Sand Springs. Ashton's mother does not want to bring up this painful past, but Ashton is determined to get the whole story out into the world. "I don't give a damn about a monetary settlement," she said. "My grandmother didn't deserve any of this. I just want to get the truth out."

As we drive around, I ask her if she knows anything about a Creek burial ground in a shopping center in Sand Springs. It sounds familiar to her. After driving around for a while, we locate it, down the block from an old K-Mart and fast food joint turned into a sports bar. "Tullahassee Creek Indian Cemetery," a sign reads. Ashton says she cannot believe she has lived her whole life in the area and never noticed that a Creek burial ground was right there, in the middle of parking lot for a strip center in Sand Springs. We get out to inspect it. Several tombstones have collapsed, but there is no contact information about who maintains the burial ground.[29] The whole scene strikes me as a metaphor for Tulsa's Creek heritage: it is hidden in plain sight but in need of some serious reparations and attention.

For the Creeks like Ashton who still live in Tulsa and preserve a collective memory of the town reborn under the Council Oak tree, it is important that everyone know that the past is not dead. The last one hundred years of Tulsa's history may have been the story of a tribal town turned upside-down by the discovery of oil and the arrival of waves of white petro-Christians, but the story does not end there.

"We are miraculously still here," a Creek woman named Tallulah Eve Smith told me recently. "The Council Oak is the birthplace of Tulsa. It is sacred and has made Tulsa strong and resilient." Tulsa Public Schools voted in the summer of 2018 to rename Robert E. Lee Elementary after the Creek meeting ground. It is a step in the right direction toward Tulsa's reconciliation with its Creek origins. Every October, Creeks gather at Council Oak for a traditional Muscogee stickball game and a feast. The event is open to everyone, not just Creeks. Despite growing up one mile from the famous tree, I never knew there was a thriving event that connected modern Tulsa to its ancient cousin in the Muscogee homeland of Alabama and Georgia. Oklahoma is the product of a forced marriage anointed in blood and oil. It has not always been a happy marriage, but it has not ended in divorce either. Ms. Indian Territory is still alive and well, having survived a century of spousal abuse. Maybe now, after all these years, Mr. Oklahoma will be ready to hear her side of the story.

CHAPTER 4

Where the Hell Is Oklahoma Anyway?

I am mostly a passive scroller of social media. Twitter and Facebook status updates are mainly distractions from doing something meaningful. I do not have many Twitter followers, and my Facebook updates are either photos of my kids or snarky remarks about Oklahoma's foibles. A meme with the outline of Oklahoma's borders and the phrase "Zero days without a national embarrassment" is a perennial favorite of mine. Recently, however, I set off a Facebook conversation that lasted for days, with far-flung acquaintances and distant relatives chiming in on what I thought was a perfectly reasonable assertion.

Before I get to that, though, we have to ask an existential question about the nation's forty-sixth state: where is Oklahoma? You can point at a political map of the United States and locate the meat cleaver above Texas, its blade dripping with the blood of the Red River, its handle a skinny rectangle squeezed in between Texas and Kansas, east of the real west: New Mexico. There it is, you would say, in the mid-south-central portion of the continental United States.

Fine. But what is it? Is it a southwestern state? A midwestern state? Is it part of the South? Is it something else entirely? The U.S. Census Bureau lumps Oklahoma in with the South. There are geographic as well as political considerations for this decision. Indian Territory courts, for example, were under the jurisdiction of Arkansas. The Five Tribes were removed from southeastern states. Generations of venerable southern historians, such as C. Vann Woodward, have said that, yes, Oklahoma is part of the South, even if it was not part of the Confederacy.[1] The state was part of the "Solid South" that resisted Civil Rights through the 1950s and 1960s.

This was the assertion I casually made on Facebook. Actually, what I said was the following: "as a Southerner, the word 'heritage' strikes me as slightly sinister, but I'm not quite sure why."

The occasion was the annual celebration of Heritage Day in Canada, a holiday created to fill up a calendar in a late summer devoid of holidays. No one is really sure what Heritage Day really means, but it is seen as an occasion to celebrate Canada's famous multicultural mosaic. Laudable enough, I suppose, but the "heritage" part makes me uneasy, in part because of a bumper sticker I used to see in Oklahoma. The left portion of the sticker displayed the Rebel flag, and the right portion read "Heritage Not Hate."

My assertion of southernness was quickly shot down by the sister of a very good friend, who happens to live in Alabama. "Oklahoma is not the South, Russ," she said. "It's the Midwest." Another friend in Georgia sprung to my defense. "I've lived in the Deep South and Chicago. Oklahoma is definitely more southern than midwestern. Still, it's not quite the South either."

A Canadian friend was confused. "Where does the South end?" he wanted to know. "Is the South synonymous with the Bible Belt?" In a famous article, one historian asserted that the best way to define the contemporary South was to examine the audience for religious television. The bigger the market share for televangelists, the more southern the place. By this calculation, Tulsa was either the buckle on the Bible Belt or at the very least one of its belt holes.

A good friend who considers a trip to Dallas to be a visit to a foreign country tried to argue that Oklahoma was its own region, that it should not be lumped together with any other state, especially not Texas. But this seemed strange, too, because there are many affinities between Texas and Oklahoma. Still, Okies have none of the bluster of Texans, and it is hard to imagine a tourism campaign with the slogan: "Oklahoma, it's like a whole other country" or "Don't Mess with Oklahoma." Okies might style themselves as red-meat cowboy conservatives like Texans, but we do not think of ourselves as arrogant. After the bombing of the Alfred P. Murrah Federal Building in Oklahoma City in 1995, Okies developed a sense of pride in the altruism that arose in the wake of the attack. The values of this new pride—the Oklahoma Standard—do sound distinctly midwestern: "service, honor, and kindness." When I was growing up, the slogan on license plates was "Oklahoma is OK." Not great, not terrible, just okay. "You're doin' fine, Oklahoma" is the phrase in *Oklahoma!* Not "You're kickin' ass, Oklahoma." So there is an element of plainspoken midwestern humility in the mythos of the place.

The Facebook thread went on for days. I could sense I was losing the argument. All the Oklahomans who posted seemed to think their native state was in the Midwest. This disturbed me, but why? It seemed to me that there was something hopelessly dull and uninteresting about being from the Midwest. Someone else, a friend in New York, agreed. "It's in the Midwest, but I would rather it be in the South," she said. Why was the South an improvement on the Midwest? Being from the South had its own set of problems. And what about the Southwest? One of our most famous museums—Gilcrease—attracts visitors because of its collection of southwestern art. Like New Mexico and Arizona, we have a sizable, visible, and vibrant indigenous presence in Oklahoma. Maybe we were southwesterners? If that was the case, why did we speak with a southern "ax-cent"?

The received wisdom on American dialects is that our rich mosaic of speech patterns and regional words has been disappearing for generations. In pop sociology, this is chalked up to a number of factors: ubiquity of television and "broadcaster speak" following World War II, invention of the interstate highway system and increased mobility of the postwar period, negative stereotypes emanating from Hollywood of people with thick accents. If you follow this line of thinking, it is only a matter of time before most dialectical differences will fade away, their traces evidenced only in old video clips. And indeed, there is some evidence that certain traits of regionalisms have disappeared: just think of Jimmy Durante pronouncing *bird* as *boid* or *curl* as *coil.* The non-rhotic *r* before a consonant used to be a defining feature of some parts of the United States (especially New York and New Orleans). Now, you would have to conduct research in nursing homes to find a substantial portion of the population that produces this sound. The truth hoits.

The idea of "newscaster speak," though, is pure bunkum. The heyday of the Standard American newscaster has come and gone, and even during its hegemony, you could hear the distinct Texanness of Dan Rather and the Canadian lilt of Peter Jennings (along with the plainspokenness of Tom Brokaw).

Trace the old Route 66 via Interstate 44, and you will eventually come to a town just across the Missouri-Oklahoma line—Joplin, Missouri— where, depending on which gas station you visit, you will hear a nasally midwestern accent or a southern accent. On the southern end of town, near the highway, locals will say "highway forty-four" but will often turn the number four into two separate syllables: *fo-er.* Linguists will tell you that this is the hallmark "southern drawl": drawing one vowel out to make it sound like two.

On the other end of town, on the road to Kansas City, I-44 becomes pronounced as *farty-far.* I can make this assertion with some authority, having traveled north and south across Missouri many times on my way to college in Iowa, which, unlike Oklahoma, suffers from no regional identity complex. Rolling hills of grain silos, perfectly red barns, and miles of corn fields signify, in no uncertain terms, the Midwest. Oh, and it is also very white. Iowa, along with Nebraska and South Dakota, has produced a disproportionate share of broadcasters, in part because the accent in these states is considered the most neutral. This is the heart-land of a type of English known as General American (sae, or Standard

American English, is another term of art for this accent), a place the linguist William Labov found to be the area most devoid of regional variations and irregular speech patterns. According to Labov's *Atlas of North American English*, General American encompasses an oval-shaped blob from eastern Nebraska and South Dakota to central Illinois, taking in much of Iowa and northern Missouri.[2] Walter Cronkite, Ronald Reagan, and Tom Brokaw all spent their formative years in General America. General America is where corporations go to test new products to see if they will succeed in the rest of the country. If all the children in Lake Wobegon (a fictional town in the Upper Midwest) are above average, all the children in General America are just average.

When I first drove across General America in the early 1990s, I was shocked to learn how different it was from Oklahoma, which I always assumed was the most generic, milquetoast place in the world. The towns of General America, however, were tidier and straighter than anything I had seen in Oklahoma. The churches—and the people—were whiter. The town squares looked like settings for Norman Rockwell paintings. So many small towns in Oklahoma looked like they had just been hit by F-5 tornadoes or served as a setting for a movie about rural meth labs.

Going back to Tulsa, I noticed that somewhere south of Kansas City, Standard American gave way to southern twang, and I eventually pinpointed Joplin as the transition zone. A 2004 study of national speech patterns boiled American dialects down to six major groupings. Northeastern Oklahoma and southern Missouri are the northwestern limits of the southern accent, while the Midland, that area from northern Missouri to Iowa, Nebraska, and Illinois, was found to be the region with the fewest deviations from Standard American.

I also assumed that anyone not from a city spoke with an Oklahoma accent, which traces its genealogy back to Appalachia—a variation on the southern dialect. When I met my first roommate, Jake, from Hawarden, Iowa (population 2,478), at the University of Iowa, I was surprised he spoke General American. He looked like a hick in his tight Wranglers, mullet, and Metallica T-shirt, and yet he spoke without a trace of an accent. I expected his accent to be something like that of Boomhauer from *King of the Hill*: a twangy, monotone slur. (The creator of the show, Mike Judge, has stated that the inspiration for Boomhauer's accent came from an unintelligible phone conversation he once had with a man from Oklahoma City.) My roommate also had three more Advanced Placement credits than I did, completing the ruin of my sense of intellectual and cultural superiority.

Even more shocking than all this was learning that I had an accent. An *ax-ee-yent*. I shared a phone with Jake and two guys from Chicago next door. The Chicagoans drank Old Style beer at 8 a.m. and skipped class to watch hockey. One day I discovered I was missing a pair of socks and asked them about it.

"You're missing what?" one of them said.

"Socks," I said. "I can't find my socks."

The one I had been talking to went to find his roommate. He brought him into the common area, where we shared a refrigerator and a telephone.

"I can't understand this guy," one Chicagoan said to the other. "What are you missing?"

"My socks!" I said. "You put them on your feet."

"Sacks," said the other one. "He's saying 'sacks.'" They laughed and then mocked me. "Saw-ahks," they said. "I cain't find my saw-ahks. Shi-yit!" To their ears, I sounded like an Alabama redneck.

So I set about detecting regionalisms in my speech and purging them one by one with the help of a fellow English major from Chicago. *Greasy* was not pronounced with a *z* sound but with an *s* sound. Words ending in *-ow* were pronounced with an *oh* sound, not with an *uh* sound. It was not *pilluh* but *pilloh*. *Pen* and *pin* were pronounced differently. My wife is still trying to help me detect the differences. I cannot. As Garth Brooks once said: "Blame it all on my roots, I showed up in boots."

Milk was one syllable, not two: *mi-yulk*.

Southern dialects, I discovered by accident, form an understudied part of our culture wars about political correctness, race, and social class. The comedian David Cross did a popular bit in 2002 about the southern drawl as a stand-in for a set of macho, racist values. "People mistakenly believe that it's just a southern thing but it's not," Cross said about the drawl. In the bit, Cross pits rednecks from California, Montana, and Georgia against one another, all of them speaking a variety of southern white working-class dialect ("Redneck Voice," he calls it). "It's all over the country," he says. "Hey fuck you, I'm from Bakersfield, California," Cross says in one instance. "No, fuck you, I'm from Bozeman, Montana," he says, escalating the conflict. "Fuck all y'all mutherfuckers," a final one says in a deep drawl, "I'm from mutherfuckin' Juneau, Alaska."

In fact, the career of Cross's comedic nemesis, Larry the Cable Guy, actually reinforces this stereotype of a singular, hegemonic dialect called "Redneck." The man behind the various iterations of "Git-r-done!" is from Nebraska, a place that is as close to Standard American as can be found. Larry's speech patterns, however, are an amalgamation of slang terms and voice inflections he observed in roommates from Texas and Georgia. An essential part of Larry's shtick is aimed at the "PC left," which he accuses of trying to censor him. Larry the Cable Guy echoes a common belief on the right that a leftist cabal of gays, media types, and liberal politicians have won the culture wars. "If you do a gay joke and you're a heterosexual white from the South?" Larry writes in *Git-R-Done*, "Oh shit, run for the hills! Now you're a homophobe and a gay basher. These are the rules of comedy in the PC world."

Taken together, we can see that patterns emerge in which southern white working-class dialect becomes a political marker of a sort of intransigent conservatism, a dialect that is in part a construction of cultural, religious, and political affiliations. No wonder I still cannot bring myself to use it in polite company.

Even if we Okies have a sort of southern accent, though, that does not make us southerners. The census bureau may designate Oklahoma as the South, but what explains the visceral reaction of Georgians and Alabamians when an Okie claims to be from Dixie? A friend of a friend from Tulsa replicated my Facebook experiment and was shot down by someone from Arkansas. "It's the Southwest," he wrote. "The South starts with Arkansas." The next person to post was confused. "Upper-central-mid-southwest?" she wrote. "Please let me know what the answer is."

Another friend of a friend who works for *Southern Living* magazine was sort of annoyed that Oklahoma was included in her lifestyle magazine. "It was a marketing decision," she said. "Everyone knows Oklahoma isn't in the real South."

But where is the real South?

There was a time in the not-too-distant past when Oklahoma politicians made a deliberate effort to make the state part of the "Solid South," a peculiar institution that guaranteed the one-party rule of the Democratic Party. The heyday of the Solid South lasted from the end of Reconstruction until the end of World War II. The strategy was all about, of course, disenfranchising Black voters and wielding monolithic political control over state politics. Danney Goble explains it this way in *The Encyclopedia of Oklahoma History and Culture*: "The fact that much of the future state was settled by immigrating southerners had great influence on Oklahoma's later politics. Its unwieldy constitution, its distrust of concentrated corporate and political power, its steady run-ins with federal authority, even its susceptibility to political corruption—all of these were qualities that the Sooner State shared with states of the Old Confederacy."[3]

The implications could shake up not only how we see Oklahoma history but U.S. history as well. Indian and Oklahoma Territories, as they evolved into statehood, *became* part of the South. The South, in the popular imagination, is a group of states that seceded from the Union to protect the institution of slavery. But, thankfully, the South lost the war and started the long and arduous process of integration. Oklahoma complicates that linear thinking about the Civil War and its aftermath. Here is Goble again on the state's early political history: "Early Oklahoma Democrats campaigned and governed just like their fellow Democrats across the South: they openly and bluntly proclaimed their racism to win power, and they used power to affirm and institutionalize their racism. It was they who mandated separate schools under the constitution; they who segregated public transportation in Oklahoma's first statute; they who countenanced 'white only' public accommodations, neighborhoods, even entire towns; they who systematically disenfranchised Blacks with racist election laws."

The end of slavery and the end of the Civil War were supposed to halt the advance of southern-style racist laws and institutions. Oklahoma—once again an American exception rather than a rule—proves otherwise. So politically and religiously, we have defied that American narrative of homogenization and become the South. But that is not the whole story.

The geographer Wilbur Zelinsky—one of the inventors of modern cultural geography—attempted to understand regional identity in the "vernacular." Zelinsky wanted to understand how everyday folks defined themselves in terms of regional identity. This was in the pre-internet age of the 1970s and 1980s, and Zelinsky focused on the Yellow Pages. The telephone book, unlike the census bureau, would give a researcher a good idea of the regional place names that people used to identify themselves and their businesses.[4]

Sorting through thousands of place names in hundreds of cities, he compiled a series of maps that showed how people identified their regions. Some of the regions were predictable: Boston businesses used a lot of terms like "New England" and "Northeastern" in their names or descriptions. "Southern" was a dominant term in phone books in Mississippi, Louisiana, and Georgia. But looking at Zelinsky's maps today, it is Oklahoma that shows the biggest regional confusion. Strangely, Zelinsky never commented on this fact. He noted that some places, like western Pennsylvania, were kind of stuck between northeastern and midwestern, but Oklahoma had the greatest amount of regional identities. Four of the twelve vernacular identities that Zelinsky came up with converged on Oklahoma. For phone books in the far southeastern part of the state, Oklahoma was southern. In the panhandle, it was the West. Along the Kansas border, it was the Midwest. From Oklahoma City to the west, it was the Southwest.

Part of the problem with Zelinsky's research, though, is that it is static. It does not take into account the way regional identities change. Minnesota was once considered the Northwest; it is now firmly ensconced in the Midwest. Maryland was once considered the South, but few people today would characterize it as anything other than the Mid-Atlantic. The Midwest, in general, seems to be gaining ground, expanding its reach beyond its western and southern boundaries. In 2006 NPR, while reporting on an outbreak of tornadoes in Tennessee, referred to the state as the

THE AMERICAN NATIONS TODAY

FIRST NATION

THE LEFT COAST
(Includes Juneau, Alaska)

THE MIDLANDS

NEW FRANCE

THE FAR WEST
(Includes Anchorage and Fairbanks, Alaska)

YANKEEDOM

NEW NETHERLAND

THE MIDLANDS

GREATER APPALACHIA

TIDEWATER

PACIFIC OCEAN

DEEP SOUTH

ATLANTIC OCEAN

EL NORTE

NEW FRANCE

3. Even an updated map of American regions does not quite account for Oklahoma's unique place at the crossroads of the South, Southwest, and Midwest. From Colin Woodard, *American Nations: A History of the Eleven Rival Regional Cultures of North America* (New York: Viking Press, 2011). Reprinted with permission of Colin Woodard.

Midwest. If the Midwest is the region of Standard American, this seems to make sense, at least on the surface. The common wisdom is that the proliferation of mainstream popular culture through TV, the internet, and social media is destroying regional identities, making us all one undifferentiated mass of Starbucks coffee shops and crappy reality television. Sociolinguists, however, have found that the opposite is true—at least in terms of regional vocabularies and dialects. New dialects are being born: California used to speak Standard American but now has its own accent, and regional variations are becoming more—not less—pronounced. Waves of Latin American immigrants have repopulated Great Plains states in recent years, giving new life to towns in western Kansas, Nebraska, and Oklahoma. These people will undoubtedly lend their own contributions to the English spoken in those regions.

I pressed people to make their own maps. Many of them revolved around dialect. The former editor of *This Land Press*, Michael Mason, sent me his map of Oklahoma overlaid with his perception of regionalisms. The western half of the state was what he called "Sparse Western," while the east (roughly the area formerly known as Indian Territory) was divided between "Southern Drawl" and "Midwestern." Other maps looked nothing like Mason's.

This brings me back to the case for the Southwest. But Oklahoma does not quite fit there either. The proper Southwest is a legacy of the territory conceded to the United States after its war with Mexico ended in 1848. This is a region that absorbed centuries of Spanish colonialism. Texas, New Mexico, Arizona, California, some of Colorado: all these places have Hispanic place names and visible relics of Spain and Mexico. Apart from the Cimarron River and El Reno—and one has to doubt that there were ever any reindeer (*reno* is Spanish for "reindeer") in central Oklahoma—there are virtually no Spanish place names in Oklahoma. Coronado apparently wandered through the Wichita Mountains and lost a few pounds of gold along the way, but there are no missions, no pueblos. Our only decent Mexican food comes from recent migration patterns; in short, we have nothing that Americans recognize as archetypes of southwestern culture. The Five Tribes share a kinship based on corn with Mesoamericans, but their relationship is about as close as Spanish culture is to Polish culture.

But wait a second. Far western Oklahoma was ground zero for the Dust Bowl. The panhandle in particular was devastated by the twin forces of bank foreclosures and dust storms during the Great Depression. Skeletons of clapboard houses dot the desolate landscape. Driving through the areas in the 1980s and 1990s felt like a trip through some postapocalyptic movie. Now, however, the region is experiencing a revival. Towns are building new banks, schools, and parks for the first time in generations. Jobs in cattle and pork feedlots, natural gas drilling, and wind energy are attracting Latino immigrants despite the state's hostile attitudes. As of 2016 Hispanics make up a majority of the population in western Oklahoma towns like Guymon. Unlike migrant workers in the Midwest, it appears that Latino immigrants to western Oklahoma are there to stay, making the region look, sound, and taste more and more like the Southwest. Again, we need to stay attentive to the dynamic forces of regionalisms. Our regional identities are constantly shifting, and it may be that far western Oklahoma is the Southwest, while eastern Oklahoma is the South.

Finally, in moments of brutal honesty, Okies will admit that their state is a variation of Texas. This is a painful admission, to be sure. "The whole state is like a suburb of Dallas," a fellow Tulsan told a Canadian friend. "It's Texas-light," someone wrote during my interminable Facebook conversation. Politically, culturally, and religiously speaking, there is a good case to be made for this assertion. Texans and Oklahomans share the same affinity for hard-right, red-meat conservative politics, and they have large populations of Southern Baptists. Western swing is a purely Texas-Oklahoma creation of Bob Wills, who belongs to both states. Both states barbecue red meat first, pork second, conserving their cowboy heritage. The accent is pretty much the same (although East Texas is more traditionally southern, while the border region has its own Tex-Mex dialect). Next, there is the massive role of oil and gas as an economic and social driver. During my childhood, my family shuttled between Houston and Tulsa as my father tried to revive the family business in oil pipelines.

And, finally, there is football. Texas and Oklahoma are football crazed, but therein lies a complication: there is no greater sports hatred than that between the Sooners and the Longhorns. I have attempted to deconstruct the annual hatefest that is the OU-Texas game for my wife, a Californian, who, before meeting me, had never watched a college football game. Part of what makes the game exciting, I told her, is that it is played on a neutral site. So it is not in Texas or Oklahoma, she asked? They play in Dallas, I said. The idea that Dallas was somehow neutral seemed ludicrous, and indeed, the more I thought about it, the more it seemed like Oklahomans had been bamboozled. We are always the poor country cousin to Texas. Mobilehoma, they call us.

So where is Oklahoma? It is in America's Heart, someone said. Well, not quite, I rebutted. If you compare the map of the continental United States to the human body, you would have to conclude that Oklahoma is America's pancreas. It is located in the mid-south-central of the body, and although the pancreas does not have the poetic resonance of the heart, it serves an important function. It breaks down proteins, carbs, and fats. The pancreas is often overlooked until something terrible happens there, like a cancer—or the bombing of a federal building. But there it is, right there in the middle of everything, trying to make sense of all the substances coming through the system. Not all the substances that come through are healthy, but the pancreas soldiers on, keeping the body running.

CHAPTER 5

The Long Goodbye to Oklahoma's Small-Town Jews

I went down to Ardmore looking for the last Jews in a town which could, if it were so inclined, lay claim to title of the Birthplace of Judaism in Oklahoma. Even before statehood, Jewish merchants had established themselves the most prominent businessmen in the fledgling town near the Texas border.

Ardmore owes existence to the advent of the railways. The tribes in Indian Territory fought to keep railroads out of their lands until Congress interceded in the 1880s. The Santa Fe Railway was one of the first to be constructed in Indian Territory, and Ardmore, surrounded by cotton fields and close to Dallas, made for as good a stop as any. It was a frontier town with opportunities, a perfect place to set up shop for Jews coming into the United States from Galveston, Texas. Alas, according to an article from the Institute for Southern Jewish Life in 2014, there were only two Jews left in this once distinctly Yiddish-flavored town. I confess that I have a certain curiosity about populations in decline. I have always been attracted to cemeteries, ghost towns, and stories about postapocalyptic survivors.

I love browsing through photos of abandoned towns on Google Maps. Decay and collapse make for fertile grounds for an active imagination. Furthermore, although I am *goyim*, I married into a Jewish family. So, I had to get down there and meet these two Jews before they joined their brethren at Mount Zion Cemetery.

The day was miserable: snow was blowing sideways and flakes were hitting my cheeks like tiny little darts. I got off Turner Turnpike and wandered down Highway 18, where the entire town of Meeker stopped for a Baptist funeral. Cell coverage was spotty; the airwaves of Tulsa's NPR affiliate gave way to something called American Family Radio. While I waited for the funeral procession to pass, I listened. An alternate reality revealed itself on AFR. According to AFR, America was under siege. Socialists, terrorists, and illegals were undermining the very fabric of our Christian civilization. President Obama was not a Christian; he did not even love his own country. The hosts of one program scoured the Bible for verses to support gun rights and a crackdown on illegal immigration and even found some quotation that supposedly supported day trading on the stock market.

When I finally made it to Stephanie's Beautique on Main Street in Ardmore, I was glad to be off Highway 18. The store's namesake, Stephanie, ran the last Jewish store in town. Stephanie and Phyllis, her best friend from high school, were happy to see me but wanted to get something straight right off the bat: there were not only two Jews left in Ardmore. That was bunk. There were at least five. Maybe even nine or ten.

It really depended on how you defined who was Jewish. There was a guy in town born Jewish, but his stepfather raised him Baptist. There were the Daubes, who had a Jewish father but a Gentile mother who took them to the Methodist Church. Then there was Phyllis's husband, Burke, a bit of an amateur historian and a self-described "closeted Jew." Even Gunner, the army vet and groundskeeper for the now-defunct Temple Emeth who wore a muscle shirt in this awful weather, "had some Jew" in him. Once again, Okie identities contained multitudes, so a melancholic story about the last two Jews of Ardmore was going to be more complicated than I bargained for.

And why did I care so much anyway, they wanted to know? That was a good question. I wondered that myself. It was kind of strange, I had to admit. I was living in Berkeley, California, and enjoying a pretty sweet phase of life with a paid sabbatical from my job. I had family in Tulsa, but driving down to Ardmore during a Winter Weather Advisory, that was pretty odd. I confessed my strange fascination with decline, abandonment. I wondered, I told them, what happens when a once-thriving community disappears. I wanted to know how the seams of the community came undone.

At the turn of the twentieth century, parts of New York City had become virtual recreations of Jewish shtetls in the Old Country. The city was so densely packed that Congress started to consider limiting Jewish immigration. The German Jewish population, which had assimilated quickly and prospered in New York's financial industry, became concerned that the new immigrants were giving Jews a bad name. A New York banker named Jacob Schiff worried that the waves of immigrants from Eastern Europe would lead to an anti-Semitic backlash, as has happened periodically in Europe. A schism opened between German Jews and eastern European Jews; Schiff worked up a plan for the newcomers.

Schiff's main idea was to reroute Jewish immigration from Ellis Island to the South. He sunk at least half a million of his own dollars into a scheme to make Galveston the new hub for eastern European Jewish immigration. For a while, the Galveston Movement seemed to work. The first steamer to arrive in the Texas port was greeted by the mayor and brass band in 1907. Rabbis came from Houston and Fort Worth to help the newcomers find a place to live. Many stayed in Texas, but others caught the Santa Fe Railroad north or west.

Phyllis's grandfather got off the Santa Fe line at Ardmore and started peddling bananas from a cart downtown. He later started a scrap metal business, which proved to be extremely lucrative when oil was discovered in southern Oklahoma in the 1920s. Two of Tulsa lawyer Coleman Robison's grandparents came over as part of the Galveston Movement. Southern Oklahoma was in the midst of its first oil boom, land was cheap, and the future seemed bright.

Nevertheless, Schiff's plan is usually remembered as a failure. The economy took a turn for the worse, and then many Texas towns started scapegoating the newcomers. For their part, the Jewish immigrants often did not recognize the South and Southwest as the America of their dreams. Many felt alienated in devoutly Christian, segregated towns. This led to infighting among Schiff and his investors and a backlash from immigration officials in Galveston. The Galveston Movement collapsed in 1914.

For most of its history, Oklahoma has been a remarkably hospitable place for Jews. Even the poor Yiddish speakers from Russia—those great unwashed that Schiff so feared—quickly worked their way into the mainstream of Oklahoma life in small towns like Ardmore and Muskogee. They were scrap metal dealers and tailors. Dry goods merchants and dressmakers. Farmers and oil men.

"I've never been ostracized from any club," Phyllis tells me.

"And Phyllis was in everything," Stephanie said with a chuckle.

This, at least, is the story Oklahoma likes to tell itself: it is a young state as ready to accept Jews and Hindus as it is Baptists and Pentecostals. There is plenty of truth to that.

Rabbi Jeremy Simons, who has spent some time traveling around Oklahoma, said he has faced more anti-Semitism in California than he has in the South. (Simons did not hesitate to include Oklahoma in his description of the South, by the way.)

In reality, though, there have been some dark moments of anti-Semitism in the state, starting with the very beginnings of statehood, when Oklahomans voted to move the capital from Guthrie to Oklahoma City. The night after the vote, Assistant Secretary of State Leo Meyer took the official state seal out of Guthrie, catching the attention of the *Guthrie Daily Leader*, which proclaimed that the "Shylocks of Oklahoma City have the state by the throat." Meyer, himself a Jew, was part of an "unparalleled conspiracy on the part of Jews and Gentiles of a rotten town to loot the State for twenty-five years." It would be at least two generations before another Jew was elected to statewide office.

This supposed conspiracy did little to damage the state's reputation as a haven. Only two years after the Guthrie incident, the *Daily Ardmoreite* ran a glowing article about the arrival of a commissioner from a Jewish Industrial and Agricultural Aid Society in New York. "Thousands of progressive and scientific Hebrew farmers may settle in the state in the present year," the article stated. Wealthy German Jews in New York were still anxious about their status in mainstream America. Congress was actively considering legislation to restrict some minority groups and the Jewish Colonization Society scoped out locales as diverse as Argentina, Oklahoma, and western Canada to found new colonies far away from the historic sites of religious persecution.

News about Ardmore spread far and wide. Even as Oklahoma City and Tulsa boomed into the state's main cities, Ardmore still counted as the second-largest Jewish town in the state. Its distinctly Yiddish flavor grew when an ex–fighter pilot from World War I showed up in town in the early 1920s. Bill Krohn spoke Yiddish growing up in eastern Pennsylvania and came to Oklahoma for a new adventure. He settled into life in Ardmore, writing a column in the local paper about oil news. Krohn did not reveal his Jewish identity to the many oil men he met, but he greeted everyone downtown with the phrase "scholem aleichem," Hebrew for "peace be upon you."

The perhaps apocryphal story goes that Krohn cajoled and wheedled wildcatters with his charisma. They took him along to discovery wells where he would get the scoop about southern Oklahoma's next big oilfield. He was a huge Ardmore booster, penning columns in the *Ardmoreite* about the riches in southern Oklahoma. One night, on a rig floor, Krohn witnessed oil spouting straight into the air. "Scholem aleichem!" he shouted to all the roughnecks, who had no idea what the expression meant. The name stuck, and Scholem Aleichem became the name of an entire oil field between Duncan and Ardmore. Krohn started a club—also called Scholem Aleichem—that met in the lobby of the Ardmore Hotel. Technically, it was a benevolent society, but in reality it was little more than an excuse to smoke cigars, drink booze, and play cards. Another Jewish Ardmore oilman became the benefactor of a literary prize at the University of Oklahoma. One Ardmore Jew, Walter Neustadt, even put the town on the global literary map by starting the Neustadt International Prize for

Literature, often considered "the American Nobel Prize." The town built a new modernist synagogue in the 1950s in preparation for a bright future.

David Halpern, a Tulsa photographer who spent years documenting rural Oklahoma Jewry in a project called "Prairie Landsmen," also heard these stories and decided to track down an old Mobil Oil sign for Scholem Aleichem. Halpern says that locals who know the area well assume it is from an indigenous—probably Chickasaw—language. Is the phrase for the wealthy oilfield Chickasaw or Yiddish? It is a question that could only be posed in Oklahoma.

However, peace was not always upon Ardmore's Jews. Krohn's rise in fame paralleled the rise of one of Oklahoma's most notorious anti-Semites, Governor "Alfalfa Bill" Murray. Krohn was, at first, a booster for Murray. They were both colorful characters: the walrus-mustachioed Murray would deliver a stump speech standing on his head. Krohn, of all people, published the governor's first biography in 1932. Murray had his sights on the Democratic nomination for president, as a Dixiecrat challenger to Franklin Delano Roosevelt. After a resounding defeat, though, Murray started to rant about a Jewish conspiracy against him. Krohn left the state for other prospects in Illinois, while Murray produced tracts like: "Palestine, Shall Arabs or Jews Control It, or America Admit 100,000 Communist Jews from behind the Iron Curtain?" Murray, who by this time was residing in a hotel in Tishomingo, argued for adoption of Adolf Eichmann's "Madagascar Plan," which would force the world's Jewish population to relocate to the African island.

As an urban-dwelling secular humanist who cringes whenever an Oklahoma politician speaks, I came to Ardmore expecting to hear of suffering and discrimination. Curiously, most anti-Semitism in Oklahoma has happened in the cities, not in the smaller towns. The Silver Legion, an American fascist group active in the 1930s, looked to Tulsa, not Ardmore, for its headquarters. Rabbi Jeremy Simons travels a circuit around the South, conducting Jewish services for communities that no longer have a temple of their own. Most of his travels take him around the Deep South, but he has also been to Seminole, where a few Jews are still hanging on. Simons, who went to rabbinical school in Los Angeles and spent most of his life outside the South, says that he is surprised by the "great lengths people in small towns go to be Jewish. The Jewish community in Ardmore survived and grew despite waves of nativist anti-Semitism. Coleman Robison, a Tulsa lawyer who left Ardmore in 1964, celebrated his bar mitzvah at Temple Emeth in 1956. He remembers the town fondly. "It was a good place to grow up," Robison told me. But he always felt like a little bit of an outsider. "We weren't in the mainstream." His mother had to pull him out of Christmas plays, and Jews were still excluded from the country club. "But that was before the separation of Church and State was recognized in Oklahoma."

By the time of Robison's youth, the Jewish community was already in decline. After World War II, the prospect of selling scrap metal or dry goods to cowboys did not seem as appealing as it once did. Most of the postwar generation moved to nearby cities—Dallas, Tulsa, or Oklahoma City—but the community raised enough money to build a new temple in 1955, and Robison was one of the few boys to have a bar mitzvah there.

The architect of the temple, Ludwig Isenberg, was also its lay rabbi. Isenberg and his parents had come over on one of the last steamships out of Homburg before the Nazis started sending Jews to concentration camps. His parents were cattle farmers who had a distant relative in Stillwater. Five years after applying for an exit visa, the Isenbergs were allowed to leave Germany in 1938. The elder Isenberg took a small Torah from the local synagogue, wrapped it in dirty clothes, and stuffed it in a trunk. The Nazis confiscated everything of value the Isenbergs had, but they missed the Torah, which found a home in Ardmore for more than half a century until its synagogue was forced to close in 2003. The Torah is now on display at the Sherwin Miller Museum for Jewish Art in Tulsa.

Temple Emeth now sits empty in downtown Ardmore. It was almost bulldozed because its insulation consisted of asbestos, an expensive material to remove. It was sold to a local businessman who eventually ended up giving it to the Goddard Center. The center's groundskeeper, Boomer, showed me around the temple, yet Phyllis refused to come with me. "It's like going to a funeral, going in there," she says. "I prefer to remember it during better days."

4. The doors of Temple Emeth shut many years ago but stand in testament to Ardmore's Jewish heritage. Photo by the author.

There was something creepy about the temple. While the asbestos had been removed, and it appeared structurally sound, some rooms looked like they were abandoned in a hurry decades ago. A few random playing cards on a table. Some matches. Boomer and I marveled over an opened package of paper straws. "Did you have these growing up?" he asked me. "Nope," I said. "That was before my time." There were other condiments in the kitchen with expiration dates twenty years ago.

On the second floor of the Sherwin Miller Museum, I saw a model synagogue put together with artifacts from a number of now-defunct Oklahoma synagogues, including Temple Emeth in Ardmore and Beth Ahaba in Muskogee. The museum displayed a bemah from Ardmore and a Torah from Muskogee. An entire wall was devoted to a dozen or so Jewish communities in small Oklahoma towns. In some, a once-sizable Jewish population has disappeared entirely. In others, like Ardmore and Seminole, there are only a few Jews left, most in their sixties and seventies.

They are people like Phyllis and Stephanie who see little chance of their children coming back to Ardmore. So their task has been to assure their "perpetual care" at Mount Zion.

Phyllis and Stephanie gave me a tour of the cemetery, which was just across the road from the Oklahoma Confederate veterans cemetery. Wandering around the graves of Fishmans, Yoffees, and Greenburgs, it was clear that Mount Zion symbolized the once and future home of Ardmore Judaism. Phyllis was dedicated to making sure the cemetery, and the people there, would not be forgotten. "We now have money for perpetual care," she said. "When there is nobody left in Ardmore, we have funds to take care of the cemetery. A trust ensures that the grass is mowed, the leaves are raked, and the trees are trimmed."

A famous rabbi, Simon Rawidowicz, once wrote that Jews are the "ever-dying people." It was precisely this fear—that the present generation may be the last—that paradoxically kept Judaism alive. I asked Rabbi Simons if it makes him sad to see Judaism disappear from small towns. "Jews have been a minority religion for at least two thousand years," he said. "Of course it's sad. It's sad for everyone, especially the last members of a community. But it's just like the human life cycle. We are born, we grow and thrive, then we get old and die."

Jews served a role in small-town Oklahoma: they were *machers*, an untranslatable Yiddish term for someone who gets stuff done, one who brokers deals or works as a "fixer"—mostly for good but occasionally for ill. Half a century ago, *machers* dotted the chamber of commerce in Muskogee, Ardmore, and Ponca City.

I picked up the day's copy of the *Daily Ardmoreite*. It had a fancy pull-out about the town's economic revival and photos of all the members of the Chamber of Commerce. Nary a Jew there. But the guy who ran the brand new La Quinta Inn off I-35, Mitesh Patel, was a hotelier looking to expand his Ardmore-based Apollo Hospitality Group into North Texas. Now that man seemed like a *macher*. Indeed, it is often said in twenty-first-century America that Indian immigrants are the new Jews, but that is another story.

Back in Tulsa, I asked Coleman Robison if he was saddened by the prospect of a purely Gentile Ardmore. "It is what it is," Robison said. He has a poster of a coffee mug in his well-appointed law office. "Oy freakin' vey," the mug reads. Robison spoke with some difficulty and walked with a cane, but his eyes still gleamed with vitality and a sense of humor. He was also on the board of the Mount Zion Cemetery Association. He went down to Ardmore occasionally to visit the graves of his parents, but now he was now more concerned about the future of the Jewish community in Tulsa than he was about Ardmore.

"The same pattern is repeating itself here," he said. "I saw the bright lights of the city and never wanted to go back." Now all Robinson's children have gone "back east," with no intention of coming back to Tulsa. "The opportunities just aren't here."

On the surface, Tulsa appears to be the most prosperous Jewish community in Oklahoma. Its Jewish population is larger than that of Oklahoma City. The Sherwin Miller Museum gleams with a new brass exterior in South Tulsa next to a swanky new retirement community and robust Jewish Community Center. Names like Kaiser, Shusterman, and Kravis are inextricably linked to the city's development and its current renaissance.

But Tulsa's Jewish population, too, is shrinking. According to the Institute for Southern Jewish Life, "About two-thirds of the Jewish children raised in Tulsa do not come back after college; while the city continues to attract new Jewish families, they are unable to offset this loss." Many Jewish Tulsans quietly speculate that the community has built up an infrastructure—an expanded museum, community center, retirement villa—that will not be supported by a declining population.

What this means and whether it even matters depends on how you see the state's identity. Oklahoma has been, at various times, a destination for displaced Native Americans, Alabama sharecroppers, Black freedmen, Jewish merchants, and Pennsylvania oilmen. All these populations have evolved. Many intermixed to contribute to our sui generis inter-American mestizo identity. Other populations moved on entirely or assimilated into the white mainstream. More recently, the state's Latino population has quadrupled, and its Asian population has doubled since 1990, giving rise to a new nativist movement that has more in common with Alfalfa Bill Murray than it would like to admit.

So, as Oklahoma says its long goodbye to its Jews, it might also want to consider how it says hello to its newcomers: Muslims, Latinos, and Hindus in all shades of brown.

CHAPTER 6

Okies in the Promised Land

When I was in high school, no course attracted as much universal loathing as Oklahoma history. My preppy little Catholic school had managed to find a way to squeeze the state's requirement for one unit of Oklahoma history into a four-week period in January known as minimester: a glorious time of sleeping, snacking, and ass-kicking punctuated by field trips to museums. The head basketball coach, Coach McBain, was the poor soul in charge of the course. He did not try to feign expertise or interest in the subject. McBain put on *The Grapes of Wrath* or *Oklahoma!* and mocked up basketball plays on a handheld whiteboard.

At some point, I plopped down from my desk and sprawled out on the short-pile Berber carpet during one of these screenings. I folded my hands across my stomach and fell asleep. McBain said nothing. The next day, I repeated the same procedure when McBain put on a documentary about the formation of Oklahoma statehood. I was down on the floor, ready for sleep to overtake me as familiar images of pioneers and cowboys flickered on screen. Then, out of nowhere, a crushing blow came down on my head. At first, I thought it was McBain taking his revenge on the somnolent mutiny that accompanied his documentary. Perhaps I was having an aneurysm. The worried face of Brian Jester appeared. He had brought down a metal chair with full force on a spot above my left eyebrow. I touched the spot. Blood was trickling into my eye. "What the hell?" I muttered.

Jester's plan to escape Oklahoma history had gone horribly wrong. He had stacked a chair on a desk to give him access to a window, so as to slip out of the classroom while McBain was occupied with basketball plays. The chair had slipped off the desk and onto my head. Jester gave me a dirty T-shirt from his backpack to stanch the bleeding. My first instinct was to punch him, but I was too dazed to do anything but stare at the screen. Jester begged me to keep the whole incident quiet. I held the T-shirt to my brow and waited.

This was how I came to learn about E. P. McCabe. According to the documentary, which referenced an out-of-print book called *Oklahoma: A History of the Sooner State* by Edwin McReynolds, McCabe was an obscure Kansas politician with a vision of Oklahoma as a refuge for former slaves. McCabe had an idea that Oklahoma could become the nation's only all-Black state. As the state auditor of Kansas, he lobbied President William Henry Harrison in the 1890s to appoint him as governor of Indian Territory, and when that did not work out, he headed down to the small town of Langston, which was already a haven for Black settlers. If the U.S. government was not going to make Oklahoma an all-Black state, McCabe would take matters into his own hands. The Sac and Fox Nation had been forced to open up their surplus land for settlement, and McCabe recruited ex-slaves and tenant farmers from Mississippi and Arkansas to out-Sooner the Sooners. They staked their claims outside Langston but found themselves in shootouts with white settlers. On one occasion, McCabe dodged five or six rounds of gunfire from a group of white settlers on Sac and Fox land. In the 1890s McCabe ran for state office as a Republican but was beaten by the Democrat. It was the white Democrats who then proceeded to build Oklahoma into a state, mirroring policies of segregation in the Deep South.

I sat there in McBain's classroom, entranced by this parallel universe. Tulsa—my little slice of it between Utica Square, Cascia Hall, and Riverside Drive—was so white. There was one Black family in my neighborhood of Maple Ridge. There were two Black students in my graduating class of 1992. My school refused to recognize Martin Luther King Jr. Day as a holiday. And here was this story of an alternate reality that could have been: had McCabe succeeded, maybe I would be the only white kid in an all-Black class right now.

The day after the injury, fully recovered from the blow to my head, I found the Reynolds book in the library. I stuck it in my backpack like some sort of contraband. Being interested in Oklahoma history was, for a high schooler, possibly one of the most uncool things one could be interested in. No, it was worse than uncool. Chemistry, trigonometry, calculus: those subjects were uncool. Oklahoma history? That was just *weird*. Weird: pronounced *wee-erd*. This *weird* was not, as the dictionary would have it, of "strange or extraordinary character" but rather deviance from social acceptability.

"That's just weird" was a statement meant not to provoke curiosity about something strange but to shut down nonconformity. And I was already weird enough. On free dress days, I sported a Hakeem Olajuwon basketball jersey and a red, black, and green Africa medallion that I had seen on the necks of my hip-hop heroes: De La Soul, Public Enemy, and A Tribe Called Quest. I spent my free time reading autobiographies of Malcolm X and Eldridge Cleaver. I really wanted to be in the Black Panther Party. An upperclassman on my basketball team called me an insult that combined "white" and the n-word. It was not so much that I wanted to be Black, I realize now, as that I wanted to be something *other*. Something other than the white, milquetoast, preppy frat-boys-in-training who surrounded me. I borrowed some elements of a punk aesthetic from my friend Jeff, who went to a public school. Jeff wore combat boots, spiked bracelets, and ripped t-shirts from the Misfits and the Exploited. I incorporated a little bit of that look into my Afro-centric look. The handful of Black students at my school had bigger problems than my furtive experiments in cultural appropriation.

My interest in Oklahoma history was secretive. At lunch, I opened the book to learn more about McCabe and his plan to make Oklahoma a Black promised land. But there was nothing there. The book—I still have it today—does mention Langston as one of Oklahoma's all-Black towns, but there was nothing about McCabe. There was no mention of Senate Bill 1 either. Nothing on the Tulsa Race "Riot" of 1921 or the criminal conspiracy at the heart of the guardianship program of Native Americans.[1] Nothing on jazz or western swing or Woody Guthrie or the Green Corn Rebellion. Lots of stuff on oil, cowboys, land runs, and our supposedly progressive constitution. No wonder the official history seemed so damn boring.

In 1907 Oklahoma became the forty-sixth state in the union. After our shotgun wedding between Mr. Oklahoma Territory and Ms. Indian Territory, the legislature got down to business. The first item on the agenda ensured that public transportation was comfortable. Senate Bill 1 promoted "the comfort of passengers of railroads, street cars, urban, interurban, and suburban cars, and at train stations."[2] It was an emergency law, and it was passed quickly, with little opposition and little discussion. So little discussion, in fact, it is hard to find information on Senate Bill 1. The purpose of the law was not comfort, as the summary of the act said, but segregation. A full reading of the bill's subsections make this clear.[3] The bill stipulated that every railway company operating in the new state should provide separate cars, waiting rooms, and bathrooms for the "white and negro races." The bill went on to discuss what materials should be used to keep the races apart ("a good and substantial wooden partition") and what fines should be issued to those people who violated the partitions (fines started at $25). The state adopted the so-called "one-drop rule," defining "the negro" as "anyone of African descent."

Before 1907 eastern Oklahoma had been Indian Territory, and the various Native American nations within the territory were all products of generations of mixing. Muscogees (Creeks), Cherokees, and Choctaws had been slave-owning tribes but had intermixed freely with poor whites and ex-slaves. No one was pure. Blood quantum was much less important than name recognition on tribal rolls. Some Muscogees (Creeks) were a mix of Scots Irish and indigenous ancestry. Some were African. In this new political setup, however, everything hinged on a drop of African blood.

I know about Senate Bill 1 because I eventually tracked down the entire text of Oklahoma's first state law in an Ardmore newspaper from a digitized internet archive. Senate Bill 1 does not feature in the musical *Oklahoma!*, where there's "plenty of hope and plenty of room to swing a rope."[4] Senate Bill 1 does not even figure into the more overtly political literature from the state—Woody Guthrie's "Dust Bowl Ballads" or John Steinbeck's *Grapes of Wrath*. The salt-of-the-earth proletariat in that literature may be the underbelly of capitalist greed, but it is a white underbelly. The fact that Oklahoma's first order of business as a state was to codify and enforce Jim Crow laws from the Old South is not proclaimed on historical plaques or advertised in tours of the state capitol. Unlike other southern states, there are few public monuments to remind anyone of any sort of historical racism here. The Confederate flag is rarely seen, even though the Civil War in Indian Territory was every bit as vicious and devastating as it was in the South. Many Tulsans are still unaware that the worst outbreak of racial violence after the Civil War occurred in their sleepy town of rolling hills and oil mansions. The history of racism in the state registers as a few blips on the internet.

We do not like to talk about anything unpleasant.

For most people, the story of the formation of this odd, butcher-knife-shaped territory is the story of the Sooners, the white settlers who arrived in waves of land runs after two territories—Oklahoma and Indian Territory—were opened for white settlement. This event, unlike Senate Bill 1, is reenacted, retold, and reinforced down to the present day. Every touchdown by the University of Oklahoma Sooners football team is celebrated by a ride around the field on the Sooner Schooner, a symbol of the covered wagons white settlers drove on their way to claim unassigned lands in the territories.

My mother's side of the family traces its roots back to these original settlers. Like most of them, they were poor and landless southerners who were trapped in tenancy agreements back in Dixie. For them, Indian Territory was not so much the Wild West as it was an unruly suburb of the

Old South. The Native Americans who had been removed there brought with them many southern practices: cotton farming, evangelicalism, grits, and, yes, slavery.[5] It was an interesting clash of southern cultures: poor southern whites invading a land where dispossessed Native Americans had held slaves and now, forced to end the institution, had intermarried with them and granted them full citizenship in the Creek, Seminole, and Cherokee Nations. Later, after the white invasion, the Five Tribes dispossessed their Black citizens (known as "freedmen"), partly as a way to assimilate into the new political reality of Jim Crow Oklahoma.

Into this strange world my great-great grandparents arrived from Tennessee. They settled in the heart of the disintegrating Muscogee (Creek) Nation, sometime in the very early twentieth century. Their quarter-section of land lay just outside the town of Checotah and adjacent to allotments granted to Creek families under the Dawes Act. I do not know what sort of relations my great-great-grandparents had with their new neighbors, but my grandmother was old enough to remember the last days of the first generation of white settlers. One day, when I was probably eight years old, she took me to the Checotah cemetery. Her grandparents, Vernon and Jordan, are buried next to a certain LeFleur family. "Creek Indians," my grandmother said of the LeFleurs. "They were treated worse than dogs. They were also my best friends."

My grandmother was a lifelong Republican who saw every Democrat as a secret communist. She loathed her poor upbringing and got out of Checotah as quickly as she could. She was the one who told me the difference between Democrats and Republicans was that Democrats were the party of poor people. If you wanted to be someone, you were Republican. But when it came to the issue of Native Americans, she was radicalized. After her first husband—my biological grandfather—died from complications of alcoholism, she took up a decades-long relationship with a Choctaw activist and artist, St. Clair Homer. I owe my middle name (St. Clair) to him.

Every anniversary of the Battle of Wounded Knee, St. Clair would declare himself on a "warpath." Naked above the waist except for a headdress, he paraded around Tulsa calling on his "red brothers" to rise up and resist white supremacy. My mom, a teenager at the time, found the whole thing embarrassing. She was a student at Central High School desperately trying gain acceptance from the "socs" (the gang of rich boys made famous by *The Outsiders*). Her stepfather, with his long braids and public stunts celebrating "red pride," was not helping her cause.

Even as a little boy I had difficulty squaring my grandmother's Southern Baptist conservatism with her devotion to this Native American radical, but that is the real Oklahoma history in a nutshell: a story of contradictions. Every summer St. Clair made cards to send to all his family and friends in anticipation of June 25, when General Custer was killed by Sitting Bull. It was a lifelong quest of his to turn Custer's 1871 "haircut" into something like a national holiday. "Red brother, rejoice!" he wrote. When St. Clair died in 1987, I think some part of my mom was relieved.

I, however, was perplexed. A new man—a white oilman with a college degree—replaced St. Clair as my grandfather. I saw this man as an interloper. I wanted my grandfather to be the Indian warrior, not the number-crunching landman. To this day, many people assume I am Latino, Mediterranean, or part Native. I am constantly bombarded with questions about my "blood." People skirt around the question, asking about heritage and culture, but what they really want to know about is this matter of blood. I speak fluent Spanish, and I stick out among the northern Europeans in Canada. My first girlfriend in college, an Australian, insisted that I was a "mulatto." I got harassed by a crowd in Sweden for being an Arab. Put together my swarthy skin with my Native grandfather figure, and I assumed that I was not quite 100 percent white. I was perfectly happy with that, since my pigment of skin seemed to be a literal manifestation of my metaphorical black sheep status in the family. I realize now that this identification with nonwhiteness sprung from a position of privilege. I never suffered discrimination or oppression based on my skin color. I never shouldered the pain of intergenerational trauma, nor did I have to attend underfunded schools or grow up in a poor neighborhood. And yet I felt, and to some degree still feel, that I am a sort of racial off-white, like that part of the paint swatch labeled seashell, ghostwhite, or parchment. Looking at the scrubbed faces, blue eyes, and golden locks of my ultra-white country club cousins, I feel a category removed from total privilege. "Another class of people," Merle Haggard sings about his Okie family, "put us somewhere just below." To the Cobbs, that is where my mother's people were from: somewhere just below the class of people who could afford membership at the country club.

It was an uncomfortably warm and humid evening in Clearwater, British Columbia more than twenty years after my graduation from high school that I once again saw Oklahoma in a different light. In a place where an August snowstorm is not uncommon, the smoke from forest fires combined with the heat to make for a smoldering afternoon. I was at the Wells Grey Diner plowing through a plate of French fries and a watery Canadian lager when Rick Jamerson came through the door. Somehow, he knew I was the person who had been persistently dogging him via email about meeting him and his gospel-revival group, the Black Pioneer Heritage Singers. I was there to watch his group of gospel singers, descended from Oklahoma immigrants, headline a Christian music festival up the highway. There were the living legacy of McCabe's dream. Jamerson was a handsome man with the look of someone two decades younger. He was followed by his equally striking wife, Junetta, the lead singer of the group. I wiped off my ketchup-stained fingers to shake their hands.

We are all Okies of a sort, I told the Jamersons. I explained to them what a weird coincidence it was that we were meeting there, in middle-of-nowhere British Columbia, when we all come from Oklahoma. But Junetta was not having it. She was not *from* Oklahoma.

"If you flew here and changed planes in Denver, would you say you come from Denver?" she asked me. Oklahoma was a stopover, she says, to their ultimate destination: Northern Alberta, the northernmost edge of farmland in North America. I persisted.

"Everyone knows about the Okies from the Great Depression," I said. "It's part of the American national mythology. Dirt farmers pulling up stakes and heading west: *The Grapes of Wrath* and the music of Woody Guthrie. You guys," I told them, "were the original Okies, but no one in Oklahoma knows your story!" They looked back at me quizzically. Only later it occurred to me that they had probably never heard the word *Okie* before.

In the early 1900s, Oklahoma seemed like the promised land for Black Americans suffering through Jim Crow in the South. E. P. McCabe's solution, resettling former slaves on Indian lands, seemed promising. McCabe's plan was to have Black settlers gather in Langston and then fan out across the state, gaining majorities in most counties. He needed to give people real incentives, so he devised a plan. In pamphlets sent out across the South, McCabe told prospective settlers that the values of the land would soon double and massive profits could be made. More importantly, though, was the idea of a self-governance. "At the present time," McCabe wrote in one pamphlet, "we are Republicans, but the time will soon come when we will be able to dictate the policy of this Territory, or state, and when that time comes we will have a negro state governed by negroes. We do not wish to antagonize the whites. They are necessary in the development of a new country but they owe my race homes, and my race owes to itself a governmental control of those homes."

With statehood, however, Oklahoma started repeating the tragedy of the rest of the South, only in fast-forward. Within a couple of years, Oklahoma had turned from Canaan to Egypt, and Blacks lost the vote and all power in state politics. Farmers like J. D. Edwards—one of the thousand or so who eventually left for Canada—paid the price.

Roving bands of white mobs terrorized small towns in the early years of statehood. White cappers, as they were known, rode out the entire Black population of Sapulpa during a single day in 1909. They lynched a man in Henryetta from a telegraph pole and then riddled the corpse with bullets. They chased an entire all-Black town to Muskogee and then burned down buildings where they thought Blacks were hiding. A race riot broke out in Okmulgee. In another country, Americans would call this wave of violence an ethnic cleansing. At the time, it was considered a civilizing mission. The *Tulsa Tribune* praised the work of the Klan in "cleaning out" Black neighborhoods like Greenwood in Tulsa. The white mobs were egged on by the editor of the *Daily Oklahoman*, Ray Stafford, an ardent racist who wanted the new state to be a part of the Solid South.

This meant purging Oklahoma of Republicans, a party that, at the time, was a biracial coalition whose platform consisted of Civil Rights and equal protection for all citizens, regardless of color, under the law. Stafford taunted Republicans for not backing Jim Crow amendments to the state constitution.

For Stafford, Oklahoma had a choice: it could take the Texas road or the Kansas road toward race relations. When Oklahoma enacted laws segregating everything from street cars to schools, as well as instituting a grandfather clause that disenfranchised virtually every Black voter, Stafford got his answer. Texas, he wrote, should be proud of Oklahoma that it did not follow the path of Republican Kansas. In the end, Stafford wrote, "a Republican politician cannot be separated from the n———."

Black Oklahomans were in a panic. McCabe disappeared from the scene. Some accused him of creating a land bubble under the guise of a Black homeland. A mysterious man named "Chief Sam" arrived in Oklahoma in 1913, promising a bright future along the Gold Coast of Africa. After one ill-fated trip in 1914 in which the migrants almost died of starvation, Chief Sam disappeared as well. Canadian immigration agents started recruiting in Oklahoma. After the discovery of oil in Bartlesville, Cushing, and modern-day Glenpool, the stakes were raised. Oklahoma was no longer a place of cheap land; it was the locus of America's black gold rush. Western Canada, on the other hand, had nothing but land, or so it seemed. With the continental United States settled, Canada promoted its new provinces of British Columbia and Alberta as "the last, best West." Land could be had for pennies. Pioneers were even granted subsidies for rail travel on the Canadian National. Somehow, word got out that Canada was warmer than Oklahoma and that Canadians had no racial prejudice at all. Glowing reports of Canada started appearing in the newspapers of all-Black towns in Oklahoma.

Henry Sneed, a man from Clearview, one of Oklahoma's dozen or so all-Black towns, decided to go scope out this place called Canada. He traveled by rail from Tulsa to Winnipeg and from there on to Edmonton. Sneed must have liked what he saw, because he returned, this time with company. Among his companions was Jefferson Davis Edwards, a cotton and tobacco farmer originally from Pine Bluff, Arkansas. Edwards, then twenty-one years old and single, made the trek from Tulsa to Winnipeg, where he had his first taste of whiskey at a saloon. In Edmonton, the men, in the words of one Alberta historian, "were seen more as curiosities than as threats."

Sneed again went back to Oklahoma and gathered up 194 men, women, and children. They sold their houses and their farms and filled two hundred rail cars with their horses and livestock. Weeks later, they arrived in Edmonton where journalists from the local paper covered their arrival.

To a newcomer, Edmonton feels like a frontier town on the northernmost boundary of civilization. At least, that is what it feels like in in the early twenty-first century. One hundred years ago, it must have felt like another planet. But the Okies did not stop in Edmonton. Canadian officials gave them land far from the city in settlements that did not appeal to white immigrants from Britain, Germany, and the Ukraine. The most notable settlement, Amber Valley, was even further flung than Edmonton, and it took weeks to get there. Edwards landed in Amber Valley and set about clearing land, mostly by hand. In the course of a week, he later estimated, he cleared a space of land for farming that was about the size of a living room.

Despite the hardships, more Black Oklahomans fled to Canada. Another group of two hundred people followed Sneed's party but was detained in Emerson, on the Minnesota-Manitoba border. Canadian officials had begun to doubt whether Blacks were suited to the climate of Canada and administered medical exams. When all the Okies passed the exam, the Canadians demanded a head tax. In Edmonton, where they had once been seen as curiosities, locals started to organize against further immigration. Black settlements were popping up all over Alberta, and local officials feared that Alberta would become a haven for the entire South. A petition by the Edmonton Board of Trade was circulated throughout town addressed to the Prime Minister:

We, the undersigned residents of the City of Edmonton, respectfully urge upon your attention and that of the Government of which you

are the head, the serious menace to the future welfare of a large portion of western Canada, by reason of the alarming influx of Negro
settlers. . . . We submit that the advent of such Negroes as are now
here was most unfortunate for the country, and that further arrivals
would be disastrous. We cannot admit as any factor the argument that
these people may be good farmers or good citizens. It is a matter of
common knowledge that it has been proved in the United States that
Negroes and whites cannot live in proximity without the occurrence
of revolting lawlessness, and the development of bitter race hatred.

About one-quarter of the city's twenty-four thousand residents signed
on. The minister of the interior, who happened to be from Edmonton,
drafted an order of council and sent it to Prime Minister Wilfred Lau-
rier for his signature. He declared that "For a period of one year from
and after the date hereof the landing in Canada shall be . . . prohibited
of any immigrants belonging to the Negro race, which race is deemed
unsuitable to the climate and requirements of Canada."

Before the Black Pioneer Heritage Singers took the stage on a little
farm outside Clearwater, the group gathered for a prayer in a tent. They
were sweating through their crisp Sunday whites, in stark contrast to the
shorts-and-tank-tops crowd that mills about eating popcorn. The band on
stage before them served up soft, sincere Christian pop, and the crowd
seemed distracted. Junetta Jamerson did not seem all that thrilled about
the venue, but once the group took the stage, it was as if this bucolic farm
in British Columbia suddenly became a Black Baptist church in the South.
Jamerson, who mostly spoke in a lilting Canadian accent punctuated with
the occasional "eh," had the entire crowd on its feet by the end of the
first song, "On the Wings of Heaven."

Between songs, Jamerson's voice started to shift. She started to sound
like a Black preacher from the South. "We don't have to wait 'til we get
to heaven, we can shout now! I've have got my shouting shoes on now,
so y'all better watch out."

By the second song, the Edwin Hawkins Singers classic, "Oh Happy
Day," the crowd was stomping and clapping, not quite in rhythm with

the gospel soul of the Heritage Singers, but enthusiastic nonetheless. It was a remarkable show, despite the fact that there was not even time for a sound check.

The next morning, back at the Wells Grey Diner, Jamerson told me that the group is often seen as a "curiosity" when they travel to the United States. "The first time I went to DC, I spoke at an event at the Smithsonian Folkways Festival," Jamerson said. "Some Black gentleman who was an African American history professor listened to me tell our story. Later, he came up to me and said, 'young lady, are you sure that what you're saying is true?' In all his learned studies, he had never heard of the Black One Thousand."

I had never heard of the Black One Thousand either. It had originally been a fear-mongering term, referring to the Black Oklahomans who had poured into the sparsely populated Canadian prairies before the government went on an anti-immigration campaign, sending agents back to Oklahoma to warn against further migration. A Black physician from Chicago, C. W. Speers, was hired to tour Oklahoma and spread the bad news about life up north. In churches and newspapers, Speers told African Americans that Canada was much colder than Oklahoma. So cold, in fact, that many immigrants were freezing or starving to death. Canadians, he said, were just as racist as Oklahomans. The land was terrible, and there was no guarantee Blacks could even secure a title to the land they struggled to clear and farm. By the outbreak of World War I, Black immigration to Alberta had stopped completely.

Some of the Alberta pioneers went back to Oklahoma, while others moved on to greener and warmer pastures in California. J. D. Edwards, after he had carved a prosperous farm out of the pine forest, went back to Oklahoma City to visit his brother, who had become a self-made millionaire selling scrap metal during World War II. Edwards tried to get around segregation on the trains by claiming he was no longer an American and wore a Union Jack in his hatband to prove it. Quenten Green, one of Edwards's great-grandsons and the keyboard player in the Heritage Singers, told me that Edwards wanted to return to Oklahoma for good. "Towards the end of his life, he was talking about going back."

The exodus of African Americans from Oklahoma created a static historical memory that remained stuck in the minds of the descendants of the settlers until recently. The Oklahoma settlers gradually gained acceptance and became fully Canadian. They moved from farming settlements to cities: Edmonton, Calgary, Vancouver. But, Jamerson said, their vision became provincial. Because Canadians came to treat them like just another immigrant group, they missed out on the cultural movements of civil rights and Black Power. When Jamerson's father, a Californian escaping the Vietnam War, came to Alberta, he found a community that had not changed in its values or beliefs in half a century. Now she is afraid that the Black settlers have completely assimilated into mainstream Canadian society. "The new generation of African-Americans here doesn't know where they come from," she said. "They don't know what kind of Black they are. If you ask them where they're from, they say, 'Nowhere.'"

Many of the descendants are not visibly Black, at least by U.S. standards. Two or three generations of intermarriage with whites have resulted in a current generation with few cultural ties to its roots in the African American experience. Furthermore, despite a sizable population, there is no Black neighborhood in Edmonton or Calgary. For years, the community revolved around a Shiloh Baptist Church, but now even that institution is thoroughly integrated into mainstream white Canadian society. Fearing a loss of African American culture in Alberta, Jamerson and her husband started the Black Pioneer Heritage Singers in the early 2000s. They play southern Black gospel, a sound that is rarely heard in western Canada. Gauging from their reception at the Christian music festival in Clearwater, British Columbia, there is a hunger among Canadian audiences for the music. Still, the Heritage Singers are as much a cultural mission about a lost chapter in American history as they are a musical group.

Jamerson told me that the first time she went to the South for a family reunion near Dallas, she was scared. The memories of violence had been passed down two generations and she feared outward racism and a society stuck in the 1950s. What she found in Texas, however, shocked her. "The infrastructure there was light years beyond what we have in Canada. We seemed like the hicks."

The older generation does not like to talk about what happened in the South, Paul Gardener, another member of the Black Pioneer Heritage Singers, told me. Gardener said that, for the older generation, Oklahoma represented Egypt and Alberta was Israel. Once they were freed from bondage, they did not look back. "Some of them were afraid that they'd be sold back into slavery if they went back," Gardener said. "This was the promised land." On their CD, the experience of the Black Oklahoma pioneers is captured in a sung poem, "Amber Valley Pine." The song pays homage to the exodus from Oklahoma while also striking a note of optimism. After fleeing the South, Black pioneers "put down some roots" in the foothills of northern Alberta.

I had imagined the Black pioneers of Alberta as the original Okies, a group rooted in Oklahoma who set out West to improve their lives. To them, however, Oklahoma was simply a stopover from the Deep South to the Far North. In her book about the Black experience in Tulsa, *They Came Searching*, Eddie Faye Gates collected dozens of oral histories of African American pioneers who saw Oklahoma as a promised land. As Jim Crow laws and mob violence turned that promised land into a nightmare, many continued on down that road, looking for another land of milk and honey, another place—California or Canada—to call home.

But maybe this is at the heart of what it means to be an Okie, to be in constant movement toward a home that is always just over the horizon. Tom Joad and Woody Guthrie left Oklahoma and never looked back. My grandmother hated going back to her old homestead on the farm. My mom also looked back with derision on her upbringing in Muskogee. When the future beckons, the past can be deadly. Orpheus died when he turned to look for Euridice in the underworld. Lot's wife refused to listen to the Lord's commandment that she should not look back at Sodom as her family fled. She disobeyed and was turned to a pillar of salt. "I'm going where there's no depression," the Carter Family sang in 1936, "to a better land that's free from care." It has always been easier to look forward than backward, to be sure. But a look in the rearview mirror reflects a reality that is closer than it appears.

CHAPTER 7

Among the Tribe of the Wannabes

Let us travel to a not-so-distant land for a visit to an understudied tribe. Before we begin our expedition, a trivia question: what do Bill Clinton, Miley Cyrus, Johnny Cash, and Elizabeth Warren all have in common? Answer: all of them have claimed to be part Cherokee at some point in their lives. Not that any of these celebrities is unique in this regard. Rare is the Oklahoman who does not proclaim some small fraction of Native American blood. My best friend from high school liked to remind me that a great-grandfather was on the Dawes Rolls of the Cherokee Nation, making him one-thirty-second Native American, like just about everyone else I knew. In the past thirty years or so, it has become a marker of cultural capital to have some Native "blood." The writer Rilla Askew remarks in her essay "Trail" that "when I left Oklahoma in 1980, no one was Indian. When I came back in the 1990s, everyone was."[1]

According to the Cherokee Nation, there are approximately 120,000 tribal members living in the state, which has a population of 3.8 million people. That means that only about 3 percent of Oklahomans are citizens of the Cherokee Nation. The tribe we are going to visit on our voyage, however, is bigger than the Cherokee Nation and perhaps even bigger than the entire state of Oklahoma. We are among the tribe of the Wannabes: non-Native Americans who insist on claiming Native heritage.

Why do Wannabes appropriate, fabricate, and invent a Native identity? Is it for financial gain? Is it part of a colonialist project to speak for the Other? An edge to gain admission to an elite college? A highly subjective existential crisis? Examining the motives of the Wannabes is a fraught subject, one where good intentions rub up against old racist habits and where narrative embroidery easily morphs into self-delusion. In Wannabe Nation, the personal is political, the political is paradoxical, and nothing is as it seems. The Native great-grandmother (*why is it always a woman who constitutes the origin of the Native ancestry?*) in the closet of a white-passing family does a lot of symbolic work: she serves as a vaccination against anyone who might question the legitimacy of white land claims in a place like Oklahoma, where many—if not most—deeds from Native Americans were gotten by unethical means. The Cherokee "princess" (there is no such title in the Cherokee Nation) also insulates whites against charges of racism while keeping open the possibility that further claims on Native land might be established in the future. She atones for the guilt of the white settler, while making him feel like he truly belongs in this place. She connects him to the founding mythology of America: the ideology of Thanksgiving, of John Smith and Pocahontas. That is a lot of symbolic work for one ancestor.

The explosion in the numbers of the tribe of the Wannabes constitutes an ironic twist in history. In the early twentieth century, actual Native Americans in Oklahoma were subject to cultural genocide: languages suppressed, families broken apart, lands stolen. If a white person wanted a particular piece of Native land, he (and it was almost always a man) could go down to the courthouse and have the Native owner declared "incompetent" by a judge. Cherokee children in particular were often taken from their biological parents and put into missionary schools or subject to forced adoption. One way for whites to get access to restricted Native American allotments was to marry into the families who owned the allotments. This led to much more mixing in Oklahoma than states with Native reservations. The list of atrocities committed against Native Americans in Oklahoma well into the 1960s would take volumes to fully document. As a result, many white-passing Okies hid their Native heritage out of fear. With that mind, we need to proceed in our journey to the Land of the Wannabes with a big caveat: many Wannabes may not be Wannabes at all but people attempting to reconnect to a culture marginalized by the white mainstream. We contain multitudes.

Our voyage begins in earnest with the case of Iron Eyes Cody, a man better known to the world as "the Crying Indian." If you watched TV at any time from the 1970s to the mid-1980s, you will remember the Crying Indian. He debuted on television on Earth Day 1971, a moment often dubbed as the birth of the modern environmental movement. The ad, produced by the advertising group the Ad Council, is one of the most emotionally powerful one-minute spots ever produced. The Ad Council, a pro-bono conglomerate that creates public service announcements, sponsored the commercial. Rosie the Riveter, Smokey Bear, "Just Say No": all public service announcements produced by the Ad Council.

The ad begins with a vague image of a man in a canoe barely visible through the leaves of a tree. He paddles gently down a river to a slow thud of drums. The fringe from his buckskin jacket, two braids of long hair, and a single feather in his headband come into view. We briefly glimpse the idyllic image of unspoiled America: pine trees, a glistening lake, and a Noble Savage in a canoe. Here is the natural man as Jean-Jacques Rousseau once imagined him: the human being at one with nature and freed from the shackles of societal conventions. Now we are face-to-face with our stoic warrior. He paddles with more vigor as the tempo of the music picks up. The camera zooms in on two pieces of garbage in the water. A brassy soundtrack starts to blare, and the camera sweeps out to reveal a factory belching smoke and more litter in the lake. Our Noble Savage drags his canoe to a shoreline littered with plastic cups and aluminum cans, his head bowed in sorrow.

The man now walks to a road filled with traffic, his once-stoic face now showing signs of a profound sadness as he watches garbage being tossed out of passing cars. An off-screen baritone narrator intones the following: "Some people have a deep, abiding respect for the natural beauty that was once this country. And some people don't." A plastic sack dropped by a motorist explodes at our Wise Elder's feet, his buckskin now soiled by fast food. The narrator pauses a beat, allowing a sense of collective shame to wash over the audience. The narrator starts back in again: "People start pollution, and people can stop it."

Now the money shot. A single tear wells up, finally rolling down the man's cheek as the screen fades to black. Many people have wondered about this tragic figure, and in his 1982 memoir, *Iron Eyes: My Life as a Hollywood Indian*, Cody purported to give a full account of his life. He tells us he was born and raised on a ranch in Oklahoma to a family of Creek and Cherokee farmers, only finding fame years later as a character actor and consultant on Indian dress and sign language to famous directors such as Cecil B. DeMille and John Ford.

Cody traced his ancestry all the way back to the Trail of Tears. During the Civil War, his Cherokee grandfather joined up with a bunch of Confederate outlaws known as Quantrill's Raiders. This mixed-race posse terrorized Missouri, Kansas, and Indian Territory, pillaging Union forces and riding off into the Ozarks with their loot. They were indomitable, submitting neither to the Confederate military brass nor to the victorious Union army. They were, in effect, professional badasses—some wearing black sombreros with silver inlays and bullet bandoliers across their chests. Among their posse was a Black man named Two Bits who acquired his nickname on account of tips he received for playing piano in whorehouses. If this is starting to sound like a Sam Peckinpah or Quentin Tarantino Western, remember that Cody's memoir is subtitled *My Life as a Hollywood Indian*. Emphasis on "Hollywood."

But Iron Eyes Cody, well, according to his memoir, was a regular old "Injun" who "wandered off the reservation into fame and fortune."[2] There are a number of issues here: Cody omits any mention of the allotment process that dissolved tribal governments and that the eastern portion of the state—which included the Cherokee area—was known not as Oklahoma

Territory (as Cody calls it) but Indian Territory. Furthermore, statehood occurred when he was two years old, possibly raising a red flag among literal-minded readers. But for the sake of our journey, let us give him a pass. We will assume he is speaking metaphorically of "the reservation." In any case, the narrative quickly shifts from an undisclosed location on an Oklahoma ranch to Hollywood, as Cody recounts a lifetime of work during the golden age of the Hollywood Western, and it is here we see the formation of the iconic American Indian take shape.

Most of the first half of the book is devoted to celebrity yarn-spinning, recalling Gary Cooper's terrible horsemanship and incorrigible playboy vices. Or John Wayne's terrible alcoholism and fear that his real name—Marion Morrison—sounded like a "fairy." More importantly, however, the book reveals the solidification of the American imaginary regarding Native Americans. Cody recalls how he butted heads with the legendary Cecil B. DeMille, insisting that Indians be represented "authentically" in the filming of *The Plainsman*. On set, Cody assembled a cast of "Indians," some belonging to local tribes but mostly white actors dressed in headdresses and war paint:

> Everybody stood at attention while he walked up and down the ranks. "Okay, take that off," he said, stopping at one end, pointing to a beaded vest. He stopped again, "Take that off, and that, and—" "Wait, wait a minute, C.B. You can't take those things off. He's gonna be a chief. Cheyenne chiefs wore vests like that. And he's a warrior, they always wore leggings. That's a medicine pouch on him. It stays." "You've got too much clothes on them." "Not for these Indians, C.B. We either do an authentic picture or I'll walk off and the Indians will come with us."[3]

Cody became the "authentic Indian," selling himself as the ultimate authority in Hollywood on the languages, customs, and beliefs of tribes as disparate as the Cherokees and the Cheyennes. Iron Eyes also taught actors a few rudimentary Plains Indian sign language gestures. Some tribes have different gestures, but Iron Eyes created a fusion, an Esperanto of hand talk. In 1970 he documented this language in a book called *Indian Talk: Hand Signals of the American Indians*. The book was reviewed positively by one of the most prestigious scholarly journals in anthropology, *American Anthropologist*, in 1972.

As Hollywood moved from the era of pure spectacle and illusion to a politicized and realistic aesthetic in the late 1960s, Iron Eyes followed suit. Working with the mercurial British actor Richard Harris on the 1970 *A Man Called Horse*, Cody began to insist on authentic portrayals of initiation rites and medicine rituals, often over the demands of the producer. Although Iron Eyes played bit parts in dozens of Westerns over five decades, it is this film that may hold the clue to his transformation from a supporting actor into America's most recognizable Indian. *A Man Called Horse* tells the story of an English aristocrat, John Morgan, who is captured by the Sioux and enslaved by them until his cunning and dogged determination wins the Natives over and he becomes a Sioux warrior. Unlike previous Westerns, however, *A Man Called Horse* spared the Armenian bole (a reddish-brown chemical often sprayed on white actors to make them look Native) and convinced many moviegoers that they were finally catching a glimpse of authentic Plains Indian culture. No one in Hollywood, apparently, considered the oxymoronic implications of a spectacle of authenticity produced without any consultation from actual Native Americans.

Some Native American activists and scholars cried foul. Among them was Ward Churchill, who pulled apart all the layers of cultural misappropriations in the film. Although *A Man Called Horse* came with words of approval from an ethnohistorian at the Smithsonian, it made a jumble of Plains cultures, depicting a people whose language is Lakota with hairstyles that went from Assiniboine to Comanche. Churchill's critique hinged on a strident defense that "authenticity" is something that can only be defined from within a given culture. Churchill, like Iron Eyes Cody, claimed part Cherokee ancestry and set about defining the parameters of Indian authenticity in books like *Fantasies of the Master Race*. This critique took a personal twist after his tenure was revoked by the University of Colorado–Boulder. Churchill, who had made a career out of debunking white constructions of authenticity for Native Americans, now had his own authenticity questioned. Many Native authors denounced Churchill for being unable to prove anything other than a sliver of indigenous ancestry, while others countered that assessing his indigeneity based on blood quantum was a trap set by white colonialism.[4] Churchill remains a vexing figure in Native American studies. Many Native American scholars see him as a fraud, others as an inspiration.[5] The question of who was and was not an indigenous person would not be clarified by the arrival of DNA kits. Genetics might be able to ferret out some practitioners of Wannabeism, but for people like Churchill, who had cultural ties to tribes and a smidge of ancestry, the issue remained as murky as ever.

During the Cold War, the Ad Council turned to blatant U.S. propaganda, urging Americans to take an active role in promoting U.S. industry in the fight against communism. At the same time, the modern environmental movement was born and urged industry to promote recycling and reuse of materials. The Ad Council countered with its own "environmental" message, which stressed the responsibility of individuals—not corporations—to fight pollution. One of the taglines of this Keep America Beautiful campaign was "People start pollution. People can stop it," which seemed benign enough but turned out to be part of a political attack on more progressive environmental groups such as the Sierra Club. Keep America Beautiful was a nonprofit group supported by bottle manufacturers to prevent bottle deposit laws and encourage more and more consumption, according to investigative journalist Ginger Strand. Bottle deposit laws—most enacted with the birth of the environmental movement—were driving down demand for new glass and aluminum. The Ad Council's Crying Indian spots tried to change the conversation, making the environmental movement a question of personal ethics, not corporate responsibility.

Iron Eyes Cody initially declined the role as the Crying Indian. The commercial required the actor to be alone in San Francisco Bay. Cody could not swim. The director promised to have a helicopter hover over him in case he tipped over. When it came time for the money shot—the tear rolling down the cheek—Cody was ready. He knew how to cry on demand for the camera, but there was a problem: his real tears did not show up well enough on camera. The director used glycerin at the last minute to create one large tear that rolled down Iron Eyes' cheek.

In 1996 the journalist Angela Aleiss revealed that the man known to the world as the Crying Indian was born Espera Oscar de Corti in the small town of Kaplan, Louisiana. Aleiss told me it was an open secret among Native American actors in Los Angeles that Cody was not Indian, but no one had thought to figure out who he really was.[6] Aleiss consulted records from a small Catholic church in the town and found that de Corti's father, Antonio, had been the victim of vicious anti-Italian sentiment in turn-of-the-century Louisiana. The decade before Oscar de Corti's father came over from Sicily, more than a dozen Italians in the state had been lynched. To make matters worse, an extortion racket commonly referred to as the Black Hand Society (an early version of the Mafia) had sprung up in southern Louisiana. Antonio de Corti had to give up his small shop and flee to Texas, where his three sons eventually joined him.

Somewhere along the way, young Oscar de Corti saw a Wild West show and became enamored with all things Native. Aleiss wrote that the de Corti family remade themselves in Texas; the father slightly anglicized his name to Tony Corti. Oscar made his way to Los Angeles in his teens, becoming Oscar Codey and finally Iron Eyes Cody. By the time Aleiss interviewed him in 1996, he had been widowed by his Native wife and brought up their two sons of indigenous heritage. When he died in 1999, everything indicated that he had convinced himself of his own lie. After he had raised two Native sons, some indigenous people shrugged their shoulders at the revelation that Cody had spent the better part of his life faking his Native American ancestry. Others saw it as one more instance of a white person appropriating Native culture for personal gain.

Iron Eyes Cody may have been a Hollywood Indian, but there is more to the tribe of the Wannabes than show business. There are many subcategories of Wannabes, but the most common member of the tribe we might call the Almost Native—the white person who claims one-thirty-second blood quantum, seemingly enough to squeak by America's arbitrary racial standards that designate who is and is not a minority.

The most famous and most controversial Almost Native of the moment

5. The Choctaw artist St. Clair Homer was a grandfather figure to the author. Courtesy of the author.

REJOICE, RED BROTHERS!
... for it was on this day
JUNE 25th, 1876
on the Little Big Horn
Lt. Colonel George Got The Point
And Quit Chasing Indians

6. and 7. The Choctaw artist St. Clair Homer (or Homma) parodied white colonialism while dating the author's grandmother for decades. Courtesy of the author.

is Oklahoma City–born Elizabeth Warren. During her 2012 campaign for the U.S. Senate in Massachusetts against incumbent Senator Scott Brown, Warren frequently described "family lore" about her Cherokee forbearers as part of her hardscrabble, coming-of-age story. Conservatives mocked her for identifying herself as a Native American minority during two stints at law schools in the 1990s. While it appears that she never benefited from affirmative action for minorities and stopped listing herself as a minority lawyer by 1995, she has refused to back away from claims of Native ancestry.

When Warren's claims to Cherokee ancestry were scrutinized closely by genealogists, no one could find her ancestors among those named on the Dawes Roll, which the government intended to be a master list of Cherokee surnames finalized in 1906. (They did find one ancestor from the territorial days who had actually boasted of killing a Cherokee.) Like many dubious narratives of whites passing for Native, Warren's story takes many twists and turns, some of which receive a gloss in her memoir,

A Fighting Chance. In the book, Warren weaves her "Native American heritage" (specific references to the Cherokees have now disappeared) into a narrative of working-class struggle, with her "mamaw and papaw" handing down stories and recipes from their days in Indian Territory.

Aunt Bee told Liz Warren that her papaw had inherited high cheekbones from his Indian ancestors but did not pass them down to the little girl. The anecdote reinforces a homespun narrative of authentic Americana: Daddy worked hard as a janitor but had a heart attack. When he recovered, he could not pay the medical bills. Mama was devoted to her family but often did not have enough money to put food on the table for the four kids. Eventually, little Liz had to work, too, before she dropped out of college at age nineteen to support her husband's professional goals. Then she picked herself up by her bootstraps and put herself through law school in the wake of a divorce. The story is like a PG-rated Loretta Lynn or Tammy Wynette song with all the cheating and drinking purged from the storylines.

A lot of people have scoffed at fair-skinned, blue-eyed Warren's claim of Native American heritage. Donald Trump resorts to the "Pocahontas" insult. Warren took Trump's bait and brought in a world-renowned genetics expert to prove whether or not she was Native American. The results only generated more outrage. For Republicans the remoteness of her Native ancestor—some six to ten generations removed—made her seem like a Wannabe. For Native Americans, the DNA test was another instance of disregard for Native traditions and sovereignty.

As an Okie myself, I instantly recognized Warren's narrative. It has an undeniable pull and a certain degree of truthiness. The mythic Native ancestor in the white settler family assuages white guilt and makes us feel like we belong. I have been there myself. Oklahoma writer Rilla Askew wades into the tricky territory of the Almost Native repeatedly in her book *Most American.* Askew has often been labeled as a Native American or Cherokee writer, and she admits that she has not always righted the record. "The fact that my family had no documentation showing Indian blood didn't bother me," she writes. If anyone asked whether I was part Indian, I'd answer with, "Well, my papaw Allie said."[7] Askew says that in the 1980s, such a logic was never questioned. She says that her first published story was labeled as Cherokee and that Native American friends even nudged her to consider herself as an Indian writer. In the era of identity politics, such a position could get one pilloried on social media.

In places like Canada, where the reserve system and government-sponsored residential schools are major sticking points in the ongoing truth and reconciliation process, Askew's position would be considered heresy. In other places in North America, there is a bright distinction between white and Native. But Oklahoma is different. Nothing there has followed a logical process; racial identity often has nothing to do with skin color and some tribes—especially the Cherokee—have staged a remarkable comeback despite the cultural genocide of the early twentieth century. Among my closest family members are Cherokee cousins. They are white passing and were decidedly silent about their heritage growing up. I was ignorant about their citizenship in the Cherokee Nation for decades. One day I asked why they had so many portraits of famous Cherokees on their walls. The fact that their license plates were issued by the Cherokee Nation and that one of them worked for the Cherokee government should have been indicators, but Okies do not think in binaries when it comes to Native identity. We think in degrees. That is because Oklahoma, if we are honest with ourselves, is a mestizo state. From the cornbread we eat, to the stories we tell, to the names of the towns we live in, we are a mixed people still digging out from under the ideologies of evangelical Christianity and white supremacy. At social dances, Native women sport traditional patchwork skirts and Oklahoma Sooners T-shirts. Native people often practice traditional ceremony and attend a Christian church. Native people often have the same Okie twang as whites but then code-switch into Creek or Cherokee. We are a mess of colonialism, hybridity, displacement, and innovation. That cultural reality does not excuse the opportunistic Wannabes, but it provides some context for the Okie phenomenon of the Almost Native.

We are still left with a nagging question for the Wannabes: Why do they do it? Why do so many white people—from Elizabeth Warren to Miley Cyrus to Iron Eyes Cody—fashion a Native identity seemingly out of thin air? I contacted Aleiss about her research to ask her if there was anything that united this unruly tribe. The one common denominator she cited was "financial opportunity." Indeed, there are many instances of whites making a buck while trafficking in a faux Native identity, but I am not totally convinced it all boils down to money. According to the 2010 census, more than a quarter of Native Americans live in poverty, compared with only 10 percent of whites. If Wannabeism is purely financial, we need to acknowledge that there is more money to be made in the white world than on the reservation.

Native identity bestows upon a white person a sort of symbolic capital that works in inverse proportion to white privilege. Fake Indian personae have allowed otherwise unpublishable white authors to achieve notoriety. There are many examples, including Forrest "Little Tree" Carter, the author of *The Education of Little Tree*. Carter turned out to not be Cherokee, as he had claimed, but a former Ku Klux Klansman from Alabama named Asa Earl Carter. The case of Carter's memoir is laden with even more ironic twists and turns than that of Iron Eyes Cody, as Carter made a name for himself in the public sphere by becoming one of Alabama's most vocal white supremacists. He is reputed to have written Alabama Governor George Wallace's cri de guerre: "Segregation now, segregation tomorrow, and segregation forever." Carter disappeared from public life only to remake himself years later as Forrest "Little Tree" Carter, an orphaned boy raised by his Cherokee grandparents, wise elders who taught the boy to live a simple, natural life until he confronted the racist system of an Indian residential school.

To this day, critics are divided about how to view *Little Tree*: is the book an opportunistic play on white America's hunger for the "authentic" Indian, or is it Carter's secret confession of guilt for having been such a vocal racist for decades? The writer Sherman Alexie summed up the contradiction. "*Little Tree* is a lovely little book," Alexie wrote, "and I sometimes wonder if it is an act of romantic atonement by a guilt-ridden white supremacist, but ultimately I think it is the racial hypocrisy of a white supremacist."[8]

There is something else at work in Wannabeism that ties it back to the foundation of Oklahoma. This might be discomfiting for Warren's folksy narrative of forbidden love between a Native and white grandparent, but it is so rooted in the formation of the state that it cannot be ignored. In the chaos of the dissolution of the tribal governments of Indian Territory and the birth of the state of Oklahoma, many Natives found themselves under not physical assault but legal and financial attack from the new settlers. Yes, sometimes an episode of Wild West violence erupted, such as Crazy Snake's Rebellion, but takeover of Indian Territory usually happened through the courts. When offers for buyouts were not accepted, whites found ways to insinuate themselves into legal claims to land, even going so far as marrying into Native families. There are many stories of predatory whites marrying Natives for money—some of the most sordid documented in David Grann's *The Killers of Flower Moon*—but none attracted as many sensational headlines as that of Jackson Barnett.

Barnett, like many "full bloods," had been left with an allotment of land that was undesirable for farming but, in an ironic twist, held riches below the soil. The oil play on Barnett's land made him into "the world's richest Indian" and a celebrity. Into his life walked Anna Laura Lowe, who made little secret of her ambition to control Barnett's riches. Lowe was considered a "fortune hunter," and the couple's application for marriage in Oklahoma was denied. Marriages such as these abounded, some of them perhaps borne from true love, but mostly as part of a larger strategy to strip Natives of their claims to land and wealth. Barnett's case was the subject of prurient media interest and an intense estate battle.

As it turns out, Elizabeth Warren probably did have a Native ancestor. Many Oklahomans do. The state has the largest population of Native Americans after California, a state with almost ten times the population. In the Tulsa metro region, 8.6 percent identifies as Native. If all the Five Tribes recognized their Black freedmen descendants, the percentage would be much higher. For every Wannabe, there are many more white-passing (sometimes called "Black Dutch") Okies out there who, because of historical trauma and discrimination, have hidden their Native ancestry.

I have one Native American ancestor some four generations removed as evidenced in a DNA test I did. This, however, does not make me any more Native American than my 16 percent British Isles DNA makes me British. Following the lead of many Native Americans, it is important that if a person claims a culture, that culture has to claim a person. We do not get to change the imagined communities of our nationhood like a pair of silk socks. The issue of Native ancestry raises two important questions for someone like Warren: one, was Native culture—religion, values, folkways, language, community—transmitted down to her identity? Two, what is the story behind her Native ancestry? Was it produced within the context of violence that led to the state of Oklahoma, or was it borne from true love? The answer to number one—in Warren's case—is clearly "no" (as it is in my case as well).

Everyone should be wary of the identity police, but it is worth remembering that the modern state of Oklahoma was founded on the swindle of Native land. The story of Oklahoma is the story of the dispossession of Indian Territory from its owners and the subsequent marginalization and oppression of Native culture, language, and identity. Through a process of transculturation, some elements of Native culture (speech patterns, foodways, etc.) filtered into the white mainstream. However, many dubious claims of Native blood quantum were submitted to the Dawes Commission to get a piece of land. Oklahoma history is replete with stories of white settlers' needling, grafting, or bullying their way onto the Dawes Rolls with the sole intent of claiming land. Warren unwittingly perpetuated that crime but eventually apologized to the Cherokee Nation.

As for the answer to number two (the question of true love versus opportunism), things are trickier. The historical record attests that there were many more Anna Laura Lowes out there hunting down Natives with allotment on top of oil patches than there were true romances between Sooners and Native Americans. We still love to mythologize our Native ancestors, and perhaps some of it comes out of a deeply held sense of guilt for what white ancestors did to Native Americans. The enduring belief in the Pocahontas mythology makes whites feel better about the original sin of colonization. In any case, there is undoubtedly something strange in the American psyche regarding the Wannabes, and I would not be telling the truth if I did not recount my own experience in being seduced by their truthy allure.

I said no Native American culture was transmitted down to my own identity, but like many white Okies, that is not entirely true. We often do not realize the way our own *mestizaje* has filtered up from below, despite the unconscious bias toward white supremacy. As a boy, I hated my middle name. Who would name their boy St. Clair? "Isn't that a girl's name?" I asked my mom one day.

My mom told me I should be proud of St. Clair, because her mother's partner was St. Clair Homer. Homer is known to the art world as Homma (the Choctaw word *homma*, which means "red," as in "Oklahoma"). Let us get this straight: Homma was no Wannabe. He traced a lineage back to Pushmataha, a general who fought the British in the War of 1812; his grandfather had been secretary of the Choctaw Nation. The thing was, I was not quite sure if Homma was actually my grandfather because after he died my grandmother started living with another man who was not Native at all. When I was three years old, though, Homma won first place in the Oklahoma Bicentennial Indian Art Exhibition at the Gilcrease Museum for a bronze sculpture called *Spirit Horse*. I was too young to remember the exhibit, but I saw it later during school field trips. I always pointed out the sculpture to my teachers and friends with pride.

What strikes me now about Homma's work is its stark defiance of much of the art in Gilcrease. There is none of the reverential Western myth-making in his work. Homma engaged in a playful mocking of cowboy culture. There was none of the rugged individualism of the American West: the white cowboy facing down the harsh environment and the Indian savages. In 1976, for the centennial of the Battle of Little Bighorn, Homma declared that he was going on "full war-path mode" and made a series of satirical postcards "commemorating" the event.

In the meantime, I had learned the truth of my connection to Homma. After my biological grandfather's failed attempt at launching a barbecue restaurant in Muskogee, he turned to drinking. He later died in poverty. My grandmother ditched him for Homma, who was already a well-known artist in Tulsa and connected to the most powerful family in the Choctaw

Nation. Homma and my grandmother lived together off and on for decades, and he practically raised my mom. His presence in my life was still there, however, especially every time anyone asked me about my middle name. My first year of college, I met a group of exchange students from Great Britain. I told them I was from Oklahoma, a place they only knew from the musicals and Westerns.

"You must be part Indian or something," one of the Brits said. I thought about this for a minute. It was not a question I had pondered before. Yes, I said, I probably was part Indian. Not only was I named after one, I was darker than most white people. The British exchange students really seemed interested. They clearly wanted to know an Indian.

"I think I'm part Choctaw," I said finally. "But only a little bit, so I'm not on any tribal rolls or anything."

There, I had done it. I felt good to be part Native American, as if I belonged to something big. Something noble, wise, and timeless. Now that I had said it, it had to be true. After all, my mother's family came from rural eastern Oklahoma, right on the dividing line between the Creek and Cherokee Nations. The family's cemetery plot in Checotah was right next to the Indian section. My grandmother's longtime lover was Native American and I was named after him. And like Liz Warren's mamaw, we had high cheekbones and swarthy complexions.

So I would belong to the tribe of the Wannabes for a while, especially during my early twenties, when I actually did not know what the hell I was. The tribe gave me a sense of identity, and it carried some instant prestige when traveling abroad. Europeans love Native Americans, I discovered.

I never fully bought in, however. I knew plenty of people who tried to cash in on some supposed Indian great-grandmother to work some advantage in school or to simply seem cooler than regular white folks. That was not me. My status in Wannabe Nation was more like a metaphor for my lowly status in the extended field of the Cobbs. There was one small problem: the only Indians I knew in Tulsa were a lot like me. They grew up on the same eighties pop music and TV shows, followed the same sports teams (even the Oklahoma Sooners, who got their name illegally stealing Native land in the late nineteenth century). They did not live in teepees or on reservations, and they did not even have cool names like Iron Eyes. They were the living legacies of generations of assimilationist policies, trying to privately honor their ancestry while making their way in a white world. Most of them were not any darker than I was, and we all spoke with the same Okie drawl. They had their own private struggles, which I was not privy to. So I did not want to be them. I wanted to be like the Indian in that commercial, stoically paddling his canoe through the American landscape, offering a rebuke to the crass commercialism of mainstream America. This was a projection, a fantasy that had nothing to do with indigenous ways and everything to do with white middle-class alienation. Working through that alienation would eventually lead me to understanding that Wannabe Nation was, in the end, nothing but a nation of fraudsters, a refuge for scoundrels. A place most Oklahoman, in other words.

ORAL ROBERTS UNIVERSITY

Educating the whole man

8. A giant statue of bronze hands in prayer greets visitors to Oral Roberts University in Tulsa. Photo by the author.

CHAPTER 8

Backward, Christian Soldier

Urban myths about Tulsa abound, but one has always rang true to me: the city is home to more churches per capita than any other U.S. city. "Coming up," raps Tulsa's own hip-hop star Steph Simon, "all I ever seen was crack fiends and some churches."

"What church y'all go to?" continues to be a polite conversation starter in some circles. There are churches in strip malls, in old warehouses, in barns. Churches in buildings that look more like a Miami Beach nightclub or an alternative music venue than a house of worship. Church on the Move boasts "artisanal coffee and tea drinks" and another one—Guts—hosted boxing tournaments for a while (that was suspended after one of the contestants died during a fight). Life.Church, founded in Oklahoma City, is a full-blown multimedia platform with video channels for different age groups, podcasts, and YouTube videos that make TED Talks look like amateur community television. Life.Church is a pioneer in lifestyle Christianity, a curious mix of self-help schtick, traditional evangelicalism, and carefully branded media. And it is all presented in the comforts of a suburban megaplex. The church claims to have the world's most popular Bible app. According to one source, Life.Church is now the third-largest church in the United States.[1]

Tulsa has an outlet of Life.Church as well. The city has played an outsized role in launching the careers of many megapreachers, including Oral Roberts, Joel Osteen, and Kenneth Copeland. The members list of the Tulsa-based Oral Roberts University board of regents until recently read like a who's who of televangelism. ORU has made its influence felt in pop culture: *The Simpsons'* Ned Flanders has a degree from the Christian university, as does Kathie Lee Gifford. Although many Okies dismiss the sprawling complex of Oral Roberts University as a place for fundamentalist holy rollers, the university is part of the reason Oklahoma, in general, has accepted evangelical Protestantism as a hegemonic force. "Have a blessed day" is a common refrain at the end of casual exchanges. There is our annual Oilfield Prayer Day, an official act proclaimed by the governor. Football games, dinner at a fast food place, coffee at Starbucks: many of these mundane events begin with a Christian prayer. Oklahoma is one of many states vying for the title of "Buckle of the Bible Belt." Nearly half of Oklahomans consider themselves evangelical Christian, a rate that is just less than that of Tennessee and Arkansas.

Churches per capita, however, turns out to be a misleading indicator of a city's religiosity. There are many towns in the Midwest that have small, obscure churches that serve a particular religious denomination. If you are interested in the overall religiosity of a population, "religious adherence" is more telling. Tulsa's metro population is just under one million people, so it was not rated in the latest U.S. Religion Census (2010). Oklahoma City, however, grabbed the number-three spot for the most religious adherents, behind Salt Lake City and Birmingham. The American Bible Society runs its own study focusing on U.S. Americans' familiarity with scripture, surveying how often people read and use the Bible in their daily lives. The society then ranks U.S. cities based on their "Bible-mindedness." While Oklahoma City scores pretty high, Tulsa is only a slightly above-average thirty-nine out of one hundred in terms of its Bible-centricity. So Tulsa might seem like the buckle on the Bible Belt on the surface, but that buckle has been unfastened for various reasons.

For all of its outward piousness, many social indicators in Oklahoma are reflective of a pretty sinful state of mind. Rates of teenage pregnancy, divorce, smoking, and drug use are all well above the mean in this most evangelical of states. Oklahoma has the second-highest rate of teenage pregnancy in the nation, a statistic that belies the evangelical emphasis on abstinence as the only method to deal with teenage sexual desires. Suicide has increased by 36 percent since 1999, while mental health spending has been slashed.[2]

African American children are twice as likely as white children in the state to die by the age of two.[3] Oklahoma also ranks third in the number of marriages that end in divorce. We come in at fourth place in the proportion of residents who smoke cigarettes on a regular basis. And yet our governor and legislators never cease to remind us how blessed we are, how our Christian values are at odds with the secular liberals of the coasts. Surely, the God of evangelical Protestantism is not blessing the great state of Oklahoma with suicide, infant mortality, divorce, and cigarette smoke.

What is going on?

The knee-jerk secular liberal critique is that evangelicals are a bunch of ignorant hypocrites. Dumb Okies. Redneck deplorables. Like the character in *Chinatown* or the protagonist in the Merle Haggard song, they are simply incapable of complex thinking. H. L. Mencken thought Okies should be sterilized. Class- and region-based snobbery has found new life. An image in my Twitter feed popped up after the 2016 election. It was an outline of the Louisiana Purchase over the contemporary political map of the United States. "Yo, France, you guys want this back? We don't need it anymore."[4] Oklahoma was on there, yes, along with most of Texas, Kansas, Nebraska, and a few more red states.

Poor Christian whites are perhaps the only group that educated white liberals continue to mock and stereotype without it becoming "problematic." Discordances between social indicators and religious views in places like Oklahoma lead to smugness and condescension among secular urban liberals. Some overweight white man holding up a misspelled sign thanking Lord Jesus for Donald Trump makes for great late-night laugh lines and internet memes. Cultural superiority is like a donut: it provides a rush of satisfaction but leads nowhere good. However, as a white progressive, I will cop to a little bit of schadenfreude when it comes to the hegemony of social conservatism in broken places like Oklahoma (or Alabama or West Virginia). "Every nation gets the government it deserves," the arch-conservative Joseph de Maistre said in the wake of the French Revolution.

Liberals have often echoed this sentiment, only directing their bitterness toward Red America. "Red States Want to Secede? Go Ahead, Make Our Day" is a typical headline for this sort of class-baiting ignorance.[5] Of course I have felt this same emotion, and a small part of me gets a perverse pleasure out of mocking Dumb Okies on Twitter. Mockery does not add up to a coherent political platform. It undercuts a basic sense of social solidarity across class lines, which is—or should be—a fundamental tenet of progressivism.

All that being said, I am genuinely curious how evangelical conservatives deal with the cognitive dissonance of having their version of Christianity experience unprecedented success in statewide politics only to watch their state slip further and further behind in social indicators. How does a committed conservative Republican Christian, for example, explain having a supermajority in the state legislature and 100 percent of statewide elected offices but declining health outcomes, a teacher exodus, and the highest level of incarceration of any state? Would he blame it on Satan? On moral failings of the state's own citizens? On a liberal conspiracy directed by George Soros?

I got one explanation from my aunt Mona. Our speaking terms fluctuate depending on her assessment of the status of my soul (she *usually* thinks I am going to hell), so we do not always have the most candid conversations. One day Mona told me why her husband outlived my dad by eighteen years, despite the fact they suffered from an identical heart disease with a genetic component. "Randy prayed hard over his illness," she told me. "Your dad never truly found his faith." For Mona, electing Christians is not sufficient. People have to truly believe in their heart of hearts. They have to pray and pray some more. I guess this is why she thinks God blesses her when she finds a parking spot only a few steps from the entrance of a Starbucks. Oklahoma might be religious on the surface of things, but it is not praying hard enough. Tulsa, in particular, is falling behind in its Bible literacy. People like my aunt Mona see the erosion of their hegemony everywhere they turn: the influx of brown Catholics, the legalization of gay marriage, marijuana, you name it.

Turning back to the wild success of Life.Church, we can see that behind the slick media presence, the idea of faith and prayer as an answer to social ills remains intact. Bobby Gruenewald, the developer of Life.Church's Bible app, told a reporter with the *Tulsa World* in 2011 that increased Bible reading has a societal impact. More people downloading the app, he predicted, would lead to more Bible literacy and ergo more clean living. If that happens, Gruenewald said, "layers of things in society will change: divorce rates, adultery, crime, deception in corporate America. . . . Parenting would change. We have a whole generation of people who haven't had parents that demonstrated a biblical worldview."[6]

I thought it might be interesting to take Gruenewald's idea seriously, so I delved into the Oklahoma Bureau of Investigations statistics on crime in the state since 2010, shortly before the app launched. On the one hand, violent crime has decreased modestly, but only at the same rate as it has decreased in more secular places like New York and California. Also, the years 2015 and 2016 witnessed a spike in violent crime, though not enough to offset the decreases of the previous years. During 2015 and 2016, lots of people started to download Life.Church's Bible app, so I do not know how we measure its effects on the violent crime rate. From an empirical worldview, it is simply ludicrous to imagine any sort of causal relationship between people consulting a Bible app on their phones and deciding to kill or not kill another person. But maybe that is not the way to approach the problem. The idea that Okies just are not praying hard enough is ridiculous enough that we do not have to take it too seriously. (What, those socialists in Vermont with their high life expectancies and low teenage pregnancy rates are praying harder than Okies?) Sorry, Mona.

Carlton Pearson has another explanation. Pearson, a former evangelical megapreacher with a socially conservative message, experimented with a turn away from fundamentalism in 2002, eventually reworking his theology completely into what he calls "the gospel of inclusion." Pearson came up through the Oral Roberts University system and managed to have a congregation of around five thousand followers at one point. He told me that he felt tortured by the idea of having to save humanity by getting strangers to convert to Christianity. His psychological struggle came to a head during the Rwandan Genocide of the 1990s, when he questioned whether the victims who were not baptized were going to hell. "I remember thinking, 'God, don't put that guilt on me. I've given you the best forty years of my life,'" he said when I interviewed him for a segment on *This American Life* in 2005. "Besides, I can't save the whole world. I'm doing the best I can. I can't save this whole world. And that's where I remember—and I believe it was God saying, precisely, 'You can't save this world. That's what we did.'"

A lot of the headlines and media fodder around Pearson's change of heart have revolved around his rejection of the notion of hell. Obviously, it would register as a shocker for someone from a fundamentalist mindset to reject a literal hell. But what has received less attention and may be more consequential in the long run is the implication for how evangelicals think about social problems. Hell, in Pearson's new thinking, is not something God imposes on the faithless but rather a social reality arising from how we treat each other. Hell is something "we do . . . to each other," he said. "And we do it to ourselves. Then I saw emergency rooms. I saw divorce court. I saw jails and prisons. I saw how we create hell on this planet for each other. For the first time in my life, I did not see God as the inventor of hell."

John Hudson, writing for the *Atlantic*, created a shortlist of famous preachers blaming natural disasters on human sin in 2010. Haiti's 2010 earthquake was the result of a "pact with the devil."[7] Jerry Falwell blamed 9/11 on gays and lesbians. John Hagee—another product of Oral Roberts University—said regarding Hurricane Katrina, "I believe that New Orleans had a level of sin that was offensive to God, and they were recipients of the judgment of God for that."[8] These statements are usually condemned by the Republican mainstream (John McCain publicly rejected Hagee's endorsement over the Katrina comments), but they represent a not-uncommon view in evangelical churches in the South. Although politicians are usually smart enough to put enough distance between themselves and these views, they are deeply rooted in the white evangelical psyche. Even among well-to-do, educated white mainstream Christianity, the social order is a divine blessing rather than a social construction. "We are so blessed" is a common refrain about everything from the weather to a football score. Mainstream educated Protestants often mock fundamentalists for their exhortations to God, but there is no clear dividing line between seeing your social position as a blessing and someone else's suffering as the opposite side of the same coin. The idea of divine retribution for natural or societal problems is way more complicated than the buffoonery of televangelist Pat Robertson. Underneath it all is a theory that things are the way they are because that is how God intended it. The earthy order of things is God's will. "God has a plan," we are told in church. This is the theological underpinning of the Great Oklahoma Swindle.

When I attended a Catholic high school in Tulsa, I was told that questions about God and religion were welcome. Part of a well-rounded education included hard questions about the Bible and, indeed, the very existence of God. I embraced the opening. Going into my junior year, I noticed that our school had a pro-life organization that got to miss a school day and travel to Oklahoma City to lobby legislators at the state capitol. Either I was naive or sadistic because I asked the headmaster if we could also form a pro-choice organization on campus. I thought through the issue enough to couch it in terms of pedagogy: the pro-life and pro-choice groups could engage in respectful debate at school, so everyone learned both sides of the argument. The headmaster looked at me in horror. In no uncertain terms would there be a pro-choice group at our Catholic school. No reason was given. It was simply the way things were.

The genius—if you can call it that—of the political turn within the modern Christian Right is narrative in nature. Climate change, LGBTQ issues, inequality, racism: reactionary positions can be naturalized into a religious story and justified through select Bible passages. Complex issues are reified into didactic morality tales. When ugly realities such as increasing levels of despair, inequality, opioid abuse, and gun violence do not fit the "blessed" narrative, they are branded as heresy, or as anti-American ideology. The problem with this is that it becomes impossible to have a debate over cause and effect or even basic facts. *You're either with us or against us*, to paraphrase George W. Bush. And if things really are not to your liking, just pray on it.

How did Oklahoma, among other places, come to embrace such a reactionary political and religious position? There are many antecedents and inspirations, of course (biblical justifications for slavery being a major one). One of the major forebearers of this reactionary political and religious thinking, though, has almost been forgotten. At his pinnacle, his use of media and politics were groundbreaking.

Oh, yes, and of course, he made his name in Tulsa, Oklahoma.

Shortly after World War II, Billy James Hargis came barreling down from the Arkansas hills—all 6 foot, 6 inches and 280 pounds of him—to a small church in Sapulpa, Oklahoma, where he set up shop as a conventional "bawl and jump" preacher ordained by the Disciples of Christ. There have always been fundamentalists, for sure, but before Hargis they mostly squawked about the end of the world and the need to repent. Many evangelicals during the first half of the twentieth century saw Christian activism in social and political affairs as pure folly. Better, these preachers said, to wait out the current corrupt kingdom by praying hard and living right. This movement came to be known as dispensationalism.[9]

But if James Brown was the godfather of soul, Hargis was the godfather of fundamentalism as a political movement. Other organizations (most notably the KKK) combined reactionary ideology and Christian rhetoric for political gain, but did so either behind closed doors or with literal masks on. None of his forebears conceived of a right-wing Christian movement as a media brand. Hargis turned the idea of a Christian nation into a media spectacle and found a receptive audience in Oklahoma, where his influence is still felt (Hargis's daughter was, until recently, the chair of the Tulsa Chamber of Commerce). Even to this day, one needs to be careful when invoking the name of Billy James Hargis.

In 1948, spurred on by a traveling preacher who gave him a pamphlet that showed a connection between communism and the NAACP, young Billy James had an epiphany: Protestant churches were being infiltrated by communists. The National Council of Churches (of which the Disciples of Christ was a member) was a Marxist organization. Liberals had kicked God out of the USA. Even President Dwight Eisenhower was a communist! The more outrageous his claims, the more audience he attracted. His evidence rested on a series of accusations of guilt by association, fake news, and statements taken out of context (sound familiar?). The politicization of Christianity took his ministry from a foundering Pentecostal church to a media conglomerate bringing in a million dollars a year (in 1950s money). Until this point, conservative preachers in the South were wary of overtly political issues. Tax-exempt status for churches is contingent on staying out of direct political campaigning. Hargis, then, was walking a fine line.

At the age of twenty-three, Hargis "stepped out in faith for the harder service as a crusader." The "harder service" was his political crusade to rid America of communism and return the nation to its Christian foundations. He came to national attention in 1953 with his Bible Balloon Project, a stunt that involved tying Bible quotations to helium balloons and floating them from West Germany to the Eastern Bloc. One hundred thousand balloons were released, and an evangelical star was born.

By 1966 Hargis had established himself in a Tulsa that had become the Hollywood of evangelical broadcasting. Not only Oral Roberts but also T. L. Osborn set up shop in Tulsa.[10] Hargis, for a while, may have been the most influential of all the megapreachers. He had a media empire that reached hundreds of TV and radio stations. At the time, Tulsa was to evangelical media as Nashville was to country music. A local ad man, L. E. "Pete" White, promoted both Roberts and Hargis and made the city a mecca for prosperity gospel preachers. Often derided as holy rollers on the fringes of American life, it has taken many years for people in the mainstream to realize the influence and impact of these televangelists on political culture. Now that the Christian Right has ensconced itself at the right hand of the Republican Party (even when the relationship gets testy), it is worth examining how this modern arrangement evolved.

Billy James Hargis published books, recorded LPs of his sermons, and claimed hundreds of thousands of readers through his *Christian Crusade* newsletter. Unlike Oral Roberts, Hargis had an explicitly political agenda. Roberts preached the gospel and could wield the Bible to alienate sexual minorities or reinforce heteronormative values, but they rendered unto Caesar what was Caesar's and to God what was God's. The more famous Billy Graham had demonstrated that anticommunism in Europe could fire up new audiences. But while Graham backed away from domestic political controversies, Hargis jumped in to a homegrown Christian crusade.

Denominationally speaking, Hargis was a Pentecostal within the Disciples of Christ. The movement had taken off in the early twentieth century in Los Angeles during the Azusa Street revival. Pentecostalism is a vividly felt version of Christianity: Preachers shout and jump. Congregants speak in tongues and collapse on the floor. Services are loud. The preacher not only reads the Bible but feels it in his soul, a soul that can, at times, be filled with demons and evil spirits. I do not think it is a stretch to see the link between African animistic religions and Pentecostalism (Pentecostalism is arguably more popular among African Americans than among whites, even though churches are often informally segregated). In any case, Pentecostals before Hargis were much more concerned with affairs of the soul than affairs of the state.

Hargis attacked some of his colleagues in the Disciples of Christ, questioning their anticommunist credentials. It was classic red-baiting, and in retaliation the church withdrew his ordination. Hargis's unprecedented foray into politics caught the attention of the IRS. The agency ruled that the Hargis's Christian Crusade organization had crossed the line from religion to politics and took away its tax-exempt status. But now Hargis was convinced that the entire federal government was infiltrated by communist stooges. The 1962 Supreme Court ruling that banned school-sponsored prayer in public schools only confirmed Hargis's conspiracy thinking.

It is important to point out that all this occurred in an era before the

Moral Majority or Focus on the Family, before politicians like Jesse Helms, Rick Santorum, and others made hard-right Christianity a feature of the modern Republican Party. So Hargis waded into new waters with his mix of McCarthyesque tactics and media-centric Christianity.

For mainline conservative Protestants, there was something unseemly about the whole thing. If Oral Roberts never quite achieved the respectability of Billy Graham, Billy Hargis never quite achieved the respectability of Oral Roberts. Mainstream newspapers liked to describe him as looking like a truck driver. There were several references to his "porcine" appearance. He never quite shook his twang, and he frequently mispronounced and misspelled words. He had spent a couple of years at Ozark Bible College in Bentonville but never completed a formal education. Hargis's holy roller shtick bordered on self-parody, his jowls shaking and his voice quivering as he denounced the communist and libertine agenda of rock music: "When the Beatles thrust their hips forwards while holding their guitars and shout, 'Oh Yeah!!!' who cannot know what they really mean!"

If his attempt to move the political needle toward hard-right Christianity did not quite work, his business boomed. His various enterprises sprawled alongside the Skelly Freeway in Tulsa, and he maintained an office downtown. Through the 1960s, as the counterculture took hold in the cities, Hargis soldiered on. In fact, the sexual and political revolutions of the second half of the decade fueled the Hargis fire, bringing in more reactionaries convinced that America was selling itself to the devil. For about fifteen years, Hargis was a one-man preaching, publishing, and media tornado, cranking out books and pamphlets with titles such as *Is the School House the Proper Place to Teach Raw Sex?*, *Thou Shalt Not Kill . . . My Babies*, and *Communist America: Must It Be?*

Occasionally, he caught the ear of someone important. He worked with a renegade military man named Major General Edwin Walker, whom he supplied with anticommunist propaganda for U.S. forces in Germany. He wrote at least one speech for Joe McCarthy. At the peak of his influence he had his own college—the American Christian College—and ran a summer camp for young Christian Crusaders, which had a choir called The All-American Kids. Hargis took a keen interest in forming a new generation of shiny coeds who would go forth and conquer communism and counterculture heathens. But maybe interest is a bit of an understatement. He really, *really* liked his students.

You probably can sense where this is going. Rumors about Hargis's sexuality circled around evangelical circles for years, but no one dared challenge the head man. Then in 1976 *Time* magazine dropped a bombshell. As it turned out, while Hargis preached against the moral decline of America, he was carrying on numerous affairs with his college students— some of them All-American Kids in the choir. According to the *Time* article, Hargis's transgressions came to light under particularly sordid circumstances. After performing a wedding for two students of his American Christian College, the bride and groom made a startling discovery: they had both had sex with President Hargis. The college's vice president, David Noebel (who went on to be a distinguished Christian culture warrior himself), started to hear tales of debauchery in Hargis's Tulsa office, at his Ozark mountain retreat, and on tour with the choir. Hargis was not only a soldier of Christ but a sexual predator with an insatiable appetite for the youth of America.

Most of the victims were male, and Hargis proved surprisingly candid about the affairs. He all but admitted them to *Time*, saying, "I have made more than my share of mistakes. I'm not proud of them. Even the Apostle Paul said, 'Christ died to save sinners, of whom I am chief.' Long ago, I made my peace with God, and my ministry continues." What might be most remarkable about the scandal, though, is that Hargis blamed his genetic makeup, rather than Satan, for his homosexuality. No one would mistake him for a gay rights advocate, but at a time when many people in the establishment still believed homosexuality was a psychiatric disorder, Hargis had another explanation. He said his sexual dalliances with the same gender had something to do with "genes and chromosomes."

While the nation chuckled at the fundamentalist Okie, the Tulsa media establishment was not amused. Despite the national attention, the scandal was too much for the *Tulsa World* and the *Tulsa Tribune*, which only mentioned the allegations to say that Hargis was retiring from the college "for health reasons." As we have seen—and will see later—media silence worked as a cover for difficult conversations in many aspects of Oklahoman life. As previously mentioned, Hargis's and Roberts's descendants have continued to play an important role in the city's political and cultural life.

Noebel, the more serious partner in Hargis's educational endeavors, hushed up the affair and sent Hargis packing with some $72,000 to his farm in the Ozarks. But, much like its big brother institution in South Tulsa—Oral Roberts University—American Christian College struggled without the charisma and fund-raising capabilities of its dear leader. In 1975 the college invited Hargis back, and he made a grand return to Oklahoma, claiming that he was "led by the Lord to come back to Tulsa." He bought a downtown building and had plans to place an eighty-five-foot sign in lights with BILLY JAMES HARGIS on top, but the city denied him the permits. At one point, he bought the historic Adams Hotel but sold it a year later, despairing that he could not find parking downtown.

With the end of the Cold War and the new crop of smiling preachers on TV, Hargis started to fade away. His college closed in 1978, and he never took to television the way he had to radio. Nevertheless, his weekly *Christian Crusade* newsletter continued to reach hundreds of thousands of readers. It was a curious little publication until Billy James Hargis Jr. died in 2013. While its headlines seem ripped from the mainstream press, the illustrations were often Counterreformation portraits of Christ suffering on the cross.

In his prime, Hargis owned a museum dedicated to Christian America, a college, a publishing house that employed seventy-six full-time workers, and a modernist cathedral. All this is gone. Hargis's offices, which lined I-44 when I grew up, were razed to make room for an expansion of the highway. Hargis's legacy, however, is alive and well. When Hargis was at the height of his power in the 1960s, he was considered a far-right extremist by Republicans and Democrats. Apart from George Wallace and a handful of Klan supporters, proto-fascists, and conspiracy theorists, no respectable politician or religious leader wanted to get near him, Southern Baptists in particular. By the 1960s, many Baptist churches were trying hard to shed their image as bastions of Southern racism while Hargis preached that it was his "conviction . . . that God ordained segregation."

A reporter once asked Hargis what he stood for. Hargis responded that he was, "anti-communism, anti-socialism, anti-welfare state, anti-Russia, anti-China, a literal interpretation of the Bible and states' rights." These positions are now staples of the conservative Republican diet. Hargis used to pound on the podium and decry the betrayal of Christian America by a bunch of elitist liberals in the media and universities. Next time Donald Trump utters a similar line, he might want to say a little prayer for this forgotten soldier of Christ.

While you would be hard pressed to find any mention of Hargis in the campaign literature of any Oklahoma politician, his legacy is alive and well. The physical descriptions of Billy James Hargis could very well fit Ralph Shortey, until recently a rising star in the Oklahoma GOP. Like Hargis did, Shortey appears built for an NFL offensive line (a photo of Shortey with this left arm embracing Donald Trump Jr. makes the presidential son look rather diminutive). I am not sure if Ralph Shortey has heard of Hargis, but the latter's story could have served as a cautionary tale had Shortey been prone to introspection.

Shortey moved to Oklahoma from Nebraska when he was six years old. He graduated from Heartland Baptist Bible College in Oklahoma City. As an unaccredited college, Heartland cannot award degrees, but it did give Shortey a diploma. After a stint in the oil and gas industry, Shortey found his way into politics at a young age, getting elected to the Oklahoma Senate in 2010 at the age of twenty-eight on a promise to create "Arizona-style" restrictions on illegal immigration in Oklahoma.

The first bill Shortey sponsored in 2011 was a "birther" law, requiring that candidates for president of the United States demonstrate their citizenship before they can appear on the ballot in Oklahoma. When Donald Trump stoked birtherism, Shortey saw a perfect ally. He became part of Trump's Oklahoma leadership team, posing for photos with Donald Trump Jr. and riling up the crowd before Trump's appearances. Shortey briefly became the source of mockery when someone at the Oklahoma State University newspaper noticed that Shortey sponsored a bill in 2012 that prohibited "the manufacture or sale of food or products which use aborted human fetuses." The story went viral. NPR, the *Atlantic,* and others sought to figure out what could have possibly triggered a bill that suggested some sort of dystopian world in which corporations used fetuses in their food. Shortey's office was barraged with questions. He only issued one statement about the bill in which he cast doubt on the logic of his own proposed law. "I don't know if it is happening in Oklahoma, it may be, it may not be. What I am saying is that if it does happen then we are not going to allow it to manufacture here."

The story, of course, was classic fake news, something ginned up from a taste test PepsiCo did that involved a widely available stem cell line from the Netherlands. The conspiratorial thinking and the total lack of evidence for a broad claim recalled classic Hargis, who once claimed that the National Education Association was rewriting American history curriculums along "Marxist-Leninist" lines.[11] Shortey lent his support to a number of reactionary measures against LGBTQ people and against a popular criminal justice reform measure to reclassify small drug possession as a misdemeanor rather than a felony. Shortey's downfall was also as shocking—and as predictable—as Hargis's.

The downfall of one of Donald Trump's biggest Oklahoma backers deserves its own narrative. The story begins with a father's call to police to report his seventeen-year-old son missing in 2017. The father suspected that his son might be involved in drugs, and police were able to track the kid to a Motel 8 in suburban Oklahoma City. The cops smelled marijuana and forced the door open, finding Shortey alone with the missing boy. Both beds were unmade and the cops found condoms and wet spots on the beds. Looking through Shortey's phone, police discovered that Shortey had used a pseudonym to solicit sex from the teenager in exchange for money. A later FBI investigation of Shortey's phone and social media revealed that he had a history of soliciting sex with young men through Craigslist, trying to stage "gangbangs." A search of an email account associated with one of his pseudonyms revealed child pornography. In fall 2017 Shortey pled guilty to child sex trafficking, but as result of the plea deal, child pornography charges were dropped.

For a long time, I wondered why Dumb Okies kept repeating history, following pastors and electing politicians who promised to create a Christian paradise of law-abiding virgins in the face of so many actual social problems that cannot be resolved by prayer. My aunt Mona thought the accusations of misconduct against Richard Roberts were the work of the devil. Plenty of people thought the sting on Shortey's sex and marijuana escapade was part of a liberal conspiracy. The FBI, after all, was an anti-Trump organization dominated by supporters of Hillary Clinton. So history would repeat itself, again, I thought, as both tragedy and farce. Richard Roberts's ouster from ORU and Shortey's guilty plea would only result in a new crop of fundamentalist swindlers. But then came a series of special elections and the revelation that Oklahoma was losing its religion.

In what was supposed to be the heart of Trump Country, people started turning their backs on the pro-business, pro-fundamentalist, anti-immigrant, anti-Obama cocktail that had swept Republicans to a total hold on every statewide office. Shortey's successor in the GOP lost to a Democratic challenger. Then came more losses for Republicans, followed by a popular teacher walkout of public schools. By June 2018 the *New Yorker* was calling it a "Democratic revival." It is a revolt against the hard-right Christianization of politics, for sure, but I think it is bigger—and more important—than a partisan pendulum swing.

Oklahoma is not only becoming a less reactionary place; it is also experiencing a wave of rising secularism. In seven short years between 2007 and 2014, the Pew Center documented a threefold rise in Oklahomans who professed "no belief in God," from 2 percent of the population to 6 percent in 2014. Those who professed "absolute certainty" in God decreased from 80 percent to 71 percent.[12] When Bill Maher showed up to do a live from Oklahoma comedy show in 2018, he seemed genuinely amazed when a crowd of Okies applauded his atheism.

I recently went to see Carlton Pearson preach again, almost thirteen years after I had last seen him at his Pentecostal church, Higher Dimensions. He was now appearing at All Souls, a Unitarian church in very white, very affluent Maple Ridge. I had been to All Souls many times over the years. While I always empathized with its social justice and ecumenical gospel, it lacked a certain vitality. The services were sleepy, and the congregation's skin tone was as white as its hair color. This time, though, I saw teenagers and millennials. And they were paying attention to a sermon about Jesus as a pro-immigrant figure. Pearson's congregation was much smaller at All Souls than it had been at Higher Dimensions but was younger and more diverse. It filled me with hope during a time of despair.

I was getting older, so some of my perception of youthfulness might have to do with my subjective bias. But it is clear that some sort of generational shift is happening in Oklahoma. This reality came into sharp focus on June 26, 2018. A referendum to legalize medical marijuana appeared on the ballot despite major opposition from Oklahoma's religious conservatives. Perhaps the state's most important rising political star on the national scene, Senator James Lankford, made a special video advocating a No vote on sq 788. Lankford is an ordained Baptist pastor and couched some of his opposition to sq 788 in traditional war-on-drugs rhetoric. He joined a religious coalition of faith leaders, saying legalized marijuana would damage the "social fabric" of the state (as if the social fabric were not already torn by years of cuts to education and health care). Despite opposition by conservative religious and faith leaders, sq 788 passed by a thirteen-point margin. Such an initiative would have been unthinkable when I was a child in Oklahoma from the 1980s to early 1990s, when organizations like DARE warned that marijuana was the gateway drug to a life on the streets.

Oklahoma has been, and will continue to be, a conservative and Christian state for some time. But the unholy alliance between evangelicalism, the oil and gas industry, and the Republican Party is showing signs of fracturing. Many Republicans marched with the striking teachers, and many Christians defied evangelical orthodoxy on sq 788. Some Oral Roberts University professors who are both scientists and evangelicals have broken with the state's mainstream thinking on climate change.

The hegemony of white petro-Christians is loosened. The result of increasing diversity and secularization of Oklahoma might not lead to a revolution anytime soon, but it makes the emergence of another Billy James Hargis or Ralph Shortey a little less likely.

CHAPTER 9

Keeping Oklahoma Weird

When I lived in Austin, Texas, for a good portion of the early aughts, I used to scoff at the ubiquitous "Keep Austin Weird" bumper stickers around town. I grew up in a place where the world's largest bronze sculpture, two hands touching in prayer, sat outside a retro-futuristic palace known as the City of Faith, housing a *Jetsons*-like Prayer Tower where Oral Roberts awaited the Lord's word to ascend into heaven. A place where a seventy-six-foot-tall crotchless roughneck stands astride an actual oil derrick. The roughneck is painted mustard yellow, built to withstand two hundred mile-per-hour winds from tornadoes that occasionally rip through town. A place where one apartment building looks like a hypodermic needle, and a local celebrity walks around downtown with a paper bag over his head, while another man, Biker Fox, cycles the city with a bald pate and mullet providing aggressive motivational speeches about the power of cycling. It is hard to sum up Biker Fox in a sentence, but we will let the director of the *Biker Fox* (2010) documentary, Jeremy Lamberton, attempt it: "Biker Fox is a mythological creature riding through the streets of Tulsa spreading love and light to the masses." This is a place where one of the top tourist draws is a crumbling concrete overpass known as the Center of the Universe. A place whose signature event is a bicycle race that includes a stretch across a quiet residential hill where naked people shake plastic baby dolls and shout obscenities at world-class cyclists, all while the music of acid-tripping jam bands fills the air. All of this in a state known for its high percentage of Christian evangelicals and pickup trucks. This is a state that hosts the only national tournament for noodling (hand-fishing for catfish) and boasts some of the longest running rattlesnake roundups in the nation. We are weird without the bluster of Austin or the hipster pretentiousness of Portland. Our weirdness runs in our rusty, oil-soaked water. We eat it up like fried pies and okra.

What can I say? Tulsa is "a slut" spelled backward.

We have given the world many well-known weirdos like Oral Roberts, Gary Busey, Leon Russell, Lee Hazlewood, Chet Baker, Larry Clark, and Anita Bryant, just to name a few. Where else in the world could a man not only have a vision of a nine-hundred-foot Jesus appear to him in the suburbs but actually build what Jesus told him to build, with gold plates covering the whole thing?

But one of our truly weird visionaries is not a household name, not even in his hometown. Once I discovered the work of Bruce Goff, I could never look at Tulsa in the same way. Long before I found myself down the Goff rabbit hole, I lived in a house built by one of his many students. The name of the architect is lost to history, since the house, like many midcentury modern gems, was bulldozed sometime in the 1990s to make way for a bloated and generic showcase luxury home. We rented the house, and the owner had made its destruction seem inevitable. According to the owner, the house was built on sand and it was slowly sliding down a hill, lacking a proper foundation to keep it anchored to the earth. We were in danger of sinking into a dry creek bed if we did not move. I begged my mom to stay in the Airplane House, whose name derived from two triangular grilles of rusted iron that protruded from the roof. The "wings" of the airplane served no practical purpose whatsoever. The house had to be the only one in Ranch Acres featuring painted cinder block walls

9. Bruce Goff's wild buildings dot the Oklahoma landscape. An early example is Tulsa's Boston Avenue United Methodist Church. Photo by the author.

that angled out from the center like a bloated airplane fuselage, accentuating the whole motif. My bedroom was a loft, and the living area had massive panes of glass on the east and west sides, almost like a modernist cathedral. Next to its down-the-street neighbor, Frank Lloyd Wright's Tulsa masterpiece Westhope, the Airplane House looked like a study in futurism on the cheap. The cinder blocks and rusted iron angling off in all sorts of directions looked like an architectural thesis built on a shoestring budget and based on *The Jetsons*. Still, for all its defects, the Airplane House stood out like a beacon against South Tulsa conformity, angling itself up against all those pseudo-colonials with fake plantation shutters, announcing a future that never quite arrived.

Maybe the Airplane House did have an early expiration date, and it was simply a matter of time before it slid off its concrete slab into the ravine. Or maybe the eccentric dwelling would never get along with its boring neighbors, and the shaky foundation was a developer's pretext to scrape a piece of avant-garde architecture.

Knowing what I now know about the madness and greed of men attached to such structures, I cannot rule out the wildest of conspiracies. In any case, living there as a twelve-year-old was the first time I can remember hearing the name Bruce Goff. If our house was an amateurish Goff imitation, what must the real thing be like? To me, the Goff buildings around Tulsa looked like they had been teleported from another universe. The Boston Avenue United Methodist Church, an early Goff building, did not so much seem like a church as it did a module for communication with alien life forms.

Oklahoma is dotted with Goff's singular works of genius, many of them houses in small towns off the main highways. Goff designed houses that seem to speak their own language (and as it turns out, Goff actually did invent, if not his own language, his own font for each house). Thirty-plus years after Goff's death, though, the architect's work is starting to resemble a dying idiom, as some of his most notable buildings fade into oblivion with no one outside a small but aging group of enthusiasts taking notice.

As something less than a household name, Bruce Goff does not have the contemporary prestige of Frank Gehry or Philip Johnson, even though both of those "starchitects" have acknowledged him as an influence. "I knew of Goff in my architectural beginnings as a shadowy mystical figure in Oklahoma who made bizarre buildings," Gehry has written. "He was an American. Like [Frank Lloyd] Wright, he was the model iconoclast, the paradigm of America. How should we have him now—this messy creature from Middle America?"

In 2011 I saw a Goff home for sale in Tulsa on South Madison. The house had two flat roofs with strange designs on the fascia that looked like indecipherable hieroglyphics in the photos. The overall effect was of a Mayan temple surrounded by Maple Ridge quaintness. I fantasized plans for making a down payment but then ran into a website that cast a shadow of doubt on its provenance. Someone on the site PrairieMod

.com seemed unconvinced that the house was a real Goff and asked for confirmation.

Nelson Brackin, an Atlanta-based architect who worked with Goff on a number of his projects late in his life, left a comment on the site that the house was, in fact, a real Goff. Brackin is the president of the Friends of Kebyar, an organization that preserves and promotes design "outside the mainstream." Brackin knows how to spot a Goff, having put together a special edition of the *Friends of Kebyar* journal dedicated to Goff in Oklahoma. Brackin said that, in the late 1950s, Goff came back to Tulsa and pointed out many of the houses he had built to a local architect, Thomas Thixton. Many of them, however, were later demolished to make way for the crosstown freeway system.

Other Goff buildings, some of them central to Tulsa's architectural identity, have either been torn down since the 1970s, or are under threat of being demolished. One such building was the Tulsa Club, which used to be a downtown institution for the rich and powerful, only to fall into disrepair and neglect in the 1990s. In 2007 the city ruled that the eleven-story building either be razed or restored to meet fire and safety codes. The building was bought by a California investor who let it deteriorate even further. Since then, the building has been the subject of years of litigation, its owner cited by the city for property code and public nuisance violations. Numerous fires have broken out, and the unique zigzag details on the walls are covered in graffiti. Crushed beer cans litter the ballroom floor. The landmark last sold for $1.1 million, the price of a modest apartment in New York City. Finally, in 2018 work began in earnest to renovate the building and turn it into a boutique hotel. By the spring of 2019, the Tulsa Club was back: it is now one of Tulsa's swankiest hotels.

I asked Brackin why Goff's work could be so esteemed by top architects and so neglected by Oklahomans. A lot of Goff's buildings, he said, date from the middle of the twentieth century. "Mid-century is seen as disposable. Goff was so singular, so unique, his architecture stood out. It didn't conform, it didn't fit in, it wasn't a rebirth of some past style or belief." I instantly recognized what Brackin meant about disposable architecture. My beloved Airplane House had been torn down as soon as my mom and I moved out in the late 1980s.

The most singular, unique, and nonconformist Goff house of them all is the Bavinger House in Norman. In a bizarre coincidence, while I was scheming various plans to buy the Goff house on South Madison, a tragic event began unfolding on the premises of the Bavinger House. At first, it appeared that a microburst of severe weather had damaged the one part of the house visible from the street: a winding, logarithmic spire held in place by a tall mast. Someone snapped a photo of the spire at a forty-five-degree angle from where it should be, and the Oklahoma City media reported "storm damage" as the cause. The next day, a story in *The Oklahoman* cast some doubt on the original reporting, claiming that "the architectural oddity in east Norman either fell to a recent microburst of high winds—or at the hand of the owner, Bob Bavinger."

Soon afterward, rumors of the house's demise started to circulate around the internet and the website for the house had a vaguely worded statement that the Bavinger House would no longer be open to the public (the website has since disappeared into the ether). Speculation about the house's destruction began to center on Bavinger, the son of the original owners and artists Eugene and Nancy Bavinger. As it turned out, Bob Bavinger had made repeated threats to destroy the house to people connected to the University of Oklahoma School of Architecture. A news crew from Oklahoma City went out to investigate, but as they stepped onto the premises a shot rang out and they retreated.

Phone calls and emails, including some from me, went unanswered, leading many to believe that Bob Bavinger, along with his son, Boz, had begun dismantling the house rock by rock. To understand how this situation came about, we need to go back to Goff's arrival in Norman in 1947 and examine his vexed relationship with the University of Oklahoma.

Bruce Goff arrived in Norman with no academic training, but he already had three decades of experience designing houses. He received his first commission at the age of twelve in Tulsa, and his sketches reveal a brilliant but quirky talent. Some designs fit with the art deco trends of the time, but others seem to be inspired by an intelligence beyond

10. Bruce Goff's Bavinger House was built on a shoestring budget using recycled materials. It was later dismantled by its owners. Courtesy of Anthony V. Thompson.

earth, or ancient civilizations. After a prolific period in Tulsa, he worked in Chicago, Ohio, and California, incorporating elements of Bauhaus, Prairie School, and the International Style into his buildings. It was in Norman, though, that Goff finally experienced the "liberation of genius," in the words of Goff scholar David DeLong. In the 1930s in Chicago, he had started to write about architecture as a design of "the continuous present," following Gertrude Stein's idea that composition never really begins or ends but flows through time. In Norman he explored the idea more fully, creating the spiral of the Bavinger House.

"What I would like to see is the clock striking thirteen around here," Goff told an audience at the University of Oklahoma in 1953. "I would like to see something strange, and new, and different . . . not to be strange, just as a name, because that will never work. What you do if you do something that we are talking about here—having an idea of your own—will naturally seem strange." Students from around the country flocked to the University of Oklahoma to study with Goff. Herb Greene, who would later become an important architect in his own right, transferred to Norman from Syracuse and did some of the first drawings for the Bavinger House. "Goff sat every student down for an hour and a half and just talked to them," he told me. "He was a great educator."

Under Goff's direction, the architecture program developed a unique sensibility. He urged students to explore radical ideas, not just in architecture but in philosophy, literature, and music. Goff introduced Greene to the Russian Constructivists and phenomenology. Although Goff cultivated a taste for the odd, eccentric, and outlandish, Greene characterized him as "the kindest man [he'd] ever known."

Summarizing what Goff did in Norman is nearly impossible, since each building is like a new school unto itself. His first house, the Ledbetter House, attracted so much attention that it was featured in a photo spread in *Life* magazine. The Ledbetter House featured a suspended carport and patio, as well as round roofs that came off looking like flying saucers. "It was the age of Sputnik, Roswell, and the space race," says Nelson Brackin. "We were thrown skyward, and the Ledbetter House reflects that."

According to Brackin, the Ledbetters loved cut glass, but costs were skyrocketing. Goff went to a dime store and bought heavy glass ashtrays and built them into the house. Goff found it amusing that, after the Ledbetter House made its debut, a rash of buildings appeared around Norman with things suspended from cables. He thought of the house as "rather conventional" and moved on to a bigger challenge: designing a house for Eugene and Nancy Bavinger for a budget of around $2,000 in the 1950s.

According to Goff, Eugene Bavinger looked like "more of a truck driver" than an art professor. One of his main hobbies was growing indoor plants, and "he liked to get out and dig and move large rocks and that sort of thing." Realizing that a bank loan for the house would be impossible, Bavinger said he would be willing to do a lot of the construction himself, recycling old materials like salvaged rope, World War I airplane parts, and Coca-Cola bottle cullets.

Goff came up with a design of a spiral-shaped house that inverted the outside and inside, turning the interior into a walled garden. The house's now-defunct website described the finished product as "a single rock wall that takes the form of a logarithmic spiral building upward toward the sky. The interior stairs, living area bowls, and closets are suspended and supported from a drill stem pipe that runs through the center of the house. A bridge on the east side of the house is used as a counter-weight for the roof to keep the drill stem pipe from bending. A buttress at the lower end of the roof keeps the roof from running away."

Like the Ledbetter House, the Bavinger House became a national sensation. The Bavingers raised money for construction by selling tickets for house tours at a dollar a head. By the time they had finished, the Bavingers had raised close to $4,000. Goff's students, including Herb Greene, came out to the property to help with the construction. During a lecture later in his life, Goff said that many well-known architects resented the house, thinking it was an abomination to make his clients live in a spiral with suspended pods instead of rooms.

Eugene Bavinger, however, always rose to Goff's defense. Goff recalled Bavinger telling off one architect in person: "It's true we never dreamed we'd live in a spiral, never thought of it. We told him what we wanted, what we liked, what we didn't like, and it ended up with a spiral, and we are damned glad it did. I really don't think it's anybody else's business."

Bavinger came to begrudge the curiosity seekers and posted trespassing signs around the property. Goff told the story of a rich man who brought his trophy wife up from Dallas to see the house years after it was built. Bavinger told the man to go away, but the man replied, "When you have a work of art you must share it with people—you shouldn't keep it all to yourself." Bavinger reportedly ogled the man's beautiful wife and asked him if he really believed that great works of art should be shared. "He never got to see the house," Goff said.

Maybe the story is apocryphal, but it gets at Bavinger's sense of ownership. A person close to the Bavingers said that Eugene always kept a gun close by. Some visitors recall seeing his "no trespassing" signs shot full of buckshot to let people know he was serious about privacy. When another Goff landmark, the Joe Price House in Bartlesville, fell victim to a mysterious case of arson in 1996, the Bavingers became convinced that their house would be next.

At this point, the relationship between Goff, his clients, and the University of Oklahoma becomes very weird and even more complicated. The Price House, perhaps Goff's second most famous building, had been deeded to the University of Oklahoma in 1985 when Joe Price decided to move his family and his unique collection of Japanese art from Bartlesville to Los Angeles. By this time, Goff had died, and his immense collection of letters, art, records, and sketches were spread out among different collections in Norman, Chicago, and Bartlesville.

The University of Oklahoma had endowed a Bruce Goff Chair in Creative Architecture, but its direction was proving to be a big disappointment to Goff's protégés, now distinguished architects in their own right. The University of Oklahoma's handling of the Price House was also causing concern. OU rented out rooms for special events, but the house's unique design, which included, among other things, goose feathers, turkey insemination rods, and blood-stained glass mosaics, was not being maintained or even insured. The Price House became so run down that the University of Oklahoma decided to sell it off, and the Friends of Shin'en Kan (the name comes from the Price House's Japanese moniker, which means "The House of the Faraway Heart") were trying to raise the money to buy it back and restore it. Goff's friends and colleagues were shocked to see the state of the house, and negotiations to restore it often ended in shouting matches with representatives from the university.

The house was sold to the highest bidder: two Bartlesville residents who outbid the Friends of Shin'en Kan but agreed to lease it to them for a dollar. Under the agreement, the buyers would then give the title to the house to the Friends of Shin'en Kan within thirteen months. It seemed to be an arrangement that Goff's protégés could live with and provided a foundation for the renovation of this landmark structure.

However, shortly after the sale, the house went up in flames. According to a later investigation, diesel fuel was used to start the blaze, and the walls, which were made of coal in places, easily caught fire. One witness, Carolyn Price, saw two figures running back and forth, dousing the sprawling complex with gas until the entire building was aflame. The house was burned to the ground, but some artifacts remained, including some brilliant blue-green glass cullets which were also part of the walls.

Brackin said that, over the years, many people have gone to Bartlesville to pilfer remnants from the fire and that there may still be some glass cullets on the property. He has seen some items from Shin'en Kan on eBay. For years, the Friends of Shin'en Kan had planned some sort of memorial to Goff on the site, but ownership was stuck in legal limbo until 2000, when the Oklahoma Supreme Court finally ruled that the Friends, and not the Bartlesville residents who bought the property at auction, owned the land. By that time, however, funds to rebuild had dried up. A recent photo from the area shows a boxy new house with vinyl siding abutting the burned foundation of Price's old home. At some point, one of Goff's students, Grant Gustafson, rescued a piece of glass and incorporated it into Goff's headstone at Graceland Cemetery in Chicago, where his ashes are interred with some of the most notable architects in history. Joe Price funded the memorial site, and Nancy Bavinger sent some earth from her house in Norman.

An investigation into the Price house arson was begun, but no one was ever charged. According to Bartlesville police captain Jay Harness, the crime is still classified as unsolved.

A few sources close to Goff put part of the blame for the tragic end of Shin'en Kan and the Bavinger House in the hands of the University of Oklahoma. Even if the university did not physically destroy the structures, one can understand the anger toward it. The University of Oklahoma had been Goff's Maecenas, but the school also very nearly ruined him. The university gave Goff the opportunity to run the School of Architecture in 1947, and for a while he made Norman an unlikely destination for avant-garde thinking. During the conformist 1950s, however, Goff butted heads with the institution, which was not willing to go along with some of Goff's more radical plans. The University of Oklahoma was an institution searching for both national respectability and cultural capital. Sometimes that search clashed with the avant-garde nature of Goff's aesthetics.

Goff had submitted designs for the nondenominational Crystal Chapel on campus in 1949, but influential donors balked. The structure would have been based on repeating diamond-shaped patterns, rose-colored glass, and a series of reflecting pools. It was, in the words of Goff scholar David DeLong, "utopian." *Architectural Forum* glowed: "Here at last is a rocket-flight use of techniques and materials never before available to realize a form of beauty and religious experience never before possible."

Finally, Fred Jones Jr., a car dealership magnate, stepped in with the money for the chapel on the condition that the building conform to a "conventional design." Goff was silently pushed aside, provoking the indignation of some of the most noted architects in the world, including Walter Gropius, Alfonso Iannelli, and Frank Lloyd Wright, who wrote letters supporting Goff.

Later, on a commission to develop a new Norman subdivision, developers took issue with Goff's plans. In retaliation for a design they did not like, they set Goff up to hurt him in the area of his life where he was most vulnerable—his sexuality. Here, too, it is hard to know exactly what transpired because the episode was quickly covered up. Builders of the subdivision, apparently outraged by Goff's quirks, contracted a teenage boy to lure Goff into a sexually charged situation. Although there was no proof that anything physical actually took place with the boy, the whiff of scandal began to undo Goff. Influential people at the University of Oklahoma called for Goff to be fired. Rumors started to circulate about Goff's relationships, some of them with male students. Herb Greene said that Goff could be indiscrete, defying the closeted norms of the time period: "It was the 1950s, and being gay was not something you talked about out in the open."

Despite the mounting pressure on Goff to resign, the University of Oklahoma's president, George Lynn Cross, tried to convince Goff to stay and fight the charges. Goff, however, was badly hurt by the episode and resigned for "health reasons," even though he was in perfect physical condition. It was then that his work with the Price family in Bartlesville led to some of the most striking midcentury architecture on the plains of northeast Oklahoma, while the School of Architecture at the University of Oklahoma slid into mediocrity. Perhaps in an attempt to rekindle the excitement that Goff brought to the University of Oklahoma in the 1950s, he was invited back in 1981 to become a visiting professor at the School of Architecture, but in an ironic twist, this time Goff actually was in poor health and died a couple of months after the academic term ended.

After the fire at the Price House in 1996, an aging Eugene Bavinger became increasingly worried about the fate of his own home. Witnessing the University of Oklahoma's treatment of his old friend Bruce Goff and botched attempt at managing Shin'en Kan made him worry that the university would eventually lead his family's house to ruin. His son, Bob Bavinger, had grown up around this vexed relationship with the University of Oklahoma, and when his father died in 1997, he started to believe that the school was actually trying to take the house away from him.

I was never able to make contact with Bavinger in person, but someone who knew him directed me to the house's Wikipedia page, which had been extensively edited by someone with an ax to grind against the university. For a brief period, it read, "the University of Oklahoma had undermined the efforts to gain funding to restore the family home."

A source with some familiarity with this situation said that the University of Oklahoma had indeed attempted to bully Bob Bavinger into letting them run the house but that he had also developed some rather wild conspiracy theories about the University of Oklahoma, the mafia, and the FBI. By the time the Oklahoma City News 9 crew made it onto the property after the collapse of the spire, Bavinger had built an armed bunker and installed security cameras around the premises.

After the shot was fired at the news crew, police made contact with Bavinger. He was not charged with a crime since the shot was fired from his property and no one had been injured (this was Oklahoma, after all). Days after the spire was toppled, Bavinger granted a rare interview to the *Norman Transcript* and said that he and his son, Boz, "were backed into a corner." Equipped with an old dump truck and jackhammer, hidden just out of view in east Norman, Bob and Boz went to work on dismantling the building art critic Hilton Kramer referred to as "one of the building marvels of our own postwar period." Something about it recalled the old line from the Vietnam War—"we had to destroy the village in order to save it." Bavinger said that the University of Oklahoma was undermining his efforts at restoration, and the only option left was to "remove the target."

Coming out of the rabbit hole, I searched up the Goff house on South Madison again. It had doubled in value in the past five years, making it way out of my price range. While I still daydream about living in a Goff myself, I have to wonder about the toll it might take on my psyche. From the Bavinger House to Shin'en Kan to the Tulsa Club, Goff's structures seem to breed extremes of the human condition: madness, greed, obsession.

Back in downtown Tulsa, a last-ditch effort was put together to save Goff's Tulsa Club building after multiple fires and vandalism earned the structure a nuisance label by city officials. The building, like the city in which it stands, had its own history of malfeasance, corruption, and bad luck. My grandfather spent the 1960s going broke while ordering cocktails from the Tulsa Club hand delivered to his office across the street. For the first decade of the twenty-first century, the Tulsa Club was a burned-out hull of a place that appeared to be destined for oblivion. Now, the Tulsa Club is slated to become a boutique hotel, and Goff's name is being celebrated around the state. Tulsa has honored Goff with a special room at the city's redesigned Equality Center, a meeting place for LGBTQ people. Everywhere I turn, it seems, Tulsa has not only preserved its history but used its unique story to create a whole new chapter, one that leaves behind the mid-America milquetoast image for good.

Perhaps that has less to do with Bruce Goff than it does with the inherent weirdness of life in these parts. Scratch underneath even the most superficially bland places in Oklahoma, and you will find some oddity. The house I grew up in was down the street from one such place, hidden by a gracious brick wall along with magnolia and oak trees. This place was in the heart of Maple Ridge, a segregated early suburb just south of downtown. Most of the neighborhood's most gracious houses were constructed during the first oil boom and reflect the aspirations of a *nouveau riche* obsessed with cultural prestige. Italianate villas, English Tudor, Georgian plantation-style houses with modest yards but ornate gardens give the neighborhood a hoity-toity feel. The whole place was—and still is—well-off, peaceful, quiet, conservative, and 99 percent white. The 1 percent that totally broke the mold was behind that brick wall and those trees.

In the 1970s, at the peak of his influence, Leon Russell bought a mansion in Maple Ridge that was a mecca and a hideout for the biggest names in rock and roll. George Harrison, Elton John, and Paul McCartney all stopped by. Eric Clapton brought on a handful of Tulsa musicians he met through Russell as his core band for about a decade. Through the 1970s, Clapton emulated the laid-back jazz twang of JJ Cale, another Tulsan in the jazz scene. In moments of honesty, the white musicians of the Tulsa Sound (Russell, Cale, Elvin Bishop, and others) copped to a truth. "There isn't really any Tulsa Sound," Cale told a reporter in 2010. "We were just trying to play the blues and didn't know how, so that's what we came up with."

In the late 1950s, Greenwood, the same area of Black Tulsa devastated by the massacre of 1921, was a crossroads for American music. Only a few blocks from Cain's Ballroom, the home of western swing, Greenwood was home to Black jazz and blues musicians. A cross-pollination of jazz, blues, country, and gospel happened at an almost-forgotten club in the neighborhood: the Flamingo Lounge. It was there that a blues guitarist named Flash Terry held court and welcomed in the white musicians. "That club and Flash didn't have any attitude at all about race or ethnicity," another Tulsa Sound pioneer, Rocky Frisco, said. "I was kind of scared to death to go there actually, but he was always really nice to me and encouraged me."[1]

It was a classic American story, of course: talented white musicians breathe in African American music and turn it into a marketable sound for mainstream audiences. But the Leon Russell story gives this narrative another twist: Russell not only helped launch the career of the seminal R&B group GAP Band but also brought Black musicians into Maple Ridge to record and party.

Russell's overt disregard for the racial conformity established between white and Black Tulsa did not stop there. Russell defied Tulsa's de-facto segregation and married Mary McCreary, a Black singer from Sly and the Family Stone. They raised a mixed-race family and made mixed-race music in the heart of white Tulsa. Much of this is documented in the off-kilter documentary about Russell and other sundry Okie weirdos in Les Blank's film, *A Poem Is a Naked Person*. In the film, an almost-naked artist paints a strange mural of a squid on the foundation of a dry pool in Russell's backyard. The hazy atmosphere of experimentation in music, drugs, and society at the Russell mansion belied the place's surface appearance as a genteel southern neighborhood.

A Poem Is a Naked Person reveals a lab of experimentation going on behind the graceful magnolia trees. We see the muralist working on the bottom of the pool, carefully capturing and releasing scorpions, while musing on the meaning of life. The film is less a music documentary than it is a window onto sundry weirdos telling ghost stories, eating glass, dancing, and generally letting their freak flags fly.

Russell's house was torn down and subdivided sometime in the 1980s when his career hit a rough patch. There are no plaques, no monuments in the neighborhood to the man and the place that gave the world the seamless blend of gospel, blues, country, and rock which came to be known as Tulsa Sound. Russell's recording studio, an old church in a hardscrabble part of town, seemed headed for the same fate until 2016 when a local developer took a chance on it. In 2017 the developer unveiled an ambitious plan to remake the boarded-up church into a recording studio, gallery, and museum preserving the legacy of the Tulsa Sound. The developer is taking cues from the people who brought the Woody Guthrie and Bob Dylan archives, slowly turning Tulsa into a destination for Americana music.

On an even rougher side of town, in Crutchfield, Danny Boy, the hype man for the hip-hop group House of Pain, has poured his soul into an almost-forgotten slice of Tulsa history. In the 1980s Francis Ford Coppola set up shop in Tulsa to shoot two films, one a moving story about marginalized teens growing up in the 1950s (*The Outsiders*) and another about a mysterious biker figure named Randy James (*Rumble Fish*). The more avant-garde film, *Rumble Fish*, became something of a cult classic with its moody Black and white expressionist scenes in midtown Tulsa. For years, *Rumble Fish* and *The Outsiders* devotees came to Tulsa on film location scavenger hunts. Europeans in particular seemed to adore these films, and I once took a group of British college students on a tour of the places where gang fights, robberies, and bar brawls were filmed. They thought Tulsa had soul. For them, Tulsa was a unique slice of Americana untouched by tourism or gentrification, while I thought Tulsa was a milquetoast small town with no history masquerading as an actual city. The Brits were right, and I would spend the next twenty years discovering what had been hidden during the first twenty years of my life.

Danny Boy (the House of Pain member) partially relocated to Tulsa to buy the house where much of *The Outsiders* was shot. He purchased the house for a few thousand dollars and started a foundation to restore it to its 1980s condition. When I showed up one warm January day in 2019, I saw a few cats on the front porch, but no other signs of life. To say the neighborhood was poor would be akin to saying a glacier was icy; Crutchfield's poverty defined the entire landscape. Carcasses of houses, broken fencing, husks of cars on vacant lots, and potholed streets dominated the area. I opened the rusted front gate to *The Outsiders* house. The cats scattered from under the 1950s-era patio furniture I remembered from the film. The renaissance of the house and the neighborhood I had read about in the local paper seemed to be on an indefinite hiatus. Tulsa's rebirth is uneven, contradictory, and occasionally ugly.

Down the street, I saw a man with knuckle tattoos smoking a cigarette and glowering at me from his front porch. Banda music rattled the windows of a beaten up Ford Taurus. Another house flew U.S. and Confederate flags from separate flagpoles at equal height. One in five houses in Crutchfield stands vacant, and the poverty rate is three times that of the rest of the city.

Sometimes Okie weirdness transitions uncomfortably into something profoundly disturbing or even tragic. Sometimes weirdness is just a survival strategy for people who do not fit into Bible Belt culture. Weirdness in Tulsa is not part of a branding image as it is in Austin but a natural product of a place that formed from the contradictions of greed, utopian visions, artistic risk-takers, and swindling money-makers.

CHAPTER 10

Cursed?

For two generations, virtually all the men in my family have contracted some form of heart disease by age fifty. Various theories have been proposed: lifestyle choices involving alcohol and drugs, genetic bad luck, or some sort of spiritual dark force. "The Cobb curse," my aunt Mona calls it. A sign that the devil walks among us. I am a firmly secular person, so I booked an appointment with a cardiologist when I turned thirty. Dr. Z seemed a little perplexed by my presence. I told him I had no symptoms of any sort, except that when I thought about my male relatives, I could feel my heart racing. Dr. Z got interested when I started to tick off the cases of heart disease in my family. Both my grandfather and my father died young from heart failure. My father's three brothers all had the same disease. Dr. Z raised an eyebrow. He sat down, ready to take notes. "Let's start with your dad," he said. "What was his particular diagnosis?"

"Cardiomyopathy," I said.

Cardiomyopathy is a disease in which the heart muscle wears itself out from too much stress. The heart becomes enlarged, like a worn-out spring. Some types of cardiomyopathy are environmental—brought on by drug use, exposure to toxic chemicals, or high blood pressure—while others are purely genetic. In hypertrophic cardiomyopathy, a healthy young person can drop dead from exertion. Dilated cardiomyopathy, on the other hand, usually means a long, slow decline of heart function ending with heart failure. "Do you know what form of cardiomyopathy he had?" Dr. Z said.

"It was idiopathic," I said.

"That means they don't know what caused it," he said.

I was at a loss. The truth was I knew very little about my dad. Fortunately, though, there was a paper trail that led to some sort of narrative of his life. I simply had to pick up the pieces and shuffle them around until they made sense. Before he came down with what seemed like the flu, my dad—who went by the name Candy—spent his free time playing tennis, poker, and lifting weights. A former high school tennis champion in Tulsa, he bore a striking resemblance to Elvis and people occasionally stopped him in the airport to ask for an autograph. With his massive jade pinky ring, solid gold cufflinks, and tailor-made shirts, he fit the part. He also had a past life he was trying to put behind him, one I would only discover two decades later. After my mom and dad eloped in Las Vegas, they moved to Houston, where he tried to revive my grandfather's failed oil business.

My grandfather had inherited a fortune from my great-grandfather's business, Cobra Oil, but had blown through it by the time my dad was a teenager. My grandfather's name was tainted by his association with a Ponzi scheme called the Home-Stake Oil Swindle, which defrauded investors out of $125 million by convincing rich people that the company was a tax shelter. As the scheme collapsed and my grandfather lost his privileges at the country club, his bouts of already heavy drinking became more severe. My grandmother ordered him out of the house, convinced he would eventually squander their last dollar. In 1968 he died penniless and alone in a veteran's hospital of heart failure, at age forty-four. Days before his death, he called his new girlfriend in Tulsa and told her to get ready for a fantastic vacation to Acapulco. Another Cobb oil well would soon renew his riches. He was, I suppose, also afflicted with a bit of Dumb Okie logic.

Among other things, my dad inherited from my grandfather this cruel optimism that wealth was just around the corner. My mom and dad moved to Houston in 1972, which had replaced Tulsa as the oil capital of the world. For a while, they fit right in with the hard-partying and big spending oil elites. My mom remembers keg and pool parties with a young George W. Bush in their condo. My dad looked around for a job in the oil pipeline business, but mostly he worked on his tennis game. Then luck hit. He found a niche reselling old oilfield pipeline at a time when petroleum prices were skyrocketing because of the Middle Eastern oil embargo in 1973. The money rolled in. My mom got pregnant with me, and they moved from their party condo into a spacious duplex in Houston's tiny Museum District. The centerpiece of the house was a chartreuse dining room adorned with a chandelier and a matching small green parrot—one of my first memories. Almost immediately after the move, though, Candy found he was increasingly breathless; he felt like he had a bad chest cold that would not go away. After a couple of weeks trying to ignore it, he could barely finish a match of tennis. He took leave from work and spent whole days in bed. His doctor diagnosed him with the flu, then pneumonia, but weeks of bed rest only seemed to make the condition worse. My grandmother came to visit during my first Christmas and dragged him to the emergency room. The ER doctor brought in a cardiologist, who diagnosed him with idiopathic cardiomyopathy.

If you had a rare, devastating heart disease as a twenty-nine-year-old in 1974, perhaps the best place in the world to have it was Houston. The Texas Medical Center, already a world leader in medical innovations, created the Texas Heart Institute only a few years before we moved to town. The institute, in turn, had become one of the top ten heart hospitals in the world. Dr. Michael DeBakey, labeled the "the greatest surgeon ever" by the *Journal of the American Medical Association*, performed the first successful bypass operation and later installed the first artificial heart pump in a patient in Houston. My dad became a patient in DeBakey's practice at the same time the surgeon was embroiled in a massive public feud with another Texas cardiologist over who should receive credit for installing the world's first total artificial heart.

The doctors associated with the famously egotistical DeBakey were at a loss over what to do with my dad. One cardiologist diagnosed my dad with cardiomyopathy but thought it came from a viral infection picked up at the gym. Damage to the heart was already too extensive for a pacemaker—a relatively new invention at the time. Surgery would not bring back the damaged heart, so the best hope was to contain any further deterioration. This meant even more bed rest. My dad's dream of bringing back the Cobb family oil fortune started to fade, and my mom went to work as a secretary for another oil man, a gentleman rancher who came to town once a week to collect his royalty checks. My parents' debts started to pile up. At one point the sheriff showed up to collect $4,500 in delinquent payments, proof that my dad could not outrun the life he had left behind in Oklahoma. Still, he felt sure he was not condemned to the same fate as my grandfather, and he made a slight improvement when doctors drained fluid from his lungs and extremities.

By the time I was out of diapers, the house was swarming with doctors and nurses. With money and options running out, we moved back to Oklahoma. We rented a cramped duplex in a treeless part of town far away from the oil mansions and country clubs. I was shuttled between grandmothers as my mom struggled to bring in a little bit of money with a part-time gig at a clothing store. My dad was in the hospital most of the time. There we watched *The Lone Ranger* together in bed. I thought it was his job. I was pretty proud of the fact that my dad worked at a fancy hospital with high-tech equipment all around him. At one point I drew a picture of him surrounded by an EKG machine and IV equipment to show my preschool class. The teachers were horrified, but my mom had accomplished her mission of making me think that our chaotic life was normal, even though she was driven to insomnia and weighed, in her estimation, about eighty pounds.

In 1977, at thirty-two years old, he became the seventy-fifth person to receive a successful heart transplant. The operation took place at Stanford, the only hospital that carried out the procedure at the time. His doctor,

Norman Shumway, was the first doctor in North America to perform a successful heart transplant in 1968. Shumway had stumbled onto the idea of heart transplantation in the early 1960s, mainly out of boredom. He had been experimenting on dogs' hearts in his lab. Shumway figured out how to isolate the organ, take it out, and put it in a special cold saline solution. One day, Shumway wondered why he could not take a sick dog's heart out and replace it with a healthy one. "We'd take the heart out of one animal and put it into another animal," he said in an interview. "To our amazement, these animals began to live. They would be jumping around the laboratory for a while."

However, the major roadblock to success was not the transplant itself but the immune system, which rejected the new organ after only a few days. Shumway felt that if doctors could find the right immunosuppressant, transplants—not an artificial heart—would be the best option for patients with heart failure. Thus, the word *successful* in relation to Dr. Shumway's 1968 surgery is, however, relative. While the recipient, a fifty-four-year-old Ohio steelworker named Mike Kasperak, lived for fourteen days and then died from, in the doctor's words, "a fantastic galaxy of complications," the procedure had turned Dr. Shumway into a celebrity. Hailed as a medical miracle in the media, the operation spurred heart surgeons from around the country to jump onto the transplantation bandwagon, and hundreds of transplants—the vast majority of them failures—were performed in the early 1970s. Many patients died within hours of their operations. The *New York Times* dubbed the trend a "medical circus" and the American Medical Association called for a moratorium.

Organ transplantation represented a quandary for Christian evangelicals. The Catholic church took a strong stand in favor of organ donation, but some evangelicals questioned whether doctors were violating the sacredness of the human body and playing God. And then there was the question of when someone was actually dead. Around the same time my dad had his transplant, there was an intense debate in evangelical communities about whether resurrection depended on the "wholeness of the body." Fundamentalists cited a passage in Corinthians that could be interpreted as an argument for the requirement of bodily wholeness to ascend into heaven. By and large, though, evangelical churches argued that organ donation represented Christian charity and compassion. Only Jehovah's Witnesses and Christian Scientists took a stance against organ donation. Despite church teachings, however, many Christians still take a dim view of organ donation. My aunt Mona goes to a church where prayer trumps modern science. When the time came for her husband to require a transplant, she was forced into a dilemma.

By this point, my dad's heart was running at 10 percent of its normal capacity, and he had suffered nine small heart attacks, each one shrinking the heart's capacity to pump blood a little less. His Tulsa doctors told him his last-ditch option was a transplant, but he would have to join a months-long waiting list. There was no guarantee he would live long enough to get his new heart. A doctor at Oral Roberts University offered his services for free. It would be a combination of modern medicine and good old-fashioned prayer. My dad was intrigued. The Cobbs' staid Episcopal church provided cold comfort for someone with terminal disease. Our family pastor, a gentle but terse man whose Yankee sobriety did not match the Cobb effusiveness, gave my parents Christian literature on theodicy.

Religion, for the extended network of the Cobbs, was background noise to the real matter of making money. The God we prayed to did not seem to intercede much in our affairs. But as my dad got sicker, he started to reconsider his faith. If the aloof God of the Common Prayer and the Nicene Creed did not hear his prayers, there was another God across town who promised much more.

My dad still cruised around town in an old black Mercedes, even though he was not supposed to drive. We ran into his cardiologist while eating cheeseburgers at a Tulsa fast food dive, and the doctor reprimanded my dad for not following his strict diet. He had a medic alert tag made up for himself listing his disease and the medications he was on. The tag was solid gold and listed Bombay Sapphire Gin with a twist among his many medicines. My dad was still considering the offer from the Oral Roberts doctor when good news arrived. In May 1977 he got a call from Shumway's secretary: his heart was ready. We were broke. My mom could not afford the plane tickets to California, but the Cobbs still had some connections. A family friend in Oklahoma with a private jet flew us out to Palo Alto, where my dad's new heart was chilling in a saline solution.

The operation was brutal. It began with a general anesthetic, followed by an incision from just below the Adam's apple all the way down to the stomach. The chest was split in half so the surgeon could divert the blood flow through a cardiopulmonary bypass machine. The diseased heart was taken out and a new heart sewn into place. The bypass machine was disconnected, and the new heart received a series of shocks to get it pumping again. The sternum was wired back together and the skin sewn up.

My dad came out of surgery and demanded a menthol cigarette, a beer, and a cheeseburger. It was as if he was reborn. Everyone celebrated. The nurses brought in the beer and cigarettes. As a parting gift, the hospital gave us T-shirts that said, "I left my heart in San Francisco." The operation itself had been a charity case at Stanford, but post-op treatment and its complications led to a medical bill of $700,000. My dad also had a story about his new heart; he had received it from a young Black man shot in the head in San Francisco. I remember him telling this story once to a horrified family friend. When I was teenager, I repeated the story. "My dad got the heart of a Black guy," I said.

My mom interrupted. No, she said. My dad had made that story up. His heart came from a white man around his same age who had been killed in a motorcycle accident. "Don't go around telling people that story," she said.

Race is a vexing issue for organ donors and recipients. In most instances, race and ethnicity have no bearing on the success of a transplant (with some notable exceptions, such as bone marrow transplants). People die on waiting lists for hearts, kidneys, and livers. And yet people hold out for hope that they can receive an organ from someone of the same race.

We moved back to Tulsa, but cardiologists there were not equipped to take care of a heart transplant patient with no money and complications from organ rejection. One cardiologist in Tulsa refused to see my dad until he paid his bills, sending my mom into a fit of rage.

My father reconsidered the offer from Dr. John Merriman, the evangelical Christian doctor across town. He was a gentle soul on a spiritual mission. Lured to Tulsa from Saskatchewan by the televangelist Oral

Roberts, Merriman was the first professor of medicine at Roberts's new medical school. In the late 1970s, Roberts injected tens of millions of dollars into a new hospital and medical school in Tulsa. The new hospital was the second-tallest building in the state, a manifestation of Roberts's vision of a nine-hundred-foot Jesus in the suburbs. Modernist buildings covered in sheets of gold metal and a sixty-foot bronze statue of two hands locked in prayer would show the world that faith healing and medical science could be reconciled.

As a modern facility that tried to integrate faith into Western medicine, Roberts's new medical school was unique in the world. For a good part of the twentieth century, Oral Roberts was the most successful preacher on television, with primetime specials on ABC. Roberts's "seed-faith" gospel touted the idea that prayer can plant a seed for material success in *this* world—demonstrated for all to see in the preacher's diamond cufflinks, silk suits, and Rolls Royce. Every week on national television, Roberts laid hands on the blind and made them see; he exorcised cancer from terminally ill patients. From the start, the school was in a constant battle with the academic mainstream over accreditation and prestige. While some of the disputes might have been about medical procedures, it was also clear that the white establishment was uneasy with Roberts's sponsorship of many African medical students, who not only studied medicine but remained in Tulsa to practice. While Roberts may have been a religious fundamentalist, he was also a truly equal-opportunity preacher, bringing thousands of students from the developing world to Tulsa.

Initially, neither of the two best hospitals in town allowed Merriman to practice there, but his colleagues back in Saskatchewan praised his radical new treatment for cardiac patients. Instead of confining patients with heart disease to bed rest, which was standard at the time, Merriman urged them to get up and exercise. For the first time since the infection, my dad started walking around with a cane, and although he was initially skeptical of the religious baggage, he started to trust Merriman. Seeing some success with Merriman's physical therapy, he decided to buy into the faith healing. My dad kept a log of his newfound faith, shakily writing down Bible passages and prayers in a journal. Many of the well-to-do

Episcopalians in the extended family found all this too much to bear and checked out entirely. I thought it was pretty spooky, but powerful too. Jesus was some kind of magician. I wanted to see his next act.

As complications from organ rejection started to mount, Merriman had my dad hospitalized. My dad passed the three-year mark with his new heart—a huge success for Shumway. For us, though, life was grim. In his hospital room, Merriman prescribed a cassette tape of Oral Roberts reading the Bible on a loop. Roberts's disembodied Oklahoma drawl made me feel like I was visiting a haunted house. Merriman urged my dad to see another visiting faith healer, Kenneth Hagin, at Roberts's new convention center, where a line of people waited for Hagin to lay his healing hands on them. By this time, my dad was confined to a roll-out bed.

My dad's twin, Randy, had deserted his brother after the transplant but now reemerged as a born-again Christian himself. Randy lent his legal services to help Oral Roberts in his many battles with city officials over planning and permits. Randy paid to have my dad driven to Hagin's faith-healing spectacle in a vehicle that would accommodate a bed. Randy's second wife also believed in Hagin's healing powers. When they arrived at the hall, security told them no beds were allowed on the convention floor, so they lifted my dad into a wheelchair and rolled him to the front of the crowd.

These Cobb boys, once preppy kids who attended mainstream white churches and private schools, were now broke and sick, one a recovering alcoholic and the other plagued with heart disease. Their father was dead and had left their mother, also an alcoholic, with $272,000 in debt to the IRS. Considering the circumstances, why not try out the healing hands of a preacher? My dad awaited Hagin's prayer with Randy at his side. "By the power of the Holy Word of Jesus Christ, I command you to get out of this wheelchair and walk!" Hagin said.

My dad tried to lift himself out but sat back down. "You win some and you lose some," Hagin whispered in his ear before he moved on.

Randy's wife could only come to one conclusion: my dad had not prayed hard enough. For most of his life, my dad had a gambler's instincts. Before he got sick, he often spent all his earnings on a football bet or at a poker table. At the end of his life, he placed his chips on God. It was a form of Pascal's wager. Since my father could not have absolute confidence in the existence or nonexistence of God, he wagered on the bet with the best outcome: eternity in heaven.

When my dad died in 1980, I was just short of my sixth birthday. I assumed the fancy technology by his bed had stopped working. I waited for someone to restart the machines that kept him alive. The official cause of death stemmed from a pneumonia that overwhelmed his feeble immune system. The house was quiet.

I assumed the magician named Jesus would bring my dad back from wherever God had put him. I asked my mom about it. She sat in silence, drinking tea and reading the newspaper. She put the Oral Roberts tapes away. My uncles took me out to get fitted for a gray flannel suit for the funeral, which was a quiet, somber affair. I never saw Jesus or talked to God, though I tried. My mom was glad to be rid of all the hollering and shouting about Jesus and the Holy Spirit. She wanted to return to the quietude of the Episcopal church. She even started reading the literature on theodicy, her favorite being *When Bad Things Happen to Good People*.

I dutifully followed my mom to church until I turned twelve and became an acolyte in the Episcopal church. I carried the perfectly polished brass cross down the aisle while dressed in a simple white robe. I memorized the Lord's Prayer, the Nicene Creed, and a few other stalwarts of the Anglican tradition. As an acolyte, I took my job of putting out the candles after communion with a silver candle extinguisher very seriously. The whole somber affair of an Episcopalian service felt weighty and important but absolutely stifling. I often felt I could not breathe in that stuffy church.

One Sunday, I had a revelation of my own while on my knees waiting for the sweet port wine that symbolized the blood of Christ. There was no God, no Jesus. The whole spectacle of church, the entire infrastructure of religion: it was one big fraud.

When I went back to Dr. Z, he gave me the good news: my heart was in perfect working order. Not a hint of a murmur, arrhythmia, or anything except borderline high cholesterol. Perhaps I had gotten lucky and

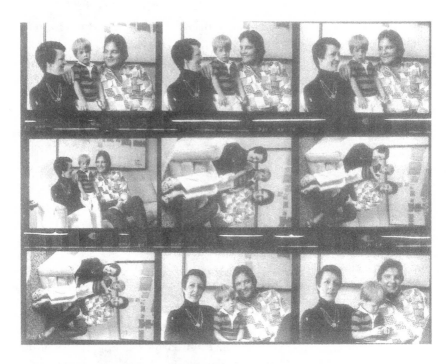

11. Pat, Russell, and Candler Cobb shortly before Candler's heart transplant at Stanford in 1977. Courtesy of the author.

inherited my mom's genes. "We can't rule that out yet," he said. "The more about your family we know, the more informed our picture will be. How about your siblings?" he asked.

"I don't have any," I said, then corrected myself. "Well, actually . . ."

My dad was barely out of high school when he had a child with a woman named Susan. They married, but Susan and the Cobbs did not mix. The relationship fell apart, and Susan took custody of their little boy. I had never met him and in fact did not even know he existed until I was almost out of high school. I saw his name on a document that paid out some of the Cobb family's dwindling oil royalties. I told my mom the company had made a mistake; they were still paying royalties to my dad when the money should go to us. This fund was supposed to pay my college tuition, after all, and I was determined to get away from home.

"That's your half brother," my mom said casually.

If my family had kept this secret from me, what else were they hiding? At the time, I did not want to know. I just wanted to get the hell out of Oklahoma. Years later, I wondered about my half brother. Had he self-destructed like other Cobb men? Had he been cursed as well? I drove to my brother's tidy, suburban colonial house. He came to the door, and we sized each other up. He was a huge man. We started to shake hands, but then he pulled me into a bear hug. My girlfriend snapped a picture, and looking at it now I am struck by how puny and insignificant I look next to this guy. We joked about the things we had in common—annoying ear hair and overbearing mothers. He knew little about his biological father, but he knew about the Cobb curse—that his biological father, all his uncles, and his grandfather had some sort of heart problem. He said his wife had been bugging him to get a full checkup but he felt fine and would someday do it. For now, the fact that he could still go jogging and biking was good enough evidence that his heart was fine. Finally, we lamented the fact that it had taken thirty years to meet. He assumed everyone on our side of the family had simply forgotten him. I did not have the nerve to tell him that decades after our father died, I found an old wallet. Inside was a picture of his first son, whom he called Baby Candy.

"Are you going to tell your mom we met?" he asked.

"Sure," I said, "At this point, I think she's pretty curious about what became of you. Are you going to tell your mom?"

"I guess I'll have to," he said. "Maybe I'll tell her when she's asleep."

He was thirty-nine years old. That was the first and last time I saw my half brother. We keep in touch, but his mother is still opposed to any contact with the Cobbs, so our conversations are usually short emails about our families and our relatively decent health. Still, I cannot quite shake the idea of a curse.

Aunt Mona once took me to a church called Guts, where young people guzzle Red Bulls and proclaim the glory of Jesus. Guts Church promotes boxing matches, poker nights, and motorcycles rallies, all in the name of the Lord. The pastor of Guts, Bill Scheer, wrote in his book *Healed: The Promise to Heal* that "sickness and premature death are from Satan and absolutely not from God." Sin, not genes or environmental factors, brings on illness, according to Scheer. For Mona, then, it was easy to understand the Cobb curse: the men drank too much, had affairs, and cheated people out of their money. The wages of sin are death, she said. The only way to cast off Satan's curse would to be reborn in Christ. My dad made a late-game bet on God, but Mona has been determined to save the rest of the family from their fate for at least thirty years. Since the 1980s, she has been working especially hard on the remaining Cobb men, dragging them to faith healings or Bible study whenever she can.

When she met Randy, he was in bad shape. His marriage was on the rocks, and his wife even pulled a gun on him at one point. He'd had scrapes with the law resulting from his consistent tax evasion and alcoholism. By the late 1980s, though, Randy was diagnosed with the same form of cardiomyopathy as his late brother, my father. He vowed to stop drinking and gave away a lot of his money to various faith-healing Pentecostal organizations. He promised to hand his life over to Jesus, only to fall off the wagon and hit the vodka bottle even harder. The few times I saw him while I was growing up, he seemed shrunken and muted, his boisterous laugh reduced to a murmur. When his heart, too, was reduced to 10 percent of its normal capacity, he was offered a place in the queue for a transplant. He refused. "He turned the decision over to the Lord," Aunt Mona said.

At Randy's funeral in 1998, Oral Roberts's son gave a eulogy and sang gospel tunes. My cousins and uncles squirmed in the pews. I rolled my eyes as Roberts performed a dramatic version of "That Old Rugged Cross" to piped-in music. My great-aunt could not conceal her high WASP disdain for all the shouting and testifying. "I know some of y'all don't like me," the preacher said. "But you want the water, you get the wet."

After Randy died in 1998, Mona remained convinced that the devil had a hold of the Cobbs. She thought Tim—the youngest of my dad's three brothers—might be next. One day, she drove him in her gold-trimmed Lexus, the license plate reading "PTL" (praise the Lord), out past Oral Roberts's now-defunct medical campus on the edge of Tulsa. They met a woman who had been "anointed by God" with a special power to break curses. Mona waited in the Lexus while the woman laid her hands on

Tim's shoulders. "Devil, you have cursed this family for generations!" she said. She shut her eyes tightly, and her body quivered a bit.

"Break these binds, Devil! In the name of your son, Jesus, break these chains and set this family free." Tim closed his eyes, too, curious about what might happen next. The Holy Ghost came over her and she broke into tongues: "*Sho sho ma fa ton so sab blu po.* Get out, Devil."

Tim reacted to the whole episode like an anthropologist. He did not believe any of it, but he was curious about the myth of the Cobb curse. He was slightly amused by the speaking in tongues and the faith healing and shrugged off the episode a few days later. Then, only a couple years later, he developed early symptoms of cardiomyopathy—dizziness and shortness of breath. As I talked to Tim about his story on Skype, however, another theory started to emerge. "We've always assumed it was some genetic bad luck or even a Cobb curse," I said. "But we also seem to have a bit of an alcohol problem on our hands."

"It sure can't be helping things," he said.

The latest frontier, the ultimate cure, is gene therapy. Theoretically, this involves the insertion of a healthy copy of a gene into afflicted cells, which would mute the problem genes. It sounds like the stuff of science fiction, but a number of research teams have produced such a thing. Ever since I stopped believing in God at age twelve, I have substituted faith in religion for faith in evidence-based medicine. My youngest son is now four years old. We shovel the Alberta snow into massive piles in the yard, then jump in it, our hearts beating like mad against the frigid cold. I have outlived my dad by eight years and have dodged the perils that tortured the other men in my family. I am also not a betting man like my father: I think Pascal's wager is a bit dishonest, actually. I tend to side with Voltaire, who thought the vague possibility of heaven insufficient proof for believing in a God who gave us the faulty tickers in the first place.

CHAPTER 11

The Fire That Time

Like generations of Oklahomans before him, Nehemiah Frank grew up thinking his future lay beyond the limited horizons of his home state. Much separates us: Frank is an African American millennial with a bespoke wardrobe; I am a white Gen Xer who prefers hoodies and sneakers. We both grew up thinking that happiness, to paraphrase an old country song, was Tulsa in the rearview mirror. Another thing we have in common: our great-grandparents came to Oklahoma seeking a promised land, while succeeding generations watched those dreams fade. Whereas I mainly griped about Tulsa's quiet mediocrity, Frank witnessed graver problems. He watched his uncles go to prison, other family members take jobs serving white people, and Black-owned shops go out of business. Before long, even close family members were telling Frank to leave for his own sake.

Frank made his way to Chicago for college. There, he found a home at Trinity United Church of Christ on the South Side. Trinity has a venerable lineage of Black liberation theology thinkers. The church had become a center of controversy during Barack Obama's first run for presidency.

Trinity's head pastor, Jeremiah Wright, had a tendency to ad-lib to his sermons and say things like "not God bless America, God damn America." Wright was vilified in the media but respected among clergy. Trinity itself was a center for progressive Christianity in the Black community. Wright said radical, even outlandish, things from time to time. It was all part of the experience, and Nehemiah Frank embraced it.

At the same time, Frank started to feel Tulsa tugging at him. Chicago has long been a hothouse for Black culture, a place where the parochialism of small-town life can be escaped for intellectual, cultural, and financial pursuits. Figures as diverse as Oprah Winfrey, Louis Farrakhan, Kanye West, and Barack Obama have all called Chicago home at one time or another. All this fit with Nehemiah Frank, but he never quite felt at home in Chicago. He kicked around ideas for going back to Oklahoma, but his extended family cautioned him against it. One Sunday at Trinity he had an uncanny experience. "I was seven rows from the front and Rev. Wright was delivering a sermon. And then he says something about the worst race massacre in American history. In Tulsa, Oklahoma! And when he said Tulsa, I was like, 'wait a second, I'm from there.'"

Wright described how the children of freed slaves created a Black homeland in Oklahoma, only to see it undone by Oklahoma's first Jim Crow laws. Black townships like Boley and Taft, once pinnacles of African American self-reliance, fell into decline. And even in cities like Tulsa and Oklahoma City, Black flight into the suburbs or bigger cities hollowed out the sense of community that once existed in Deep Greenwood and Deep Deuce. Seven out of his nine uncles had been convicted of felonies, some for minor drug offenses. Locally owned businesses were failing, and police brutality continued unabated.

Wright described how, in the face of Jim Crow laws, African Americans had built a Black Wall Street out of sheer will. Before 1921 the neighborhood of Greenwood had become a model of Black excellence just two generations out of slavery. There were hotels, juke joints, law offices, movie theaters, and a newspaper. Dr. A. C. Jackson, deemed the most "able Negro surgeon in America" by the Mayo brothers, established his practice in town. Greenwood was a mecca for Blacks fleeing small-town oppression. The neighborhood grew so fast that it bumped up against the newly christened Oil Capital of the World. The lines between Black and white Tulsa became blurry. Whites went to Greenwood to dance and drink; Blacks came to white Tulsa to work. White women formed relationships with Black men. Resentment at Black success became a major talking point in the *Tulsa Tribune*, which advocated a "clean up" of Greenwood. Then, during two days and nights in the spring of 1921, Greenwood was completely burned down. And this brings me to one last thing Nehemiah Frank and I have in common: despite our profound ties to Tulsa, both of us grew up ignorant about the events of 1921 until well into adulthood. Finding out the truth has reshaped our entire relationship with our hometown.

Wright told the story of the rise and fall of Greenwood as if it were a prefiguring of Wakanda. The story had Frank on the edge of his pew. Coincidentally, Wright was preaching out of the book of Nehemiah. "Whenever Reverend Wright would say 'Nehemiah,' people would turn around and look at me. It was like he was preaching directly to me."

Frank felt like some part of his identity shifted. Odd pieces of family history started to fit together. Frank remembered his grandfather saying something about a great fire and the Klan coming to Tulsa, but it was all vague. The Franks had bought a home from the father of David Duke, the Klansman. For the most part, though, Frank's family had kept quiet about their troubles in Tulsa. To this day, he says, there is a sense among the Black community that the tragedy of 1921 could happen again. The Black community has reason to worry. In 2012 white terror surfaced again. On Good Friday, two men drove around North Tulsa in a pickup truck, shooting randomly targeted Black people. The men shot five people, killing three. Eric Harris and Terence Crutcher were unarmed Black men killed by the Tulsa police in 2015 and 2016, respectively. For generations, Black Tulsa has lived in fear of white Tulsa. It is only in the past decade that Tulsans have started talking openly about what took place nearly one hundred years ago. Frank wanted to be part of that conversation but had no idea how to get involved.

By 2016 Frank was back in Tulsa teaching gymnastics at a private club in the affluent suburb of Jenks. He took on another job at a predominately Black charter school downtown. The stark contrast between these two worlds was brought home to him one day when a girl at the school asked how she could get into the gymnastics club. "I looked at this beautiful Black girl and knew there was no way her parents would be able to afford an expensive sport like gymnastics, especially with all the traveling," Frank said.

Every day, Frank traveled across a divide that few Tulsans paused to consider. On the North Side, where Frank lived, the average life expectancy is about two years less than in North Korea.[1] One of the only public pools on the North Side had been shut down due to budget cuts. In Jenks, where he taught gymnastics, private pool parties and ski trips to Colorado were the norm. He grew frustrated by the lack of awareness of this disparity, yet he was reticent to take his political frustration public. It was only after the 2016 election, in which Donald Trump won Oklahoma by thirty-six points, that he felt he needed to say something. He started a blog called *Black Wall Street Times*. "My first post was a badly written ramble about Trump. I had to get it off my chest," he said.

The post was lost in a sea of online despair. Then Frank started to write about hyper-local events in North Tulsa. The turning point was a post about the city's sale of a piece of land to a dollar store. Frank said the sale would exacerbate the community's food desert. The post caught the attention of some community leaders, who started to push for an ordinance against the close conglomeration of dollar stores. An African American city councilman who dismissed Frank's complaint lost his reelection bid to a friend of Frank's, Vanessa Hall-Harper. Hall-Harper pushed the anti–dollar store initiative through city council. Hall-Harper started pushing for other things as well, like an independent monitor of racial bias at the police department. A new mayor announced that the city would finally get serious about identifying mass graves from the 1921 massacre. Suddenly, things in Tulsa were changing, and the *Black Wall Street Times* gained tens of thousands of followers. The spark for Black Wall Street's second renaissance had been lit.

The turning point for Nehemiah Frank was the trial of Betty Shelby, the Tulsa police officer who shot Terence Crutcher. In September of 2016, for unknown reasons, Crutcher had abandoned his car in the middle of Thirty-Sixth Street North. He was walking away from his car when police showed up on the scene after an onlooker had called 911. A police helicopter overhead warned that Crutcher looked like "a bad dude." The two officers on the scene demanded that Crutcher show his hands. He walked slowly back to his car. One officer hit him with a Taser. Then Shelby shot him. Crutcher died later from the gunshot wound.

A major portion of Shelby's defense revolved around the fact that Crutcher had not obeyed the officers' commands and had drugs in his body. When Shelby was found innocent, Frank was at home. He had a glass of water in his hand. He threw it against the wall and it shattered. "I had to find a more productive outlet for my rage," he said.

Frank posted a piece on the *Black Wall Street Times* titled "Who's on Trial, Terence Crutcher or Betty Shelby?" The piece centered on the criminalization of Black lives, as evidenced by the "bad dude" comment from the police in the helicopter hundreds of feet away. The fact that Crutcher had his hands in the air and had no weapon seemed to take a backseat at trial to the idea that the very presence of a large Black man on a road constituted a threat to be dealt with by lethal force. "White people too often deem Black lives as criminal and predatorial based on what they see and hear on television," Frank wrote.[2]

Frank's piece channeled a sense of outrage missing from the local media. The post went viral, then national outlets like NBC started contacting him. Terence Crutcher's sister, Tiffany, invited Frank to speak at a news conference to help get the story of Crutcher's life out there. Crutcher had been a troubled young man but reenrolled as a student at Tulsa Community College to study his passion: music. He was also a father, a son, and a church-going man who liked to barbecue and belt out gospel songs. He had served time for drug trafficking years before, but his family and friends were convinced that "Big Crutch" was turning his life around.

Frank started to connect the dots to Tulsa's past. This was not the first time the white establishment had justified the taking of a Black life by blaming its victim. In fact, causation was at the heart of the debate about the Tulsa Race Massacre of 1921. The very word *riot* was the frame by which Tulsa, as a political entity, had managed to escape any legal consequences for its actions generations ago. The more Frank researched the topic, the more the events of 1921 did not seem like a riot at all. And the *Black Wall Street Times* was no longer a blog but a publication for Black voices outside the mainstream. Frank and his team now took on the single biggest stain in Tulsa's history.

One of the site's new writers, Orisabiyi Oyin Williams, wrote that the word *riot* was used by the Tulsa Real Estate Exchange Commission so that it would seem like Black Tulsa had provoked the violence. The exchange described the tragedy as a "riot" since that word "implied two parties were involved with malicious intent," Williams wrote. "Using this term caused insurance claims to be denied because of policy holders' participation in the event. Without insurance settlements, the citizens of Greenwood had no money to rebuild their homes and businesses."[3] Early scholars of the massacre held the same view: a few well-armed Blacks started the violence. African American intervention, in their view, set off a "race riot." The word *riot* had become the frame by which Tulsans understood the tragedy. It was an episode of spontaneous mob violence that only the National Guard was able to quell.

Black Wall Street Times challenged the dominant narrative and urged Tulsans to reframe this tragedy as a massacre. As Tulsa draws closer to the centenary of 1921, Frank's *Black Wall Street Times* has found itself the touchstone for the debate around what to call the event and how to commemorate it. The publication's push to rename the tragedy has come at an interesting time. After generations of sweeping the history of 1921 under the rug, the collective memory of the event is shifting. Some historians have labeled it "ethnic cleansing," a "pogrom," or even "a cultural genocide." Meanwhile, the Tulsa Race Riot Centennial Commission changed its name to the Tulsa Race Massacre Centennial Commission in November 2018 after pushback from activists.

The commission was announced by U.S. senator James Lankford, a white Republican, and state senator Kevin Matthews, a Black Democrat, in 2017. The pairing symbolizes the ultimate goal of reconciliation, but the commission's mission statement strikes an odd note. "The Tulsa Race Massacre Commission," the group's homepage states, "will leverage the rich history surrounding the 1921 Tulsa Race Riot by facilitating actions, activities, and events that commemorate and educate all citizens."[4] Using a tragic event as "leverage" strikes many people as discordant. The phrase implies that a certain version of a story can, like financial capital, be used to buy out other versions of a story. If control of the history of 1921 is indeed like a private equity firm, it is clear that the commission has economic and political clout. Senator Lankford, for his part, is aiming to set the terms of the conversation. In 2016 he gave a speech on the floor of the U.S. Senate, anticipating the coming debate about the meaning of 1921.

"In five years," Lankford said, "the entire country will pause and look at Oklahoma and ask a very good question, 'what have we learned in a hundred years?'" Lankford said that the country needed to do something. As to what, he left that open.[5] More text on the commission's homepage perhaps provides a clue. Apart from education, the commission is committed to "fostering sustainable entrepreneurship and heritage tourism." It is worth noting that the original commission to study the massacre urged Oklahoma to pay reparations to survivors and their children, to establish special scholarships for descendants, and to create a special economic opportunity zone in Greenwood. That was in 2001. In the years since, almost all survivors have died, and flight from Greenwood has only gotten worse since Frank's childhood. While he eventually returned to Tulsa, many talented African Americans did not.

All of this worries Nehemiah Frank. In winter 2018 Frank wrote in the *Black Wall Street Times* that the divisions from 1921 were being replayed nearly a century later. In white spaces, he said, it was still a riot, even though in Black spaces, Tulsans called it a massacre. It was not just semantics: North Tulsa still struggles to find fresh food, decent city services, fair representation, and protection from police brutality. The legacy of the 1921 attack could be felt in the deaths of not only Terence Crutcher, but also Elliot Williams and Eric Harris, Black men who died at the hands of public institutions that were supposed to protect the community. "We still don't have a seat at the table," Frank told me.

On an overpass that cuts through the heart of Greenwood, Black artists commemorate the cultural legacy of the community. Much of the street art celebrates Greenwood's jazz legacy. One piece, however, made reference to the Tulsa Race Massacre. Someone painted over "race massacre" in black paint. Frank said the graffiti artists came back to rewrite the phrase Tulsa Race Massacre, but again vandals covered the phrase with paint of their own. This time, the vandals put their own phrase. "Love Tulsa," it read. Someone was sending a message: talk of a "massacre" went too far. And it was not only a message from a few vandals. Despite Frank's pleas to the *Tulsa World*, the newspaper announced that it, too, would continue to refer to the event as a riot, although it would no longer capitalize it as the Tulsa Race Riot. The managing editor, Mike Strain, wanted to put some critical distance between the present moment and the newspaper's past coverage while not provoking the readership of the newspaper. Even this minor change, however, set some white Tulsans off. One reader wrote to the paper to say that "The Tulsa 1921 Race Riot was not in any way a massacre, and by people today trying to make it known as a massacre . . . just to get more attention for the readers of your paper."[6] Rumbling about reframing the events of 1921 bled over into other toxic debates around names of prominent buildings. Robert E. Lee Elementary School and the Brady District were two ongoing points of contention.[7] All of this was happening within a larger context, of course, that revolved around the politics of memory in the United States. From the Confederate flags and statues to Columbus Day, the discussion of riot versus massacre took place within a wholesale reconsideration of the meaning of America. Such a conversation requires an intense reading of primary sources and historical context. In this case, we need to know who, exactly, was responsible for the destruction of Greenwood. Only then can we consider how much of Black Tulsa's ongoing inequality with white Tulsa is a direct legacy of 1921. Despite the newfound openness about race relations in Tulsa, these questions are far from settled. The more we learn about the history of 1921 and its aftermath, the more questions arise.

12. Nehemiah Frank contemplates the tragic past and uncertain future of Tulsa's Greenwood District. Photo by the author.

When I was a graduate student in Texas, I chanced upon Scott Ellsworth's *Death in a Promised Land.* I called my friend Lonnie, who grew up in North Tulsa and never shied away from discussing racism with me. Did Lonnie know what had happened in 1921? Like Nehemiah Frank, he had heard some folk tales about a big fire and the Klan. That was it.

I devoured the book. It was like discovering that my family held a secret so dark it changed how I saw them. I still cannot believe it all took place in what I thought was a sleepy town in Middle America.

Less than three years after the end of the Great War, Tulsa prepared for a massive Memorial Day parade. Soldiers of every color wanted to march. Black soldiers had fought valiantly and proven their worth in the U.S. military. In the run-up to war, Black and white soldiers had walked the streets of Tulsa together, signing up recruits of all races. Black veterans wanted recognition, but the sight of armed African Americans was too much for the white elite, which mainly consisted of southerners who had been instrumental in making Oklahoma part of the Solid South. Added to this tension was the Ku Klux Klan, which invaded the state from other parts of the South and signed up close to two thousand Tulsans by spring 1921.[8] The editor of the *Tulsa Tribune*, if not a member of the KKK himself, was a vocal promoter of the Klan's agenda.

Downtown, in the Drexel Building, a young man named "Diamond" Dick Rowland worked as a shoe-shiner. Rowland got his nickname for his side hustle running number games. Although Tulsa was segregated, whites often flowed into Greenwood at night for jazz shows, "choc" beer, and dancing. Other cities vied for the title of Black Wall Street, but Tulsa's rise was unparalleled in the South. African Americans migrated from all over to Greenwood to set up shop. One of the first Black surgeons worked there along with the renowned lawyer B. C. Franklin (father of the historian John Hope Franklin). Greenwood and downtown Tulsa boomed together, but they also butted up against each other, so segregation was more of a political than a cultural reality.

Sarah Page was a white girl acquainted with Rowland, perhaps romantically—the historical record is unclear. In any case, Rowland took the elevator up to the "colored" bathroom at the top of the Drexel Building and met Page. On the way down, something happened. When the elevator doors opened, Page tripped and the two bumped into one another. What took place in the elevator is a matter of intense and frustratingly unclear speculation. What happened after the doors opened, though, is documented. After they bumped into each other, Page yelled that Rowland had attacked her. As people gathered around her, she accused Rowland of attempted rape, and Rowland fled on foot back across Archer to Greenwood before he could be arrested.

Gossip about the attempted rape of a white girl spread quickly, and reporters for the City edition of the *Tulsa Tribune* prepared a story with the headline, "Nab Negro for Attacking Girl in Elevator." The article played up the races of the two parties involved. A mob formed. Rowland was shortly apprehended by Tulsa's only Black police officer, Barney Cleaver, and brought to the county jail just a mile from the Greenwood District.

The *Tulsa Tribune* might have been the most proximate cause for the attack that followed. The newspaper, known for a sensationalist style that contrasted with the more sober *Tulsa World*, had been started by Charles Page as the *Tulsa Democrat*, and Page leveraged the paper to his advantage until he sold it to a friend, Richard Lloyd Jones, in 1919.[9] Jones was a newcomer to Tulsa but an established figure on the national stage. He was a prominent public figure in Wisconsin where he had clashed with his former friend and political ally, Senator Robert La Follette. During World War I, Senator La Follette became a vocal critic of the Wilson administration's decision to enter the conflict. Jones's disagreement with La Follette led to a complete fallout. Jones sold his *Wisconsin State Journal* and moved to Tulsa, where he threw himself into a two-front crusade as editor. One front amounted to all-out boosterism for the so-called Oil Capital of the World. In 1920 Jones took out a half-page ad in the *New York Times* for his paper and his adopted city. With Jones's face front and center, the ad proclaimed that Tulsa had the highest per-capita income of any city in the United States and that virtually every home received a copy of the *Tulsa Tribune*. On the other front, Jones railed against the town's lawlessness and corruption. Tulsa was a center for "gambling and bootlegging and 'hi-jacking.'" He feuded with the less inflammatory newspaper, the *Tulsa World*, and endorsed an aggressive nativism in the run-up to World War I. Along with his friend and colleague Charles Page, Jones sought to remake Tulsa as a bastion of whiteness, piousness, and prohibition. Law enforcement had been lax, and of particular concern was "Little Africa," where white and Black commingled over jazz and choc beer.

Jones may never have been an official member of the Klan, but he did endorse its mission. A February 1921 *Tulsa Tribune* story proclaimed the work of the Klan in maintaining, "the supremacy of the white race in social, political, and governmental affairs of the nation."[10] During May of that year, the *Tribune* beat a drum denouncing pernicious ideas about racial equality in the booming neighborhood of Greenwood. On May 15 the paper ran a small item on a Black man named Gilbert Irge who was arrested for riding a white streetcar in Tulsa. The Black man "thought he owned the car," ran the headline. A front-page story on May 21 made the case against racial equality more explicitly. An ad-hoc commission of a white pastor, a former judge, and a private detective told of their undercover adventures in Greenwood to the *Tribune*. Liquor was available at every hotel and rooming-house they visited. At hotels Black porters offered to connect the men to prostitutes, some of them white women. The committee visited a roadhouse where they "found whites and Negroes singing and dancing together."

A subversive new kind of music—jazz—filled the air. A milky, boozy concoction called choc beer, invented by Choctaw people, flowed freely. "Young white girls were dancing while Negroes played the piano."[11] The prospect of racial equality was itself a threat in a young state that had yoked itself to the Jim Crow laws of the Old South. But throw in the element of white girls enjoying themselves in the company of newly wealthy Black men, abetted by jazz and liquor, and the *Tribune* had the city's attention. The situation was intolerable.

Jones certainly sympathized with the blatant white supremacy fostered by the KKK. He later wrote a special column for the *Des Moines Register* in which he proclaimed the vice of "N——town" to be the root cause for the destruction in the spring of 1921. "The bad black man is a bad man," he wrote. "He drinks the cheapest and vilest whiskey. He breaks every law to get it. He is a dope fiend. He holds life lightly."[12]

The equation of Black men with criminality, then, did not start with Betty Jo Shelby's defense for shooting Terence Crutcher, the "bad dude." It was rooted deep in the psyche of Tulsa. Tulsa had been fertile ground for the rapid rise of the Ku Klux Klan. One of the most powerful men in town was Tate Brady, a former Klansman obsessed with the Old South. Brady had a mansion resembling Robert E. Lee's house built on a hill overlooking downtown and Greenwood. Down from the hill lies Brady Heights, the Tulsa Arts District (until 2017 known as the Brady District), and the Brady Theater (recently renamed the Tulsa Theater). For all of Tulsa's racial animosity, the city had not witnessed a race-based lynching, even as such occurrences took place all over the state of Oklahoma. But mass hysteria about the supposed rape of Sarah Page and the racism embedded in the young city's foundations threatened to change that. The mob outside the county jail demanded rough justice, but the sheriff held firm. He deployed officers with shotguns to the steps of the jail in the event the mob decided to break in.

Back in Greenwood, news spread about the possible lynching. Many World War I veterans volunteered to go to the county jail and serve as added protection for Rowland. A carload of armed Black men then headed south, where they put themselves between the white mob and the doors to the jail. At this point, then, Tulsa was the stage for an unusual situation for a town that, for all intents and purposes, had recreated the power structures of the Deep South: a small but heavily armed contingent of Black men held at bay a large but mostly unarmed white mob, intent on lynching a Black man.

At this point Sheriff Willard McCullough addressed the crowd. He told them there would be no lynching. Slurs were directed at the contingent of African Americans, who stood firm. A small scuffle broke out between the two groups. A white man tried to wrestle away a gun from a Black man and a shot rang out. At this point the white mob closed in on the Blacks, who retreated to their car and fled back to Greenwood.[13]

By the evening of May 30, white rage was no longer focused on Dick Rowland, who still sat in a Tulsa jail cell, but on the very existence of Greenwood itself. Sarah Page, for her part, left town. She declined to press charges, leading many to believe that her claims of rape had been fabricated from the start. The *Tribune*'s afternoon article about Rowland's supposed rape (the *Tribune* called it an "assault," code for rape) of Page lit a spark. But it was an editorial, possibly written by Jones, that turned that spark into a conflagration.

The editorial is one of the great mysteries of the event. Multiple Black and white eyewitnesses remember an editorial inside the *Tribune* with a headline along the lines of "To Lynch Negro Tonight." The later edition of the paper, the State edition, did not run the editorial, but the City edition may have.[14] The problem is that all extant copies of the City edition of the *Tulsa Tribune* from May 30, 1921, had part of the editorial page ripped out. A reward circulated early in the twenty-first century to find the editorial turned up nothing.

University of Tulsa Special Collections librarian Marc Carlson entertains the notion that the disappearance of the editorial might have resulted from poor handling of the actual newspaper, and indeed other newspapers are in bad condition.[15] Following the massacre, however, Jones seemed to implicate his paper in the attack. He insisted that he would make "no apology" to city officials for urging them to clean up Greenwood. Furthermore, he wrote, the burning of Greenwood should be seen as an opportunity. In the June 4 edition of the *Tribune*, he wrote that "such a district as old 'N——town' must never be allowed in Tulsa again."[16]

The Oklahoma Race Riot Commission, a governor-appointed agency to study and make recommendations about the event, was likewise unable to track down the original editorial supposedly calling for lynching. If we are to believe the survivors, though, the editorial pointed toward a concerted effort from the Tulsa elite to invade and destroy Greenwood. Part of that effort involved turpentine bombs thrown from airplanes and a fire department that only acted to hold the flames inside the boundaries of Deep Greenwood. The police department, meanwhile, marshaled ordinary citizens who themselves had already started rioting in white Tulsa. They broke into hardware and sporting goods stores, seeking all sorts of weapons—baseball bats, lead pipes, anything. Carloads of armed whites massed just off the railroad tracks near First Street.

In Greenwood, a small contingent of African Americans took up defensive positions, sensing an invasion was coming. Greenwood Avenue itself was a commercial district, filled with hotels, restaurants, and a new movie theater, the Dreamland. Heading west, the district began to merge with white businesses, and there was not a clear dividing line between white and Black as there was to the south, where the Frisco train track created a clear barrier.

The proximity and growth of Black Tulsa made whites envious and nervous. The city was booming and needed room to expand. To the south, many Creek people still held on to their allotments. A separate but equally devastating takeover of Indian land was occurring there, slowed only by legal holdups. The graft and theft connected with Tulsa's expansion to the east and south has been documented by Angie Debo and recounted earlier in this book. But it has only been considered in isolation by historians, as if the dissolution of Native sovereignty and the Tulsa Race Massacre were not connected. The sheer brutality of the massacre is shocking to learn, but it did not happen in a vacuum. It cannot be a mere coincidence that many of the most brazen thefts of allotments—including the kidnapping and assault of Millie Naharkey and the Osage Reign of Terror—happened around the same time as the massacre.

The riches under the Oklahoma red dirt had become a matter of intense speculation. The white elite sought to reorganize society around oil extraction, an industry that still indirectly contributes to around one-quarter of the state's economy. In the teens and early twenties of the 1900s, many eastern oil men and their companies relocated to Tulsa—Harry Sinclair, J. Paul Getty, and Josh Cosden among them. It was also around the time of the massacre that Tulsa proclaimed itself "The Oil Capital of the World." Booster clubs traveled the country promoting the "Magic City" that, only two decades before, had been little more than a trading post at the crossroads of the southern plains and the Ozarks. All us Oklahomans are part of a forced marriage consummated in blood and oil.

Oil, then, was remaking Tulsa, bringing whites and Blacks to town and enriching the elites of both races but leading white Tulsa to view Black Tulsa with jealousy and suspicion. With some one thousand armed whites amassing near the railroad tracks and with Black snipers taking up defensive positions in Greenwood, Tulsa must have looked like a battlefield. As shots rang out, a train pulled into Union Station. It was riddled with bullets. Whites started fires around Greenwood, but the fire department only responded to contain the fires from spreading to white homes and businesses. Planes circled overhead. Multiple witnesses said that the planes swept down low and dropped fire balls. Parents rushed children out of their houses in the middle of the night, ducking gunfire and fleeing blazes.

With Greenwood now on fire, the white mob advanced in pickup trucks and cars and on foot. A few were shot by snipers in two- or three-story buildings on Greenwood Avenue. Most of the population fled in terror, grabbing what they could. The lucky ones had cars and headed toward relatives' homes. There are many all-Black towns in eastern Oklahoma, a legacy of the brief era before statehood when Indian and Oklahoma Territories appeared to be promised land for the descendants of freed slaves. Now, of course, the new state was a living hell for African Americans, a site of frequent lynchings and now a full-fledged attack on the nation's most prosperous Black community.

One by one, white invaders ransacked Black homes and businesses. Those who resisted were shot, and some who submitted willingly were killed as well. One of the most tragic incidents of this type involved A. C. Jackson, the Mayo Clinic–trained surgeon. Jackson was taken at gunpoint by a white militia with his hands in the air but then was inexplicably shot and killed on his way to an internment camp. The main church, Mount Zion, was burned by white mobs, many of them sheriff's deputies. The attackers invaded houses to steal what they could before everything burned to the ground. Oral histories recount tales of African Americans who, many years later, would notice a stolen necklace or ring on a white citizen while downtown.[17]

The photos taken early in the morning of June 1, 1921, reveal a city on fire, black smoke enveloping the area just north and east of downtown. Still the fire department refused to intervene, and the police department mainly served to facilitate the invasion. Some whites, of course, were appalled. Some of those who employed Black servants went to the Brady Theater or McNulty Field, a baseball stadium now the grounds of the new Robert E. Lee Elementary School, to find their employees and get them out.[18]

The mayor, T. D. Evans, cabled the governor. There was a sense that, as much as white Tulsa resented Black Tulsa, things had gotten out of hand. The governor called in the National Guard, which mainly worked to protect white lives and property near Greenwood. By this time newspapers had heard about the burning of Tulsa and dispatched reporters to cover the story. By the end of June 1, the battle had mostly subsided, with dozens of square blocks of Greenwood burned to the ground and most of the entire Black population, around ten thousand people, interned.

Blacks could only leave if they were given special cards issued by white employers. Rich oil men and women went to detention camps to release their servants. Richard Lloyd Jones, whose newspaper had been a touchstone for the violence, reportedly hid his Black servants in his basement.

Meanwhile, bodies were heaped in piles on flatbed trucks. Some of the bodies were burned beyond recognition. Some were dumped in mass burial sites. The gruesomeness of the attack was transformed into mementos by photographers who sold the images of death and destruction as postcards, with titles like "Little Africa On Fire," or "Running the Negro out of Tulsa." One of the few mostly white organizations to help out was the Red Cross, which saved the lives of many gunshot and burn victims.

How many people actually perished in the massacre? It is matter of intense speculation, with best guesses between seventy-two and three hundred people, the majority, though not all, Black. Why, after so much attention and research into the Tulsa massacre, is it still so hard to know how many people died? Was what took place the product of a well-organized and planned invasion of Greenwood? Or was the Tulsa Race Riot really, in fact, a riot—in other words, a chaotic explosion of violence that no one could really control? If the events of 1921 were the former, it can be argued that Tulsa was the site of domestic ethnic cleansing or even attempted genocide that year. If the latter, the event was still tragic, and the blame for it still—mostly—resides with white Tulsa, but the implications for white Tulsa today are somewhat tempered. This is why words matter. Riot or massacre? The words themselves will shape the collective memory of the event for generations to come, filtering down into civic decisions about white Tulsa's responsibility for the ongoing troubles of North Tulsa, a place in need of a vibrant business district.

Oral testimonies tell of bodies dumped in the Arkansas River, as well as mass graves in Oaklawn Cemetery (south of downtown) and Newblock Park (west of downtown). Life insurance claims and property claims were denied after the attack. A district court dismissed lawsuits against the city for neglecting to hold off the real rioters, the whites, in 1937. As national attention focused on the tragedy of Tulsa, city leaders sought to downplay the extent of the destruction or place the blame on Greenwood's defenders. Leading papers from Los Angeles to New York ran front-page headlines about Tulsa's "race war." *The Nation* magazine pointed to "Tulsa's shame."

Leading Tulsans, from Mayor Evans to Richard Lloyd Jones, may not have recognized the human tragedy of the event, but they did understand the gravity of a public relations nightmare. Jones, after all, had come to Tulsa determined to put the city on the map. Boosters toured the country talking up the "Oil Capital of the World" and "Magic City." Richard Lloyd Jones promised that "N——town" would never exist again. He also made sure the *Tribune* would bury the event. It would be decades before any mention of Tulsa's massacre appeared in the local papers again.

As the local media and government sought to distance itself from its role in stoking the attack, *riot* became a convenient word. Dictionary definitions of *riot* denote actions of a few lawless individuals acting outside the law. As we have seen in previous chapters detailing the years of graft after the dissolution of tribal governments in Oklahoma the law itself often provided cover for widespread theft. Often we talk of "domestic terrorism" to describe the actions of white nationalists who attack the institutions of the state. The case of Tulsa, however, represents something else: state-sponsored terrorism directed at minorities. This is what might approach something resembling an objective description of what took place, though I realize such a thing is impossible.

The facts of the Tulsa Massacre of 1921 do not match with any conventional definition of the word *riot*. The massacre was stoked by sensationalist stories in the press and by greed for land. The resulting mass violence, partially endorsed and sponsored by the state, resulted in the absolute devastation of a neighborhood. When one thinks of a riot, images spring to mind of football fans going berserk and smashing windows after a Super Bowl win. Even if a riot has a political dimension, it is usually spontaneous, uncontrolled, and unplanned. Searching for recent historical analogies to Tulsa in 1921 leads us to Bosnian Serb intimidation and violence against Muslims in the Balkans in the 1990s. It also leads us to the ethnic Russian violence and intimidation of Ukrainians in the eastern part of Ukraine. Another analogy might be Apartheid South

Africa's collaboration with mercenaries in Namibia to protect German settlers in the 1970s. In any case, all these actions have the potent combination of intimidation, state-sponsored violence, and local cover-ups that characterized the Massacre of Tulsa in 1921. States that sponsored the persecution were not so much conservative in nature as *reactionary*. The ethnic nationalism of Putin's Russia, Serbia of the 1990s, and Apartheid South Africa cannot rightly be considered conservative but, rather, reactionary. This, I think, is what sets Oklahoma apart from other conservative states: its repeated endorsement of reactionary violence as a means of social control.[19]

The United States has seen localized and militarized movements based on white ethnic nationalism: the insurgency of the Confederacy, the rise of the KKK in the 1920s, in the Midwest, and the draft riots in New York City, as well as smaller movements like the Sovereign Citizen movement in the West and the Texas Rangers' persecution of the Comanches. But in Oklahoma the reactionary movement encompassed a whole state within the union and started during territory days with the incursions of "Boomers," who are still a symbol of heroism, and extended well into the 1920s, when raids on all-Black towns, lynchings, and dispossession of Native lands were executed with the complicity of the law. From the Tulsa Race Massacre, to the Osage Reign of Terror, to a policy of mass incarceration that has made Oklahoma the "world's prison capital," we are not just a conservative state but a reactionary one.

"What makes Oklahoma so special?" my friend Daniel asked me. "Isn't it just like Alabama or West Virginia? All those states blend together."

Daniel is Quebecois. He speaks French as a first language, so I do not have to lecture him on the importance of local differences within homogenizing national narratives. He also spent some quality time in Santa Cruz and San Francisco, hanging out with leftist academics, tech entrepreneurs, and hipsters. When he drove across the United States, he traveled the width of Oklahoma on I-40, noticing the gradual change from red dirt country in the west to the rolling hills of the east. He got off in Oklahoma City to see the house of Flaming Lips singer Wayne Coyne, had a steak, and then moved on to the Arkansas Ozarks without giving Oklahoma much of a thought.

Most outsiders, when they consider Oklahoma at all, lump the state in with other conservative red states with a history of racism and poverty. It is true that us Okies do not have a monopoly on belligerent white ethnic nationalism, fundamentalism, and intractable social problems. Around the time of the Tulsa Race Massacre, other race "riots" flared up in Chicago, Little Rock, and elsewhere. But in Rosewood, Florida, where another tragic massacre took place, reparations were paid. The attacks were not as violent, nor was the cover-up as blatant and all-encompassing as it was in Tulsa. Oklahoma, unlike other places in the South, was once a promised land for Black settlers and a homeland for indigenous nations with fully functioning governments. Nowhere else in the nation were the experiments in Black and Native self-government so promising and so quickly and thoroughly devastated by white settlers.

Destruction, violence, and oppression are not the whole story. Despite Richard Lloyd Jones's encomiums against Greenwood and its citizens, Black Tulsa rose again. The hotels, theaters, tailors, and churches were reborn. The lawyer B. C. Franklin, father of historian John Hope Franklin, fought racist building codes in court and won. A place called the Flamingo Lounge became a hotspot for white and Black musicians steeped in the unique blend of country, blues, and jazz that would become known as the Tulsa Sound. The funk pioneers the GAP Band referenced the traditional boundaries of Black Tulsa in its name: Greenwood, Archer, and Pine. Only twenty years after the massacre, the western swing pioneer Bob Wills would sing the district's praises in the country standard "Take Me Back to Tulsa." Examine the lyrics beyond the repetitive refrain of the title, and you find some subversive ideas. In the song, Wills recognizes that while the "Black man picks the cotton," it is the white man who reaps the profits. Despite it all, Wills says, he wants to go back to a particular area of Tulsa: Black Tulsa. "Let me off at Archer," he sings, "I'll walk down to Greenwood."

Greenwood was nothing if not resilient. More long-lasting damage to the neighborhood's identity might have been done by desegregation and urban renewal in the late 1960s than the massacre. By then, I-244 cut a swath right through Deep Greenwood, and many Blacks joined the exodus to the suburbs or bigger cities like Chicago or Los Angeles. By the 1980s most buildings on Greenwood Avenue were vacant, and some were in danger of being bulldozed. Only during the second decade of the twenty-first century did Greenwood rise for the third time. This time, however, the renaissance was complicated by gentrification. Nearly one hundred years after the massacre, it is an influx of white capital, not mob violence, that is the existential threat to Greenwood's Black character. A software startup has moved next to Wanda J's soul food restaurant. There are fights over whether Greenwood's arts and cultural centers should be exclusively Black or integrated. How much white money and influence will Black Tulsans accept as the town's rebirth filters into its North Side?

Since returning back to his hometown, Nehemiah Frank has been at the center of this debate, walking a fine line between promoting dialogue and equality while also fighting to conserve the living culture of Black Tulsa just north of downtown. A student of history might see the creeping revitalization of white Tulsa as another attempt to control Black-owned lands. An optimist might see this newest stage in Greenwood's history as a chance at reconciliation. Ricco Wright, the chair of Black Wall Street Arts, has purposely paired white and Black artists in a gallery. The effort is part of a *Conciliation* series. Tulsa, Wright says, was never properly "conciliated" in the first place, so talk of reconciliation is still premature. But history is not destiny for Wright. He thinks desegregating the arts is one way to finally make positive change. Other Black activists, including Frank, wonder if such initiatives might repeat the same cycle of oppression that came from Jim Crow, urban revitalization, and white flight. One thing is certainly different this time: people are sticking around. Tulsans of different races and political orientations might be hashing out their differences in the public square, but they are not leaving for some other promised land. They are here to stay.

Taking all this in, even for a child of relative privilege, is hard for me. Rilla Askew wrote that finding out about the massacre was, for her, like learning that her parents were not her parents: "you think you know who you are, but you don't."[20] Watching what was once a blighted area remade by a new ballpark, microbreweries, and boutique hotels gives me mixed emotions. It simultaneously gives me hope for the renaissance of Tulsa and fear that capitalism will do what racism could not: destroy the unique character of Greenwood. When I discovered Scott Ellison's *Death in a Promised Land* all those years ago in an Austin, Texas, library, I assumed that Tulsa's history was forgotten. Until that moment, I assumed my hometown was midsized Anytown, USA. A place for test-marketers, backyard football, and pursuers of the American Dream. Before I learned about the tragedy of 1921, Tulsa may have been boring, but it was innocent. Little did I understand that innocence was a ruse designed to keep people from questioning the foundation of white supremacy. "But it is not permissible that the authors of devastation should also be innocent," James Baldwin wrote in *The Fire Next Time*. "It is the innocence which constitutes the crime."[21]

Whatever Tulsa becomes in the twenty-first century, it will never be innocent again.

CHAPTER 12

Uncommon Commons

It was one of those steam baths of a late August night. Cicadas were rev-ving up their engines in the post oaks and sycamores. Stealthy mosquitoes feasted on my ankles. The corner of Thirty-Third Street and Riverside Drive had been officially closed to traffic for almost three years, but there was still a desire line through the front yard of a house on the corner. The cicadas were the only sound on this once-bustling section of the scenic boulevard that winds its way alongside the Arkansas River through Tulsa. The river smelled like dead fish. I walked north and came to a high cyclone fence bearing a construction zone sign. Ambling on through, I hummed that last verse of "This Land Is Your Land." You know, the infamous one with the communitarian spirit, about how the other side of the "No Trespassing" sign was made for you and me?

When I first came to Thirty-Third Street and Riverside Drive in the summer of 2015, the other side of the fence was an unholy mess of dirt, weeds, and steel pipes. It stayed that way for more than three years. Now the area is known as Gathering Place, one of the most stunning and expensive parks ever built in America. It is the crowning achievement of Tulsa's twenty-first-century renaissance. A cause for celebration, to be sure.

I guess I was trespassing back in 2015, but this was supposed to be a public park. Or was it? Now that the park is open and attracting visitors from all over the world, the issue is far from settled. A sign at Gathering Place states that "the open or concealed carry of guns, knives, or other weapons is strictly prohibited." Second Amendment enthusiasts wasted no time in defying this ban, on the grounds that the state of Oklahoma's law allowing the open carry of guns also applied to Gathering Place. The city attorney's office realized that Gathering Place existed in a gray area between public and private. To stave off a legal fight, the city's police force decided not to enforce the ban on weapons. That job would be left to the park's private security force. The gun issue is a metaphor for a more profound issue involving public land in twenty-first-century America.

Economists acknowledge that the United States is in the midst of a New Gilded Age, one that has only accelerated since the election of Donald Trump. In an effort to patch over the holes in the frayed safety net, a few megawealthy individuals, such as Mark Zuckerburg, Bill Gates, and Warren Buffett are giving billions of dollars to causes that used to be the sole domain of government institutions—public education and public health. This has given rise to a phenomenon called "philanthrocapital-ism." The word is a mouthful. It is useful, however, for describing this new economic model in which the rich avoid a tax bill by giving away their billions, either to charities or philanthropic LLCs, and then position themselves as the saviors for a dysfunctional government. Oklahoma has its own megawealthy philanthrocapitalist, George Kaiser, who has turned his efforts to the revitalization of public space. Kaiser has been the financier behind the Tulsa renaissance, and the city has responded with adoration. At least one hip store downtown sells T-shirts that say "Thanks, George!" Gathering Place is Kaiser's crowning achievement, one that he hopes will shift the center of gravity of the city away from sprawl and back toward the river. In the process, he hopes that the park will improve public health, bring the segregated communities of Tulsa together in a shared space, and lure young talent away from hipper cities like Austin. One could make the argument that the half-billion-dollar park is almost utopian in scope. Oh, and it happens to be located about a football field away from my childhood home.

In the midst of the park's construction, I had a long conversation with Jeff Stava, the COO of the George Kaiser Family Foundation.[1] It is a complicated arrangement, he explained. Kaiser's foundation created a GKFF Park Conservancy, an LLC that essentially loaned the park to the River Parks Authority for one hundred years. The LLC remains in charge of the maintenance and programming of the park. This arrangement gets trickier because the River Parks Authority is not technically part of the city or county government but rather another public-private partnership created in 1974 during Tulsa's last monumental attempt to transform the nature of the Arkansas River, the prairie river that runs through it.

Gathering Place then, is a public-private partnership whose public partner is a public-private partner whose public partner is Tulsa and whose private side is a subsidiary of a foundation known for its public-private partnerships. Stava, on occasion, referred to the park as "my project." It has its own security force.

You tell me who owns it.

The massive scale of the project—$350 million over the first five years—put some people in the quiet, affluent neighborhood of Maple Ridge on edge in 2015. Some moved out entirely, annoyed at the closure of their main artery to the big box stores in South Tulsa. Residents around the park engaged in skirmishes with GKFF and its partners in the project about road closures, sidewalk access, and construction noise. NIMBY stuff, basically. Many residents are staunch libertarians who fought the city twenty years ago to make Riverside Drive, one of the main roads connecting downtown to South Tulsa, inaccessible to public transit. Go back even further and you will find that the neighborhood was planned in the 1920s as Tulsa's first "restricted"—read, "segregated"—and master-planned community. The neighborhood had a bylaw in force until the 1960s that prohibited anyone of "the negro race" from living in Sunset Terrace, except in servants' quarters.

To his credit, Stava pounded the pavement, reassuring neighbors that the unwashed hordes would not be pouring into their leafy midtown enclave and parking on their lawns. According to the neighbors I spoke to, the foundation was unexpectedly responsive to their concerns. So for all Stava's imperiousness (when I simply talked with neighbors, he accused me of "going behind his back"), he turned out to be a sympathetic figure to many. There are some cranks in the neighborhood, for sure, but the big question is what the park will mean for the future of the city. Is Gathering Place becoming the city's central square, where all races, classes, and age groups will finally come together? Or is its amorphous public-private status leading it to become the "One Percent Park," the private playground of one of Tulsa's most exclusive neighborhoods? That's what I really wanted to find out.

The idea for Gathering Place first appeared in the "fiery crash memo" that Kaiser periodically shares with his staff at the George Kaiser Family Foundation. With more than $3 billion in assets, the GKFF is one of the richest and most influential charities of its type in the country. The memo tells the foundation how Kaiser wants his money spent in the event of the philanthropist's untimely demise—hence the fiery crash. Until recently, Kaiser directed most of his efforts toward helping "those left behind by the accident of birth."[2] Kaiser is ardently in favor of equal opportunity and has stepped in to fill the void left by a state government that has favored tax cuts over investment in early childhood education. Kaiser played a vocal role in 2014 in opposing preferential tax treatment for oil and gas drilling, even though his business roots are in the Oklahoma oil patch. By the standards of Oklahoma's reactionary good ol' boy politics, Kaiser is a progressive.

By all accounts, Kaiser's investments have paid dividends. Both presidential candidates, Barack Obama in 2007 and Hillary Clinton in 2014, detoured to the reddest of red states to see Educare, a model early childhood education program fostered by Kaiser and his staff, in action at a Tulsa school.[3] During her 2016 campaign, Clinton expressed a desire to implement Kaiser's ideas on a national scale. A few years ago, however, Kaiser noticed that many talented, educated people left Tulsa for cities like Austin or Chicago. Tulsa, to them, was a small town with an airport and a handful of skyscrapers. I can relate to this. When I was growing up in the 1980s and 1990s, my number-one priority after graduating high school was getting as far away from Tulsa as possible. Among my small group of friends, there was a prejudice toward those who did not leave or who came back. Returning to Tulsa, for creative or liberal types, felt like surrendering to conformity. Oklahoma continues to bleed college graduates to other states with bigger and more diverse economies. Kaiser, on some level, recognized this. It was clear that the city was not retaining human capital, and the trend would only accelerate during the Great Recession.

"If you look at all the great cities of the world, New York, Paris, San Francisco, all of them have a central park," Stava said. "Tulsa doesn't. This is something George felt should happen." Including Tulsa in the phrase "greatest cities in the world" might seem hubristic, but this is a city that ordained itself the "Oil Capital of the World" when it was just a fledgling town of about seventy-five thousand people on the southern plains. Tulsa is a town where the "Center of the Universe" sits atop a decaying concrete bridge and where a televangelist once built the world's tallest hospital, sixty stories tall, before it went bankrupt eight years later. Tulsa's civic dreams often outstrip reality as a midsized city with a population size comparable to Dayton or Albuquerque. But that did not stop some Tulsans from seriously considering a bid for the 2024 Summer Olympics.[4]

Kaiser's initial gift of $350 million to create a vast park on the east bank of the Arkansas River was not, then, out of keeping with Tulsa's character. It was the largest sum ever given to a public park in American history. And it has created something of a snowball effect, with other foundations and corporations donating to the park, endowing programming, and securing naming rights to different parts of the park. Many of Tulsa's big names in business like Williams Companies, QuikTrip, and ONEOK have since joined Kaiser in giving to the park.

The ambition of the project turned heads around the world. The *New York Times* squeezed Tulsa between Shanghai and Rome as one of the "52 Places to Go in 2015." Owners at vacation rental sites like Airbnb touted proximity to Gathering Place as a selling point years before it was open.

"Tulsa's at this critical point of deciding what its future is going to be," Chris Gates told me while the park was still being built. Gates was the project lead for the park's architectural firm, Michael Van Valkenburgh Associates (MVVA). "Not all cities have a great foundation like the Kaiser Foundation to help push things along. But they've helped Tulsa decide it was not going to be left behind. We want to make our city as livable as can be. Parks and open space are a big thing."

Stava and the GKFF in general have been so passionate about the project from the beginning because "this is their town," Gates said. "They know this is for everyone." Listening to the rhetoric of the people building the park, you get the sense that there is something idealistic, even utopian behind all the plans. Tulsa's socioeconomic trends point to increasing income inequality, entrenched racial segregation, and obesity. The park provides at least a partial answer to all of these problems.

Stava himself got emotional about the potential for the park to bridge the divides that have plagued Tulsa for generations. He rarely sat still as he led me around the model of the park in a tower in South Tulsa. For years, he has been seen in the media wearing a hard hat on the site. When we met, though, he was dressed in business casual attire: pressed khakis and a button-down shirt, no tie. He had a boyish charm but bristled at any criticism of Kaiser's projects.

The idea to create a park with lots of cultural and physical programing started with an earlier GKFF project, the Guthrie Green. The Guthrie Green is an urban entertainment space that was partially planned, paid for, and developed by GKFF to help revive a dormant industrial area. That neighborhood also houses the Woody Guthrie Center and its extensive music archive across the street. In 2016 GKFF acquired Bob Dylan's archives, to be stored at an arts center down the street from the Guthrie Center. Boosterism for Tulsa's new golden age is everywhere. In late 2018 GKFF launched a program to give remote entrepreneurs $10,000 to relocate to Tulsa for one year. Thanks, George, indeed.

Behind the cheerleading is an idea that is quite radical for red-meat-and-guns Oklahoma: the idea of the commons. It is obviously not something that Kaiser or anyone in his organization wants to play up in a place where private property is sacred, but it is there. The mission statement on the MVVA website places the idea front and center: "Our parks are founded on the idea of the commons—democratic, inclusive spaces that anchor neighborhoods and serve as focal points in the daily rhythms of their users while promoting ecological, programmatic, experiential, and social diversity."

Gathering Place, in other words, is not simply a place to play softball and climb a jungle gym. It is at the heart of a concept that economists have been debating for centuries: the notion that any shared public space (the commons) could be overused and abused by citizens wanting to freeload or maximize their own well-being. Sheep overgrazing on common land is the frequent metaphor. "The tragedy of the commons" became a catch-phrase among libertarians describing the seemingly inevitable decline of shared public resources. This is why many Maple Ridgers, even those who did not read their Milton Friedman, balked at the park. Freeloaders and criminals would seize upon the shared space and it would become a social dystopia: Central Park in the 1970s.

The Nobel Prize winner Elinor Ostrom, however, debunked the tragedy of the commons by studying societies that managed to govern common-pool resources without depleting them. A common-pool resource is something all people use: the air we breathe, the water we drink, the streets we drive on. Public grazing land. Depending on how far you want to take it, the commons can become a form of socialism. Oklahoma had an early tradition of agrarian socialism that led the Socialist Party to win many local elections and become, for a brief time, the largest socialist party in the nation. Woody Guthrie was, depending on whose account you buy, either a communist or a socialist. So Okies have a deep communitarian streak that runs against the grain of the political establishment. But the idea that any kind of socialism might be associated with the park would give the GKFF nightmares.

In any case, Gathering Place, with its reliance on private money for everything from events to infrastructure, is something new—certainly not socialist. It is a hybridized version of the commons—something you might call a "private commons." With an enervated public sector and a slate of politicians unwilling to raise taxes of any sort, let alone to fund large public works projects, philanthrocapitalism may be the only way forward for a state like Oklahoma.

But there are costs to the philanthrocapitalist model of common-pool resource management. Money that might have gone into the public treasury through capital gains or estate taxes is instead shifted to charities, who answer not to a ballot box but to select donors. Years after my initial research into the making of Gathering Place, I called and emailed staff with follow-up questions. They went unanswered until I dropped an important name. A few people have interpreted the rise of GKFF as a sort of conspiracy to undermine democracy. I do not entertain that notion, but it is important to be skeptical about a philanthrocapitalist future.

To understand how the City of Tulsa, River Parks, and GKFF worked out an unprecedented deal to build Gathering Place, you have to understand Tulsa's complicated relationship with its river. Generations of Tulsans have looked over the bluff where the Muscogee (Creek) people settled Tvlahasse-Locvpokv in the 1830s and experienced a strange and contradictory mix of sensations.

The river brought the first Native migrants to Tulsa. Later, the river provided a home for oil refineries and water treatment plants. It also flooded. It flooded so much that Tulsa was declared a federal disaster area nine times in fifteen years through the 1970s and 1980s.[5] I remember the river smelling like burning tar on humid summer nights. It was a place that, as a boy in the 1980s, I was taught to avoid. Bacterial infections and a dangerous undertow, when there was water in the Arkansas River, awaited those foolish enough to set foot in it. Talking about the similarly often-dry Trinity River, Oklahoma's Will Rogers once told the leaders of Dallas they "ought to go right ahead and pave it." He could have been speaking for Tulsa. Three decades have now passed since the last major flood. Water quality is improving. Tulsans now want to be close to the river and even, God forbid, play in it. As former mayor Kathy Taylor put it to me, "How do we make the Arkansas River more attractive? It's been the subject of lore."

In 2006 Kaiser threw his weight behind an initiative to develop the Arkansas River with an ambitious plan to keep the river full of water, improve the parks alongside it, and encourage active engagement by Tulsans on adjacent trails, playgrounds, and athletic fields. Kaiser vowed to match public funds with his foundation's own money but a proposed increase in Tulsa County's sales tax turned voters away from the project.[6]

The generosity of the donation itself may have also backfired. Oklahoma City pollster Bill Shapard said that even the plan's supporters wondered, "If he's going to put up all that money, why doesn't he just pay for all of it?"[7] As Tulsa and the nation fell into a recession in 2008, it appeared that any plans to rejuvenate the Arkansas were dead in the mud-red water. Then-mayor Taylor did not know that Kaiser was still pondering river redevelopment. Her time was spent making sure basic public services still functioned.

Even as Tulsa went through a period of public austerity in which Taylor had the lights along city highways turned off, Kaiser and the board of GKFF pondered a brighter future. Stava told me that for a time the foundation got stuck in a rut. The idea of the river improvement faded away; "we felt like we were pushing our own ideas around. The economy was bad."

One GKFF board member, Phil Frolich, heard that the Buford family might be interested in selling the Blair Mansion, a white, southern plantation-style mansion that faced the Arkansas on a plot of thirty acres in the Maple Ridge neighborhood. It was centrally located, two to three miles south of the center of downtown Tulsa and three to four miles north of the general transition of the sprawling beast known simply as South Tulsa. This set the foundation in motion. Another board member knew someone who owned the Sundance Apartments a few blocks down river on Riverside Drive. The apartment complex next door, Place One, had gone into foreclosure after a California real estate company could not pay the bills. Between the Blair land and the apartments was a slice of River Parks land with a lot and a lawn that basically collected dog poop. Connect all these disparate places and suddenly there appears a nearly hundred-acre swath of land big enough for a major park.

At this point, GKFF started to move quickly. Buford moved out, and the mansion was slated for demolition on February 1, 2014, sparking a hue and cry from some longtime Tulsans.[8] The *Tulsa World* published an online comments section that lit up with posts urging Stava to include the "historic" mansion in the new park. Amateur historians were quick to point out that, while the mansion appeared historic, it was only completed in the early 1960s. The house was modeled on Beauvoir, Jefferson Davis's home in Biloxi, Mississippi. A relatively new building built in homage to an apologist for slavery was not deemed worth saving, so the foundation razed it with little fanfare.

Along the way, George Kaiser got the idea to hold a competition for building a transformative new park. The foundation got the word out to the top landscape architecture firms about a park in Tulsa. The scale of the project attracted the attention of the best of the best around the world. With ninety-six firms on the line, the foundation staged a two-hour conference call. Stava said it was bordering on chaos, "with questions being simultaneously interpreted in all different languages."

By the summer of 2011, the foundation had developed a shortlist of four firms. Each received a stipend of $50,000 toward a bid presentation for the board of directors. Stava said that every firm came up with something original, but Michael Van Valkenburg caught everyone's attention with the idea of long, gently sloping land bridges across Riverside. "There are all these barriers on the old site that divide up the space. There's Thirty-First Street, Crow Creek, Riverside Drive, and the Blair Mansion. None of it was very seamless."

MVVA found a way to smooth over these divisions in the landscape by having a wide piece of land extend across Riverside, thus submerging traffic and opening up a vista to the river and beyond. Even if knocking down the Blair Mansion was the best decision, many residents started to feel like the project was moving forward without enough public input. In response, Stava knocked on doors and organized public forums that brought city engineers, councilmen, and architects together. The forums were not always pretty. At one meeting in September 2014, at All Souls Unitarian Church, the attendees were loud and diverse in their views. Some residents of Maple Ridge started accusing Stava of ramming the park down their throats. The scale of construction was going to destroy the character of the neighborhood. People complained about the closure of two major thoroughfares and the construction of a twenty-foot-high metal building. Internet message boards lit up with wild accusations of a conspiracy to make the temporary construction headquarters permanent. Others warmly welcomed the park.

Martha Cantrell, who has lived in Maple Ridge since 1970, remembered one resident finally getting up to speak and asking whether the people of Maple Ridge had lost their minds. She said it was like a scene out of a Frank Capra movie where a common man stands up for basic civic decency. "This is an amazing park we are getting," Cantrell remembered the man saying. "We all need to remember that."

Cantrell said the situation grew volatile. City councilman Blake Ewing arose. With a bald head, beard, and size 52 chest width, Ewing looks more like a nightclub bouncer or NFL lineman than a wonky politician. He reminded Maple Ridgers that they were getting a project that many urban dwellers only dream about. At the end of two years, he said, Maple Ridge would not only have a new park but would also have new streets, sidewalks, and water lines. Two years dragged on into four, though, and people grew weary.

"I went to the unveiling of the model," Cantrell said. "Our house was on the actual model. Most people were delighted. But a lot of people were upset about the Blair Mansion. There's this little distrust about what people hear and what they see. The original plan didn't call for Riverside Drive to be closed for two years. But putting up with this inconvenience will be worth it because we're going to have a world-class park in our backyard."

J. D. Colbert has been trying to get GKFF to honor the land's original gatherers, the Creek people who relocated their ancestral tribal town to Tulsa after removal. After Creeks were forced to cede their communal lands for private allotment around the turn of the twentieth century, the area just south of Gathering Place was deeded to a Creek man named Tuckabache and his son, Ned. Tuckabache lived through the most traumatic moments of the nineteenth century (removal and the Civil War) and was given a 160-acre allotment; his land encompasses the footprint of Gathering Place and other parts of Maple Ridge. Tuckabache's cabin sat at the present-day intersection of Hazel Boulevard and Cincinnati Avenue, directly behind the park opposite the river, and he got his water from the natural springs that have since been paved over by city streets. For decades, Tuckabache roamed the eastern bank of the Arkansas River, hunting deer with his dogs. His family's cemetery, where he and at least seventeen of his relatives were buried, sits under Twenty-Eighth Street and Cincinnati, a stone's throw from the park. When Tuckabache died in 1910, he was well into his nineties. Shortly before dying, he told a reporter that he had only one regret in life: granting an easement on his land for the white man to build a railroad, the tracks of which form the original path for the Midland Valley Trail. There have been some efforts to rename the park after Tuckabache, including one initiative that went before city council. For the most part, though, Tuckabache remains "the dead Indian," a cloud in a title, an inconvenience for those wanting to make money off the land.

J. D. Colbert, like most Tulsans, is excited about the park. He has had discussions with Jeff Stava and still hopes the Kaiser Foundation does something to honor the land's Creek heritage. There's a catch, however. "A lot of that rests on whether the Muscogee Creek Nation becomes a major sponsor of the park," Colbert said. He was told that a historical marker was "pretty much a given," but the park has yet to do anything to commemorate its Creek origins. Four years after the initial discussions, there is still no public acknowledgment of Tuckabache, anything or anyone Creek at Gathering Place.

A building with information about the land's Native history, however, would cost money. Potentially a lot of money. Colbert said the tribe has had "an open invitation" to discuss the Creek presence there, but a significant presence with a museum would cost about $10 million. Other Creek people said they were invited to an early focus group about the history of the land, but nothing was ever done. The fact that the land was sold out from under the Creek people a hundred years ago seems to be an irrelevant, or even inconvenient, historical fact. In the model of philanthrocapitalism, history can be written by those with the means to do it. For example, in Tulsa, the city's 2012 masterplan for the revitalization of the area that is home to Guthrie Green and the Woody Guthrie Center, aka the Brady District (since renamed the Tulsa Arts District), contained but one passing mention of the Race Massacre of 1921. That event did as much as the discovery of oil to shape the social development of the city in the past hundred years.

Maple Ridge is one of the most solidly white and well-to-do neighborhoods in Tulsa. As a child in the neighborhood, I remember the first Black family moving into a house on the corner of Cincinnati and Twenty-Seventh Street in the early 1980s and the hushed tones of the grown-ups wondering what would happen next. At the time, my block was filled with plumbers, electricians, and teachers. Maple Ridge is close enough to downtown and the primarily African American neighborhoods of North Tulsa that many whites fretted openly about integration. Although this not-so-subtle racism has fortunately abated, it is still just below the surface. Look up any *Tulsa World* article about the park, and you will find dozens of screeds in the comments section about an impending "ghetto" or "invasion." Access to the park, not the park itself, may be the thorniest issue that the Kaiser Foundation has had to deal with. The foundation is caught between two competing desires: those, especially on the North and East Sides, who want more access to the park, and some in Maple Ridge who only see thousands of the Great Unwashed strolling across their lawns and blocking their driveways.

This opposition flared up when the city unveiled its plans to create a new sidewalk on the east side of Riverside Drive to facilitate access to the park. From a Smart Growth perspective, the sidewalk was a no-brainer: it would lead pedestrians from downtown straight into the park without having to cross the pseudo-freeway of Riverside Drive. Artist renderings of the sidewalk show a broad concrete path with a low brick wall and metal fencing separating the sidewalk from private property, a feature rather typical of urban parks.

But in October 2014, Mayor Dewey Bartlett signed an executive order rescinding the designs for the sidewalk. Bartlett's ties to Maple Ridge ran deep. One of his business partners had a house in the neighborhood in

question. In November plans for the broad, landscaped sidewalk leading through Maple Ridge to the park simply disappeared. After some
residents cried foul, Bartlett conceded that he had nixed them due to
"safety issues." Bartlett said that pedestrians should be kept to the west
of the road. Residents of some of the older, statelier mansions on the
north end of Maple Ridge put together a professional-looking video that
argued, in an interesting twist of logic, that the sidewalk would pose a
threat to pedestrians. A representative of the Maple Ridge Homeowner's
Association wondered to News on 6 about the character of the pedestrians
streaming to the neighborhood. "Where is the parking that supports this
sidewalk? Where are these people coming from?" he said.[9]

Driving into the park, visitors come to the Williams Lodge (named after
the Williams Companies, one of the biggest donors and a long-standing
Tulsa company but which was recently acquired by Energy Transfer Equity,
a Dallas-based energy company). The lodge has a community room that
accommodates up to three hundred people and provides shelter from
Tulsa's extremes: heat, snow, and rain. The idea of the lodge is something
like a large living room for the city, with a huge fireplace, furniture, and
smaller areas for meetings and events. The back of the lodge has a series
of terraces with moveable tables and chairs and a built-in playground for
young kids.

Moving west through the park, there is Mist Mountain, a water feature
designed by the same architect who designed the Bellagio Fountains in
Las Vegas. Interconnected pathways go from koi ponds to lily pad gardens to a main water feature that shoots water above and around visitors.
The water then cascades down a stone wall. The playground area covers
five acres on its own. There are essentially seven different "rooms," each
gauged for a different age group, starting with Cloverville for babies and
toddlers and staffed by child development professionals. River Giants,
another of the rooms, has equipment being produced by a Danish company called Monstrum. Like much of Gathering Place, this playground
is at the vanguard of design and contemporary thinking about parks. A
New York Times profile of Monstrum described the company's playgrounds
as "elaborate, enormous and highly imaginative. Their designs often

feature giant creatures, both natural and fantastical, that children can climb, swing from, slide down and incorporate into their play."[10] The structures in Tulsa represent Monstrum's entry into the United States and the company's largest work to date. The playground's massive geese, which have slides jutting out from their wings, have already become an iconic image of Tulsa, along with our Golden Driller and Praying Hands.

Chris Gates told me that his firm has tried to pay homage to Oklahoma's rich diversity of habitats and ecosystems. There is a forty-five-foot-long replica of a prehistoric billfish found at the bottom of the Arkansas River. "The kids can climb up and on the billfish." Gates said he and Michael Van Valkenburg were inspired by the limestone bluffs at nearby Chandler Park and the native grasses at the Tallgrass Prairie Preserve in adjacent Osage County. They have found ways to introduce elements from both of those parks on the site.

In sum: only a cynic or a curmudgeon would not feel awed by the wonder and creativity of the park. And only the most fiercely libertarian individualist could oppose it. Yet its very ambitiousness raises a difficult question about the nature of public parks. By Stava's own admission, Tulsa's city parks can barely stay afloat based on the city's meager tax base. Philanthrocapitalists might see a return on investment in a neighborhood where they own properties, but what about Tulsa's marginalized parks? Who will save them? An even bigger question: who owns public space in twenty-first-century America?

When the nation's great urban parks were founded, it was clear who owned them: no one. Golden Gate Park, Central Park, Balboa Park—these parks were, in the words of Frederick Law Olmstead, "the lungs of the city." Densely populated cities need big parks not just to breathe but to thrive. They create a sense of identity among city dwellers and an outlet for recreation. And they level the playing field. In the 1960s, however, parks became the space of confrontation between police and protesters and between private property owners and hippies. Many of the most violent episodes of the social upheaval of the 1960s took place in parks: Grant Park in Chicago and People's Park in Berkeley were the scene of very public riots, all well documented by television and beamed into the homes of terrified suburbanites. By the early 1980s, public parks in big cities became synonymous with urban decay and crime.

During this time, New York's Central Park had deteriorated to such a point that roving bands of teenagers circulated through the park mugging tourists. One group of bandits stabbed patrons inside the park's most prestigious restaurant, Tavern on the Green. Central Park was a no-go zone after dark. In 1980 New York threw up its hands and turned the park over to the Central Park Conservancy, a semiprivate group of philanthropists and urban planners who began to turn the park around. Miraculously, crime went down, and the park's natural beauty was restored. As a public-private model, the Central Park Conservancy resembles the Tulsa River Parks Authority and many other organizations around the country; the injection of private money has led to a revitalization of scores of urban parks. Thanks in part to private donations, Central Park is once again a destination for locals and tourists, even after dark.

But what would happen if a public-private partnership created Central Park today? Welcoming more private than public money into the public space and giving unaccountable private persons the lead role may create its own problems. Beth Gazley, a professor at Indiana University who has studied public-private partnerships extensively, has written that the influx of money into what used to be the sphere of public services can create a "virtual Pandora's box of potential ripple effects." These include "reduced public accountability and citizen access, less donor transparency, more-challenging power dynamics, and less stable public services."

Gazley cited Chicago's Millennium Park as an example. While residents are generally happy with their new park, there have been conflicts around its hybrid public-private nature. The Jay Pritzker Pavilion, for instance, has been closed on occasion for private functions for those who can afford to rent it for dinners, weddings, and marketing or fund-raising events, leaving park-goers wondering if the space belongs to them or only to the 1 percent. The preponderance of private donations has also meant that donors were able to follow their whims and fancies without public input. Corporations like Boeing, AT&T, Chase, the Tribune Company, and Wrigley have splashed their brand names across parts of the park.

Kaiser is, by all accounts, a benevolent philanthrocapitalist with the best of intentions. He has been the catalyst for Tulsa's twenty-first-century renaissance. As someone who continues to own property in Tulsa, I guess I should thank Kaiser for increased property values. But even a philanthropist with his heart in all the right places cannot help but spot a good business venture when he sees one. In 2013 Bloomberg reported that over $1 billion of Kaiser's nonprofit largesse was invested in ways that benefited Kaiser's for-profit endeavors. According to a Bloomberg analysis of the George Kaiser Family Foundation's 2011 tax return, "the charity invests alongside the billionaire's stakes in some companies. In other instances, it directs funds in ways that support his for-profit businesses."

Kaiser's connection to a scandal involving a solar panel manufacturer made him a frequent target in the national conservative media. The company, Solyndra, won a half-billion-dollar government-backed loan to work on solar energy innovation with help from the Obama administration. Kaiser's charity, along with his private equity firm, had the biggest stakes in Solyndra's solar panel venture. When the company went bankrupt, Republicans charged that Kaiser had pressured the White House for the loan through President Obama's stimulus plan. After wading through pages of emails and congressional testimonies, it does not appear that Kaiser did anything unethical or illegal. He simply made a bad bet on U.S. solar panels at a time when the Chinese had established themselves as industry leaders.

When I first started researching Gathering Place, I was told that mentioning this overlap of private and nonprofit interests should be squashed. Kaiser and his second-in-command hated the *Bloomberg* piece in particular. Through an intermediary, I exchanged emails with a higher-up in the Kaiser Foundation. Was the *Bloomberg* report factually incorrect, I asked? It was not so much that it was incorrect but rather what it implied, I was told. As I dug deeper into Kaiser's impact on the city, I found that, for such a liberal-minded organization, it did not like dissent. A fellow journalist—who will remain nameless here because they fear professional reprisals—started a large-scale investigation into the foundation but decided not to publish his findings. Quietly, many North Tulsans bemoaned some heavy-handed efforts by the Kaiser people to further their own agenda regarding redevelopment in the area.

All of this, of course, has led to some conspiracy theories about a Jewish liberal carrying out an experiment in social engineering in the Heartland. That is bunkum. A more dispassionate criticism however, is to analyze the legal framework that has incentivized charities to act like corporations. Peter Buffett, the son of Warren, made a forceful case in the *New York Times* in 2013 that charities were doing precious little to address the underlying crises of our time: inequality and global warming. And yet our political system now desperately turns to private money as the silver-bullet solution to the problems capitalism created in the first place. "With more business-minded folks getting into the act," Buffett wrote, "business principles are trumpeted as an important element to add to the philanthropic sector. I now hear people ask, 'what's the R.O.I.?' when it comes to alleviating human suffering, as if return on investment were the only measure of success." Kaiser's own giving pledge discusses his attempts to "leverage other resources, public and private, by our example." Financial jargon mingles uncomfortably with the discourse of social justice.

More recent critiques, such as Anand Giridharadas's 2018 book *Winners Take All* and David Callahan's 2017 *The Givers*, point to a breakdown in our political culture. Our society has turned to what Giridharadas calls "Market World" (billionaires and their foundations) to solve public problems. We look for easy solutions that reinforce a status quo. The powerful, then, get to praise themselves for finding win-win solutions to problems for which they are at least partly responsible.

This dynamic is easy to see in Tulsa. The Tulsa Community Foundation—an umbrella organization that works closely with the GKFF—punches way above its weight for a city of Tulsa's size. In terms of assets, with its $3.8 billion, the TCF is richer than the New York or Chicago Community Trusts. Only the Silicon Valley Community Foundation is richer.[11] This means the stakes for public-private partnerships are even higher here.

As inequality increases, Tulsa leans on people like Kaiser—the richest of the rich—to solve the problems the political class ignores. Tulsa is indeed lucky to have Kaiser, a man that by all indications is committed to noble causes. But his foundation is appointed, not elected. His money is his, not the public's. No one on his board, no one in his private equity partnership, is elected by citizens.

On the other hand, voters in Oklahoma have proven to be an unpredictable bunch. Many urban liberals, in private company, say they would prefer a benevolent dictatorship run by someone like George Kaiser to democratically elected know-nothing legislators like Ralph Shortey. The question of the public's role in Kaiser's developments vexes people who might sympathize with the ultimate objectives but feel sidelined by the private process.

"In a public-private partnership," Kathy Taylor says, "the public has to have a role. It has to have a say." Taylor, like most Tulsans, was excited about the future of Gathering Place. Taylor told me that city leadership lagged behind the ambitions of the Kaiser Foundation. In particular, she cites access to the site via public transit as a problem. "The regional leadership needs to ensure that everyone can get there. We need to have a regional discussion about transit."

Those conversations have become more and more complicated as the "private commons" expands into new areas. But in at least one case, due to Tulsa's blurred lines, the conversation has been pretty easy. City councilor Phil Lakin has proven to be a one-man, walking, talking public-private partnership. In addition to his salary as an elected official, he is the chief executive officer of the Tulsa Community Foundation. In those dual roles, he influenced both the public and private sides of public-private partnerships. And by the way, Lakin is also on the board of the George Kaiser Family Foundation.

Chris Gates told me that building a park for Tulsa, even one as vast and diverse as Gathering Place, was a completely different challenge than it would be in New York. "Tulsa is essentially a suburban city," he said. "People are used to paradise in their backyards." The city has never had a park that functioned as a commons, where teenagers, adults, and small children all interact in the same space. This means that part of Gates's job has been to change the mindset of Tulsans. If Gathering Place functions like Stava, Gates, and others think it will, it will represent Tulsa's biggest shift from suburban to urban living, a change that is in line with a larger demographic trend across North America. Millennials, especially the upwardly mobile, college-educated ones, are increasingly forsaking their crabgrass kingdoms for the conveniences of city life. When I asked Stava what Tulsa would look like in 2020, he told me to look even further down the road. "By 2030, you're going to see dense living up and down Riverside Drive. Restaurants, cafes, all the way from downtown to the park."

It is no secret that the generosity of corporations is not simply an altruistic gesture but an investment. Stava highlighted this point. "All the CEOs of QuikTrip, Williams Companies, and ONEOK need young professionals to stay here. They really believe that this is an investment."[12]

There may be also a bit of greenwashing going on as well. Many, if not all, landscape architects now plan into the future with the understanding that climate change will dramatically reshape the places they design. While Oklahoma politicians are busy denouncing climate change as a hoax, landscape architects are preparing for unprecedented flooding. New parks in Boston are being redesigned for sea level rise. There is nary a mention of climate change or earthquake preparedness in any of Gathering Place literature, which is not surprising considering many of its major donors are oil and gas companies. That force of nature was on full display in the spring of 2019 as floods ripped apart some of the park's infrastructure near the Arkansas River. Whether the political class wants to admit it or not, climate change will bring more frequent and severe flooding in the years ahead.

Antoine Harris, for his part, is not so sure the park is going to benefit those who need it the most: people in areas of Tulsa where they struggle to keep their parks' lawns mowed and their pools filled with water. Harris is a lifelong Tulsan who heads Alfresco Community Development, a 501(c)(3) nonprofit. He has studied community development plans in San Francisco and Cleveland that have been successful models of integrated redevelopment projects and wants to bring that kind of development to Tulsa. But he said he has been pushed aside by the "good ol' boys."

Like many African Americans in Tulsa, Harris had mixed feelings about the redevelopment of downtown and the riverfront. As someone with an immense amount of civic pride but who sees North Tulsa being perpetually left behind, all of this was bittersweet. At several points during our conversation, Harris stopped to reassure me he was not against the park. "The park is going to put Tulsa on the map," Harris said. "And that's a good thing. I want to make it clear I'm for the park. But is it a bridge-builder? I don't see it, yet."

A cynic would say the mega park will be one more way the rich will get richer, pushing up property values along the river and pushing out those who cannot afford rising rent. Those people will have to drive long distances or use Tulsa's notoriously bad transit system to access the park. I am definitely a leftist and a tad bit cynical. I suspect, like Peter Buffett does, that there may be a bit of "consciousness laundering" going on. Much of Tulsey Town was obtained by hook or crook by white folks a little over a century ago. I am also the owner of two properties within spitting distance of Gathering Place. I grew up in Maple Ridge, when a preschool teacher like my mother could afford a house there.

So, yes, I might have been trespassing as I tramped through the weeds to a place where I took my first girlfriend to watch fireworks on the pedestrian bridge. But this is how we Maple Ridge kids always rolled. Private property be damned. We cut through the backyards and alleys of the neighborhood, carefully avoiding the threat of Mr. Stoghill's shotgun to get to the Midland Valley Trail, where I played hooky and smoked my first doobie. We trespassed through the Blair property and got into all kinds of trouble by the low-level dam. And it certainly was no golden age of "the commons." We did not expect or want anything from our civic leaders. We just wanted to be left alone at Southroads Mall and a nearby QuikTrip.

By all means, count Gathering Place as a win not only for Tulsa but the entire state of Oklahoma. It won a Readers' Choice award from *USA Today* for the best new attraction in the United States in 2018. The park attracts a more diverse set of people than you will see anywhere outside a DMV office. But it remains a thorny test case for how we relate to public land in twenty-first-century America. Is it made for you and me? Is it made for Tuckabache's descendants and the grandchildren of the Tulsa Race Massacre victims? Is it made for Muslim immigrants and Latino day laborers or for upper-middle-class Maple Ridge ladies in yoga pants? I think it is made for all of them, even though some nearby residents sneer at people of color parking in front of their houses.

In some sense, I still consider Tulsa home, even though I live thousands of miles away and have not had a permanent address in Oklahoma in a quarter century. I was once one of those young folks who thought happiness was Tulsa in my rearview mirror. So I am kind of jealous of all those kids who will spend their years roaming freely from playground to garden, from game to game, and even down to the rocky beach of the river that brought the first Tulsans to their original gathering place.

Epilogue

Even as the nation slowly worked itself out of the Great Recession in the second decade of the twenty-first century, Oklahoma seemed stuck. The state had witnessed a decade of declining health outcomes, increasing poverty, and cuts to education and social services during the so-called recovery. Finally, in the spring of 2018, Okies decided they had had enough. The first signs of a revolution began with a series of special elections the year before, when seats in solidly Republican districts in the state legislature were won by Democrats after the election of Donald Trump.

One such candidate broke all the molds of the Oklahoma political establishment. In a district that went to Trump by almost forty points, a little-known and underfunded woman named Allison Ikley-Freeman beat the Republican candidate by just thirty-one votes. During the campaign, Ikley-Freeman did not shy away from her identity as a lesbian mother who had once been homeless, who had worked her way up the ladder to become a mental health counselor. Despite having little help from the Democratic establishment, Ikley-Freeman managed to relate to the struggles of working-class Okies without making the election a referendum on Trump. At a town hall meeting with constituents in the blue-collar town of Prattville in 2018, one voter said he was amazed that, for the first time, he was able to ask a direct question of a sitting politician. "Dan [the resigned incumbent] never came to meet with us," said a man who worked part-time at a prison. The teachers' walkout, which began as an informal discussion among teachers on Facebook, soon captivated the whole state as tens of thousands of education professionals filled the normally sleepy state capitol. More than one hundred education professionals (teachers, administrators, support personnel) threw their hat in the ring during the primary in spring 2018. Curiously, not all teachers running for office were liberal Democrats. About half were actually Republicans who felt their party had finally gone too far for tax breaks. During the primaries, the educators eliminated all but five of the incumbent politicians who had opposed their demands. Many won their primaries.

The *New Yorker* ran a long think-piece on a "Democratic revival" in this deep red state. Elections in 2016 and 2018 showed that there was more complexity to Oklahoma's political scene than Donald Trump's whopping thirty-six-point margin of victory in the presidential election. In the case of medical marijuana and criminal justice reform, Oklahomans sided with liberal or even progressive causes in popular referenda while electing Republican candidates who opposed the very same measures they supported. Once again, we were contradicting ourselves and containing multitudes.

School districts hundreds of miles from Oklahoma City created walking groups, taking over highways to march to the state capital. When the teachers arrived, they met legislators who were clearly unprepared to deal with them. Tensions between the governor, legislators, and the teachers ran high. Governor Mary Fallin promised a meager pay raise but shut down all talk about funding for new infrastructure or new programs. Teachers countered that Oklahoma needed to fully fund education, not just throw a bone to teachers. Fallin told the media that the teachers were "behaving like teenagers who want a new car." Another legislator said, "I won't vote for another stinkin' measure when they're acting the way they're acting." It seemed like the hour of the teachers had arrived to a state in which Donald Trump won every single county. Leading up to the midterms in November, there was talk of a "blue wave" in Republican strongholds like Oklahoma, Arizona, Kentucky, and West Virginia.

Many teachers, parents, and students seemed crestfallen as Republicans actually increased their majority in the state legislature. In an election that was supposed to be a referendum on education, the results were mixed at best. There were some bright spots, with a few teachers winning seats over incumbents. The teacher walkout mobilized a demoralized profession, instilled new hope in young people, and demonstrated the importance of public education to a polarized electorate. It could not, however, flip an entire state from one party to another.

The single biggest surprise nationwide on election night happened right in America's Heartland in a Oklahoma City district where Kendra Horn, a Democrat who no one gave a chance at winning, won a seat in the U.S. House of Representatives by beating a Trump-supporting incumbent. It was a shocker to those who followed Washington politics. At one point, Horn was given an 8 percent chance of winning, but she pushed on, avoiding talk about Trump and emphasizing the importance of education. The national media called Horn's win a surprise, but Horn had an easy explanation. "What we were hearing about was not the president," she said. "It was about education."

For the first time in decades, the Great Oklahoma Swindle had been exposed. The promise of more tax cuts magically transforming into gains for working-class people was rarely uttered. The Democratic challenger, Drew Edmondson, appeared to be within striking distance of Kevin Stitt, the Republican. Stitt, however, learned a lesson. Rather than demonizing teachers, as Fallin had done, he promised the moon.

Under his plan, Stitt said Oklahoma would become a "top ten" state in education. When pressed on how he would achieve this ranking, Stitt made it clear that he opposed the teachers' walkout and any tax increases. Stitt cited a rising price in oil, a return to prosperity, and a cutting of "red tape." To people who followed education policy, Stitt's program sounded like a vague plan based on wishful thinking (or just an extension of Dumb Okie logic). To a majority of Oklahomans, though, it sounded good enough. The supposedly tight race between Stitt and Edmondson turned out to be a blowout, with the Republican winning by twelve points. I was not shocked at all. The foundation of the Great Oklahoma Swindle had cracked open during the walkout. Powerful interests made sure the crack got covered up for another few years.

One through-line in this book is the idea of Oklahoma as either an American microcosm or an American exception. One of my heroes, Angie Debo, insisted that her native state was the former. Okie writer Rilla Askew, whose latest book about Oklahoma bears the title *Most American*, seems to agree. I have to respectfully disagree. The more intensely I have fine-tuned my microscope on the state, the more it seems to defy many of the trends that define U.S. American political culture. I am more persuaded by George Milburn's argument that there is something inherently odd about the state. "Oklahoma is to sociology as Australia is to zoology," Milburn wrote. "It is a place where the trials and errors of men, instead of nature, have been made only yesterday, and the results are as egregious as a duckbill, or a kangaroo. Oklahoma is filled with man-made contradictions, perversities and monstrosities."[1] Recent political developments have only reinforced this view.

Local politics in Tulsa and Oklahoma City make the contradictory political landscape even stranger. The mayors of Oklahoma City and Tulsa are Republicans who have adopted some select progressive causes. In 2018 David Holt, the Oklahoma City mayor, proclaimed October 8 as Indigenous Peoples Day rather than Columbus Day. G. T. Bynum, the Tulsa mayor, seems to represent the supposedly extinct species of the RINO (Republican In Name Only) with youthful vigor and widespread popularity. Bynum has supported LGBTQ rights, reopened investigations into mass graves from the Race Massacre of 1921, and supported the teacher walkout. Meanwhile, many of the state's Native American elected officials, such as Representatives Tom Cole and Markwayne Mullin, descended from people who were the original victims of the Great Oklahoma Swindle, have sided with Trump. Nationally, we hear stories about how Americans are increasingly sorting themselves into ideological bubbles that correlate with everything from car makes to beer preferences. In Oklahoma, such neat categories have never worked.

In *Red Dirt* Roxanne Dunbar-Ortiz tracks a strange (but familiar) political journey in her poor Okie family, from agrarian socialism to reactionary Republicanism. Before World War I, Oklahoma had one of the strongest socialist parties in the nation. A 1907 ballot gave voters three options for straight-ticket voting: Democrat, Republican, and Socialist. Oklahoma was a hotbed of socialist activity for the first decade of its existence. The culmination of Okie radicalism was the Green Corn Rebellion of 1917 in which white tenant farmers bonded together with African Americans and Native Americans to march to Washington DC to put an end to the draft and maybe overthrow President Woodrow Wilson. The rebellion sprung from the activism of the Working Class Union, a socialist, direct-action organization whose tactics often involved violence. The Working Class Union claimed tens of thousands of members in eastern Oklahoma, drawing support from farmers who were subjected to high rents from large landowners to operate their subsistence farms. Historians have cast doubt on the WCU's claim of thirty-five thousand members statewide, but it is clear that the widespread disaffection with traditional two-party politics had given rise to a popular movement.

The Socialist Party picked up on this dissatisfaction. During the first decade of statehood, the party's growth led some historians to argue that the Oklahoma Socialist Party was the strongest state branch of the national party. In 1914 the Socialist candidate won 21 percent of the popular vote. The German-born socialist, rabble-rouser, and journalist Oscar Ameringer came to Oklahoma to start a newspaper and form an alliance between farmers and workers. He fell in love with his adopted home. But Ameringer was shocked by the conditions of Oklahoma farmers, writing that they were much worse than the sweatshops and tenements of the Lower East Side of Manhattan. He found fertile ground for the socialist ideals of the time: a progressive land tax, cooperative farming, and protections from high interest rates. Ameringer found that he had to walk a tightrope between Marxism and Christianity. Rural Okies were amenable to socialist ideals, but they were most receptive to them when they came in a biblical package. Rural people were the most supporting of socialism. Tenant farmers, especially, stood ready to organize and rally for socialism. These people were dismissed as dirt farmers by wealthy city dwellers, and even some unions saw them as a class apart from proletarian. Ameringer chronicled the prejudice he initially held against poor Oklahoma farmers in his autobiography, *If You Don't Weaken*. The Green Corn Rebellion, then, was born out of frustration with mainstream labor and became a true grassroots rebellion. The rebellion began on a farm in southern Oklahoma, with rebels cutting down telegraph lines and burning bridges. As they marched, they sustained themselves on grilled green corn, choc beer, and barbecue beef, a true Okie combination.

Local police, landowners, and prowar citizens quickly mobilized and engaged the rebels in battle. On August 3 the rebels met a posse of lawman and vigilantes. It was not much of a fight. A handful of combatants were killed and hundreds of rebels were arrested, making for an anticlimactic end to the Green Corn Rebellion.[2] In its wake, a wave of nationalist hysteria enveloped the land. The Working Class Union, the Industrial Workers of the World, and the Socialist Party of Oklahoma all had different ideas about democracy, organizing, and ultimate goals. They often disagreed with each other about the nature of the proletariat and the means of shifting power to the marginalized. But no matter: to the conservative press, the oil industry, and the political class that controlled the state, all those groups were lumped in together as "disloyal" to the United States. The coming of the KKK provided vigilante justice to anyone who questioned white supremacy and militarism.

Where is the spirit of the Green Corn Rebellion today? For a long time, people who think they are white believed that the imperial drive toward assimilation, civilization, and progress would eventually win out for everyone. I do not doubt their sincerity or even their good intentions. But we, I mean we who believe ourselves to be white, have clung to this belief at our own peril. It has meant erasing a painful history of invasions, massacres, and oppression right here in the Heartland. More intimately, though, it has led to a trap in our own sense of self. "A vast amount of the white anguish," James Baldwin wrote, "is rooted in the white man's equally profound need to be seen as he is, to be released from the tyranny of his mirror."[3]

We white Okies suffer from a particular type of internal tyranny based on racial and class insecurity. We strive to divest ourselves of our accents, and of any cultural markers that might signify redneck, white trash, or hillbilly to metropolitans. Secular liberals are embarrassed by our Bible-thumping aunts who speak in tongues.[4] I remember the mixed emotions I felt the time a New Yorker said to me, as if patting me on the back, "You don't even have an accent," and the time a Californian responded "I'm sorry" when I told him I was from Oklahoma. We take our big city friends to our Italianate museums and show off our handsome neighborhoods of English Tudor and neoclassical houses. We talk about our "world-class" and "progressive" cities.

We know, however, that we do not quite measure up to the standards of pure Anglo civilization, which passed from London to New York and then skipped over the Great American Desert on its way to sunny California. The rise of Heartland socialism and the fleeting Green Corn Rebellion were attempts at proto–social justice movements that rejected the terms of the Great Oklahoma Swindle. We would do well to study them and redefine our own history in the work toward a reconciliation based on racial, economic, and environmental justice. Releasing ourselves from the tyranny of white supremacy means rethinking our identity. It can be disconcerting to learn the place that formed you is not what you were told. That your forefathers were not only heroes but also perpetrators of great crimes. That the legacy of those crimes was papered over and recast as just the way things are.

I felt anger and bitterness for years about the toxic mix of religion, conservatism, and outright lies that formed the basis of my youth. But releasing myself from the tyranny of white supremacy has been a form of liberation. So much unconscious labor goes into maintaining a sense of superiority, a sense that, as a white person (especially as a white man from a well-known family), I deserve what I have inherited in terms of privilege, land, and wealth. White people in the United States have the luxury of not thinking about the crimes upon which their society was founded. When we do think about it, however, we strive to prove that we deserve what we have, that what is ours was earned, fair and square. To learn, as I did, that the fortunes of white Oklahoma were created by a series of legalized swindles can be disconcerting. The result can be a miserable feeling of guilt. But disavowing the Great Oklahoma Swindle can result in a new way forward, a way to build a foundation for new relationships, new ways of thinking about our relation to the land we share with others for this brief moment of time on earth.

NOTES

PROLOGUE

1. Quoted in Michael Wallis, *Way Down Yonder in the Indian Nation: Writings from America's Heartland* (Norman: University of Oklahoma Press, 2007), 7.

2. Danney Goble, *Progressive Oklahoma: The Making of a New Kind of State* (Norman: University of Oklahoma Press, 2015), 20.

3. For reasons that I discuss in chapter 12, I have chosen to describe the events of 1921 as a *massacre* rather than using the more mainstream and common term *riot*.

1. VOYAGE TO DEMENTIATOWN

1. Thomas B. Edsall and Mary D. Edsall, *Chain Reaction: The Impact of Race, Rights, and Taxes on American Politics* (New York: Norton, 1992).

2. Scott Cohn, "America's 10 Worst States to Live in 2017," CNBC, July 11, 2017, https://www.cnbc.com/2017/07/11/americas-10-worst-states-to-live-in-2017.html.

3. James N. Gregory, *American Exodus: The Dust Bowl Migration and Okie Culture in California* (New York: Oxford University Press, 1991), 102.

4. Quoted in Donald Worster, *The Dust Bowl: The Southern Plains in the 1930s* (New York: Oxford University Press, 1979), 53.

5. Jasmine Song, "Oklahoma Educators Quash Attempt to Ban AP U.S. History," *NEA Today*, March 17, 2015, http://neatoday.org/2015/03/16/oklahoma-educators-quash-effort-ban-ap-u-s-history/.

6. Lisa Gutierrez, "Oklahoma, Florida Lawmakers Say 'In God We Trust' Sign Belongs in Every Public School," *Kansas City Star*, February 27, 2018, http://www.kansascity.com/news/article202353564.html.

7. John T. Parry, "Oklahoma's Save Our State Amendment and the Conflict of Laws," *SSRN Electronic Journal*, 2011, doi:10.2139/ssrn.1893707.

8. *Chinatown*, directed by Roman Polanski (Los Angeles: Paramount-Penthouse, 1974).

9. Anne Case and Sir Angus Deaton, "Mortality and Morbidity in the 21st Century," Brookings, August 30, 2017, https://www.brookings.edu/bpea-articles/mortality-and-morbidity-in-the-21st-century/.

10. *Real Time with Bill Maher*, Episode 411, January 20, 2017, HBO, https://www.hbo
.com/real-time-with-bill-maher/2017/1-january-20-2017.

11. Thomas B. Edsall, "Opinion: Sex, Drugs and Poverty in Red and Blue America,"
New York Times, May 6, 2015, https://www.nytimes.com/2015/05/06/opinion/sex
-drugs-and-poverty-in-red-and-blue-america.html.

2. YOU'RE NOT DOING FINE

1. Carly Putnam, "Four-Day School Weeks Could Leave Thousands of Oklahoma
Kids Hungry," Oklahoma Policy Institute, April 13, 2016, https://okpolicy.org
/four-day-school-weeks-put-low-income-students-risk-hunger/.

2. Another glimmer of hope here: in June 2018 Bridenstine announced that he
came to believe that climate change was real and that human activity played a
significant role in its occurrence.

3. Adam McCann, "Most and Least Politically Engaged States," *WalletHub*, October
18, 2018, https://wallethub.com/edu/most-least-politically-engaged-states/7782
/#main-findings.

4. Silas Allen, "Life Expectancy Dips in One Oklahoma County, Barely Improves
Elsewhere, Study Shows," *Daily Oklahoman*, May 14, 2017, https://newsok.com
/article/5548921/life-expectancy-dips-in-one-oklahoma-county-barely-improves
-elsewhere-study-shows.

5. Rosa E. Brooks, "Failed States, or the State as Failure?" *University of Chicago Law
Review* 72, no. 4 (2005): 1159–96, http://www.jstor.org/stable/4495527.

6. Peter Wagner and Wendy Sawyer, "States of Incarceration: The Global Context
2018," Prison Policy Initiative, June 2018, https://www.prisonpolicy.org/global
/2018.html.

7. See Ruth Seydlitz, Pamela Jenkins, and Valerie Gunter, "Impact of Petroleum
Development on Lethal Violence," *Impact Assessment and Project Appraisal* 17, no.
2 (June 1999).

8. Actually, North Korea's average life expectancy of 70.1 years (according to the
CIA Fact Book) is slightly higher than North Tulsa's 69.7 years (according to the
Tulsa Health Department).

3. THE ROAD TO HELL

1. Max Nichols, "'Marriage' Merges Two Territories Symbolic Ceremony Part
of Statehood Day," *Daily Oklahoman*, October 27, 2002, https://newsok.com
/article/2812746/marriage-merges-two-territories-symbolic-ceremony-part-of
-statehood-day.

2. "Indians Centennial Protest Walk," *Daily Oklahoman*, November 5, 2007, https://
newsok.com/article/3164749/indians-plan-centennial-protest-walk.

3. See Angie Debo, *And Still the Waters Run: The Betrayal of the Five Civilized Tribes* (Princeton: Princeton University Press, 1973).

4. David Brody, "Unraveling the 'Weaponization' of the EPA Is Top Priority for Scott Pruitt," CBN News, February 26, 2018, https://www1.cbn.com/cbnnews/us/2018/february/unraveling-the-weaponization-of-the-epa-is-top-priority-for-scott-pruitt.

5. Derek Hawkins, "Oklahoma Gov. Mary Fallin Says All Faiths, Not Just Christians, Should Observe 'Oilfield Prayer Day,'" *Washington Post*, October 11, 2016, https://www.washingtonpost.com/news/morning-mix/wp/2016/10/11/okla-gov-mary-fallin-says-all-faiths-not-just-christians-should-observe-oilfield-prayer-day/.

6. Jerald C. Walker, "The Difficulty of Celebrating an Invasion," in *An Oklahoma I Had Never Seen Before: Alternative Views of Oklahoma History*, ed. Davis D. Joyce (Norman: University of Oklahoma Press, 1994), 20.

7. I am indebted to Darren Dochuk for this term: Darren Dochuk, "Blessed by Oil, Cursed with Crude: God and Black Gold in the American Southwest," *Journal of American History* 99, no. 1 (2012): 51–61, https://doi.org/10.1093/jahist/jas100.

8. Angie Debo, *From Creek Town to Oil Capital* (Norman: University of Oklahoma Press, 1943), 3–4.

9. Debo, *From Creek Town to Oil Capital*, 3–4.

10. The *v* in the Creek alphabet is pronounced with an *uh* sound, roughly.

11. I have used the most common English transcription, but the name in more contemporary Mvskoke can be rendered as Tokvpvcce, Tvkvbvche, or Tvkvpvtce.

12. Sidney Harring, "Crazy Snake Uprising (1901)," in *Encyclopedia of United States Indian Policy and Law*, ed. Paul Finkelman and Tim A. Garrison (Thousand Oaks CA: CQ Press, 2009), http://dx.doi.org/10.4135/9781604265767.n151.

13. "Crazy Snake's War," *New York Times*, March 30, 1909, 8.

14. Debo, *From Creek Town to Oil Capital*, 96.

15. "Indian Burial Near Tulsa," *Sallisaw Democrat-American*, April 1, 1910, 2.

16. "State News Condensed," *Muldrow Press*, 1910.

17. Kent Carter, "Snakes and Scribes, Part 2, The Dawes Commission and the Enrollment of the Creeks," *Prologue*, 1997, https://www.archives.gov/publications/prologue/1997/spring/dawes-commission-2.html.

18. The fall of the Cobb fortune was more spectacular than its rise and is the subject of chapter 10.

19. Glenda Carlile, "Oil Heroines," *Oklahoma Today*, July–August 1997.

20. Debo, *And Still the Waters Run*, 106.

21. Debo, *And Still the Waters Run*, 305.

22. Bobby D. Weaver, "Cushing-Drumright Field," in *The Encyclopedia of Oklahoma History and Culture*, http://www.okhistory.org/publications/enc/entry.php?entry=CU008.

23. Opal Clark, *A Fool's Enterprise: The Life of Charles Page* (Sand Springs: Dexter Publishing, 1988).

24. "Charles Page Says He Bribed Two City Commissioners in Purchasing Ball Park," *Morning Tulsa Daily World*, October 9, 1917, 1.

25. "She's Heir to a Fortune, Lives Like a Pauper," *Muskogee Times-Democrat*, October 5, 1922, 1.

26. "Government Is Trying to Disbar Oklahoma Lawyer," *Springfield Leader-Press*, January 11, 1925, 5.

27. "Government Is Trying to Disbar Oklahoma Lawyer," 5.

28. Gertrude Bonnin [Zitkála-Šá], Charles H. Fabens, and Matthew K. Sniffen, *Oklahoma's Poor Rich Indians: An Orgy of Graft and Exploitation of the Five Civilized Tribes—Legalized Robbery* (Philadelphia: Office of the Indian Rights Association, 1924), 26.

29. I told you Oklahoma was weird: where else will you find a Native American burial ground in a parking lot between an abandoned K-Mart and a sports bar?

4. WHERE IS OKLAHOMA ANYWAY?

1. Even this assertion, one made by many southerners to exclude Oklahoma from their club, is not entirely true. Many of the nations in Indian Territory sided with the Confederacy for reasons we shall explore later in this book. Opening this Pandora's box right now might lead to the world's longest footnote.

2. "Welcome to the Home Page of the TELSUR PROJECT at the Linguistics Laboratory, University of Pennsylvania," Linguistics 001—Language Change and Historical Reconstruction, http://www.ling.upenn.edu/phono_atlas/home.html#regional.

3. Danney Goble, "Government and Politics," in *The Encyclopedia of Oklahoma History and Culture*, https://www.okhistory.org/publications/enc/entry.php?entryname=GOVERNMENT%20AND%20POLITICS.

4. Wilbur Zelinsky, "North America's Vernacular Regions," *Annals of the Association of American Geographers* 70, no. 11980 (1980): 1–16.

6. OKIES IN THE PROMISED LAND

1. As I will discuss in depth later, the understanding of what took place in Tulsa in 1921 is now understood to be a massacre, rather than a riot. Because *riot* was the term used until recently, I have reproduced it when attempting to recreate the thinking of this episode in the recent past.

2. Oklahoma Senate, *Proceedings of the Senate of the First Legislature of the State of Oklahoma* (Muskogee OK: Muskogee Printing Company, 1909), http://www.oksenate.gov/publications/senate_journals/archived/sj1907v1.pdf.

3. "Emergency Laws," *Daily Ardmoreite*, January 30, 1908, 3, http://gateway.okhistory
.org/ark:/67531/metadc80655/m1/3/zoom/.

4. Other kinds of rope were indeed swinging. Lynching was a common occurrence
in the state.

5. How and why the Five Tribes engaged in slavery is a matter of debate among
historians and a subject deserving of its own research project. While some form
of slavery did exist precontact among the Creek peoples, historians have documented that it was quite different from plantation slavery as practiced by the
English-speaking whites. Furthermore, many Creeks adopted and intermarried
African slaves. Finally, there were marked differences in slavery between traditionalist Upper Creeks and Lower Creeks who had assimilated English, Christianity,
and other white practices. See Claudio Saunt, "'The English Has Now a Mind
to Make Slaves of Them All': Creeks, Seminoles, and the Problem of Slavery,"
American Indian Quarterly 22, no. 1/2 (1998): 157–80, http://www.jstor.org/stable
/1185115.

7. THE TRIBE OF THE WANNABES

1. Rilla Askew, *Most American: Notes from a Wounded Place* (Norman: University of
Oklahoma Press, 2017), 113.

2. Iron Eyes Cody and Collin Perry, *Iron Eyes: My Life as a Hollywood Indian* (New
York: Everest House Publishing, 1982).

3. Cody and Perry, *Iron Eyes*, 195.

4. Casey Ryan Kelly, "Blood-Speak: Ward Churchill and the Racialization of American
Indian Identity," *Communication and Critical/Cultural Studies* 8, no. 3 (September
2011): 240–65.

5. See, for example, Susan Shown Harjo, "Ward Churchill Went Tribe Shopping,"
Indianz.com, February 11, 2005, https://www.indianz.com/News/2005/02/11
/suzan_shown_har.asp.

6. Angela Aleiss, "Native Son," *Times-Picayune*, May 26, 1996, D1.

7. Askew, *Most American*, 30–31.

8. Hillel Italie, "Disputed Book Pulled from Oprah Web Site," *Washington Post*,
November 6, 2007, http://www.washingtonpost.com/wp-dyn/content/article
/2007/11/06/AR2007110601431_pf.html.

8. BACKWARD, CHRISTIAN SOLDIER

1. Dallas Franklin, "Life Church in Edmond Named 3rd Largest Church in America,"
Oklahoma's News 4, October 13, 2017, https://kfor.com/2017/10/13/life-church
-in-edmond-named-3rd-largest-church-in-america/.

2. Jackie Fortier, "Oklahoma Suicide Rate Up 36 Percent since 1999," *StateImpact Oklahoma*, June 7, 2018, https://stateimpact.npr.org/oklahoma/2018/06/07/oklahoma-suicide-rate-up-36-percent-since-1999/.

3. Jackie Fortier, "CDC: Oklahoma Is One of the Worst States for Black Infant Mortality," *StateImpact Oklahoma*, January 4, 2018, https://stateimpact.npr.org/oklahoma/2018/01/04/cdc-oklahoma-is-one-of-the-worst-states-for-black-infant-mortality.

4. "Yo, France You Guys Want This Back? We Don't Need It Anymore," Me.me, https://me.me/i/yo-france-you-guys-want-this-back-we-dont-need-it-3842537.

5. Miles Mogulescu, "Red States Want to Secede? Go Ahead. Make Our Day," *Huffington Post*, December 5, 2012, https://www.huffingtonpost.com/miles-mogulescu/secession-petitions_b_2246000.html.

6. Bill Sherman, "Lifechurch.tv's Bible App Attracts Millions of Users," *Tulsa World*, January 4, 2011, https://www.tulsaworld.com/lifestyles/lifechurch-tv-s-bible-app-attracts-millions-of-users/article_f16b0a3f-2599-5eac-9a25-b0ffec1d1adb.html.

7. John Hudson, "Pat Robertson Blames Natural Disaster Victims," *Atlantic*, January 14, 2010, https://www.theatlantic.com/technology/archive/2010/01/pat-robertson-blames-natural-disaster-victims/341489/.

8. Hudson, "Pat Robertson Blames Natural Disaster Victims."

9. See George M. Marsden, *Understanding Fundamentalism and Evangelicalism* (Grand Rapids: Eerdmans, 1991).

10. Although largely forgotten today, it was often said that T. L. Osborn preached in person to more people than anyone in history. His crusades in Latin America and Africa regularly drew more than one hundred thousand people a service. He died in relative obscurity in 2013.

11. Thomas Wayne Dehanas, "America's Modern Day Messiah: Billy James Hargis and His Christian Crusade—A Case Study in Extremism" (MA Thesis, Oklahoma State University, 1964), https://shareok.org/bitstream/handle/11244/26769/Thesis-1966-D322a.pdf.

12. "Adults in Oklahoma," Pew Research Center, http://www.pewforum.org/religious-landscape-study/state/oklahoma/.

9. KEEPING OKLAHOMA WEIRD

1. Andy Wheeler, "Sounding Off on Eric Clapton and the Tulsa Sound," *Tulsa People*, http://www.tulsapeople.com/Tulsa-People/March-2010/Tulsa-Sound-Sounding-off-on-Eric-Clapton-and-the-Tulsa-Sound/.

11. THE FIRE THAT TIME

1. See "Life Expectancy at Birth," World Bank Data, accessed January 15, 2019, https://data.worldbank.org/indicator/SP.DYN.LE00.IN; and Mike Overall, "Shorter

Lifespan Hangs over North Tulsa Zip," *Tulsa World*, September 14, 2015, https://www.tulsaworld.com/shorter-life-span-hangs-over-north-tulsa-zip/article_5a7b31e1-94ed-5ec6-ac63-dbaa95170a2f.html.

2. Nehemiah Frank, "Who's on Trial, Terence Crutcher or Betty Shelby?" *Black Wall Street Times*, May 14, 2017, https://theblackwallsttimes.com/2017/05/14/whos-on-trial-terence-crutcher-or-betty-shelby-2/.

3. Orisabiyi Williams, "On the 1921 Greenwood Massacre—Don't Call It a Riot," *Black Wall Street Times*, April 11, 2017, https://theblackwallsttimes.com/2017/03/31/on-the-1921-greenwood-massacre-dont-call-it-a-riot/.

4. Home page, 1921 Tulsa Race Riot, https://www.tulsa2021.org/.

5. "Senator Lankford Speaks on the Tulsa Race Riot on the Senate Floor," YouTube, May 25, 2016, https://www.youtube.com/watch?v=Lezj-fjf-hA.

6. Mike Strain, "We Changed How We Refer to the 'Tulsa Race Riot.' Here's Why," *Tulsa World*, July 14, 2018, https://www.tulsaworld.com/news/columnists/mikestrain/mike-strain-we-changed-how-we-refer-to-the-tulsa/article_4d3a3a0a-dad3-563f-8411-6d1ee6803eb9.html.

7. The Brady District, now known as the Tulsa Arts District, was named after W. Tate Brady, an early Tulsa booster and businessman who idealized the Confederacy and built his mansion to look like Robert E. Lee's. He joined the Klan, cosponsored Confederate veterans meetings in Tulsa, and, by some accounts, participated in the destruction of 1921. If we were not southern during the Civil War, we certainly had become southern by the onset of the Depression.

8. Larry O'Dell, "Ku Klux Klan," in *The Encyclopedia of Oklahoma History and Culture*, https://www.okhistory.org/publications/enc/entry.php?entry=KU001.

9. The R. L. Jones Jr. Airport in the Tulsa suburb of Jenks is named after Jones's son.

10. Tim Madigan, *The Burning: Massacre, Destruction, and the Tulsa Race Riot of 1921* (New York: St. Martin's, 2001), 32.

11. State of Oklahoma, "Final Report of the Oklahoma Commission to Study the Tulsa Race Riot of 1921," February 21, 2001, 55.

12. Richard Lloyd Jones, "Police Dodged Chance to Halt War of Races," *Des Moines Register*, June 2, 1921, 1.

13. The narrative here follows the general outline as detailed in the "Final Report of the Oklahoma Commission to Study the Tulsa Race Riot of 1921," released in February 2001.

14. I am indebted to Marc Carlson for the detailed explanation of this mystery.

15. Scott Ellsworth, *Death in a Promised Land: The Tulsa Race Riot of 1921* (Baton Rouge: Louisiana State University Press, 1982), 48.

16. Quoted in Madigan, *The Burning*.

17. See Madigan, *The Burning*.

18. In 2018 Robert E. Lee Elementary School was renamed Council Oak School.
19. Oklahoma is not entirely unique in this regard, of course. Slavery, once again, represents a decent indicator of a state's proclivity toward reactionary, as opposed to merely conservative, political cultures.
20. Askew, *Most American*, 50.
21. James Baldwin, *The Fire Next Time* (New York: Vintage Books, 1993), 5.

12. UNCOMMON COMMONS

1. Stava expressed displeasure that I was talking to people "behind his back." I explained to him that it was a journalist's duty to get as many angles as possible. ("You got Stava-ed," another journalist told me.)
2. "George Kaiser," Inside Philanthropy, http://www.insidephilanthropy.com/wall -street-donors/george-kaiser.html.
3. Mike Averill, "Hillary Clinton Touts New Child-Development Initiative during Tulsa Visit," *Tulsa World*, March 25, 2014, http://www.tulsaworld.com/news/education /hillary-clinton-touts-new-child-development-initiative-during-tulsa-visit/article _b651b674-7798-53eb-ae04-4837c310fcd6.html.
4. Mary Pilon, "London. Tokyo. Athens. Tulsa? A Heartland Olympic Dream," *New York Times*, June 30, 2013, http://www.nytimes.com/2013/07/01/sports/olympics /london-tokyo-athens-tulsa-a-mid-american-olympic-dream.html.
5. Ann Patton, "Readers Forum: Lessons Learned from the 1986 Flood," *Tulsa World*, October 1, 2006, http://www.tulsaworld.com/archives/readers-forum-lessons -learned-from-the-flood/article_53f032fe-4ced-580f-9e5d-63a8cb8b44a0.html.
6. "EXCLUSIVE: George Kaiser Talks about the River Tax Proposal," News on 6, December 29, 2007, http://www.newson6.com/story/7513009/exclusive-george -kaiser-talks-about-the-river-tax-proposal.
7. "Kaiser Talks about the River Tax Proposal."
8. Kevin Canfield, "Blair Mansion Set for Demolition," *Tulsa World*, January 31, 2014, http://www.tulsaworld.com/homepagelatest/blair-mansion-set-for-demolition /article_6132fb68-8ad4-11e3-914a-001a4bcf6878.html.
9. Emory Bryan, "Proposed Gathering Place Sidewalk Causing Controversy," News on 6, October 23, 2014, http://www.newson6.com/story/26879303/proposed -gathering-place-sidewalk-causing-controversy.
10. Jessica Gross, "Kids at Play," *New York Times*, October 10, 2014, http://www.nytimes .com/2014/10/12/magazine/kids-at-play.html.
11. "Foundation Stats," Foundation Center: Knowledge to Build On, October 2014, http://foundationcenter.org/findfunders/topfunders/top25assets.html.
12. Jeff Stava, interview with the author, April 2015.

1. George Milburn, "Oklahoma," in *An Oklahoma I Had Never Seen Before: Alternative Views of Oklahoma History*, ed. Davis D. Joyce (Norman: University of Oklahoma Press, 1994), 5.

2. "Green Corn Rebellion," in *The Encyclopedia of Oklahoma History and Culture*, https://www.okhistory.org/publications/enc/entry.php?entry=GR022.

3. *New Yorker Magazine, The 6os: The Story of a Decade* (New York: Modern Library, 2016), 27.

4. Even Okie-style Pentecostalism has African American roots, which have been whitewashed out of official history. See Randall J. Stephens, *The Fire Spreads: Holiness and Pentecostalism in the American South* (Harvard: Harvard University Press, 2008).

INDEX

CPSIA information can be obtained
at www.ICGtesting.com
Printed in the USA
LVHW031040280122
709278LV00001B/1